AF905030

Economic Growth and the Environment

Yoram Krozer

Economic Growth and the Environment

Assessment of Changes Toward Sustainable Development with Statistical Data and Experiences

Springer

Yoram Krozer
Sustainable Innovations Academy
Amsterdam, The Netherlands

ISBN 978-3-031-99180-6 ISBN 978-3-031-99181-3 (eBook)
https://doi.org/10.1007/978-3-031-99181-3

© The Editor(s) (if applicable) and The Author(s), under exclusive license to Springer Nature Switzerland AG 2025

This work is subject to copyright. All rights are solely and exclusively licensed by the Publisher, whether the whole or part of the material is concerned, specifically the rights of translation, reprinting, reuse of illustrations, recitation, broadcasting, reproduction on microfilms or in any other physical way, and transmission or information storage and retrieval, electronic adaptation, computer software, or by similar or dissimilar methodology now known or hereafter developed.
The use of general descriptive names, registered names, trademarks, service marks, etc. in this publication does not imply, even in the absence of a specific statement, that such names are exempt from the relevant protective laws and regulations and therefore free for general use.
The publisher, the authors and the editors are safe to assume that the advice and information in this book are believed to be true and accurate at the date of publication. Neither the publisher nor the authors or the editors give a warranty, expressed or implied, with respect to the material contained herein or for any errors or omissions that may have been made. The publisher remains neutral with regard to jurisdictional claims in published maps and institutional affiliations.

This Springer imprint is published by the registered company Springer Nature Switzerland AG
The registered company address is: Gewerbestrasse 11, 6330 Cham, Switzerland

If disposing of this product, please recycle the paper.

Preface

This study shows growing demands for better economic, social and environmental performances across countries, along with improvements in the last decades, as well as capabilities of businesses, citizens' initiatives, and governances for the future improvements. It is a data-based assessment of economic growth and maintaining availability of environmental qualities. Opportunities for innovations are presented, which enable sustainable development if human greed is tamed.

This book is the result of work by many people. I am grateful to them for uses of their ideas, while deficiencies and mistakes are my responsibility. Major changes and additions in the book are made thanks to several experts mentioned below in the alphabetic order. Maarten Arentsen, former professor political science at the University of Twente, insisted on bolder expression of opinions and policy recommendations. I am grateful to Jacqueline Cramer, former Minister of Housing, Spatial Planning and Environment and emeritus professor sustainable innovation at the Utrecht University, for her comments about interactions between businesses and policies. I enjoyed the discussions about the capabilities with Elzbieta Gończ, Polish member of the Club of Rome. Lucas Reijnders, former advisor to the National Environmental Forum and professor Environmental science at the University of Amsterdam delivered instructive comments on the indicators for sustainable development. Subhas Sikdar, former Associate Director Research at the USA Environmental Protection Agency, crunched several disputable ideas about sustainability. Finally, Jan-Kees Vis, former Global Director Sustainable Sourcing Development at Unilever, was helpful with insights for businesses. I appreciated cooperation with Margaret Deignan Senior Editor at Springer Nature Group and discussions about the relevance with Mira Krozer, my daughter and experts at the Governance and Integrity.

The experts and author of this book experienced and participated in the rise of ideas and practices for sustainable development throughout the last half century. We could experience improvements, but new generations confront the global political turmoil. I truly hope that my grandchildren will be able to experience a better world in the course of this century.

For Juka and Lea

Amsterdam, The Netherlands Yoram Krozer

Competing Interests The author has no competing interests to declare that are relevant to the content of this manuscript.

Contents

Chapter 1
Introduction

Can economies grow and improve environmental qualities? A positive answer is based on experiences during the last decades with the use of statistical data for all countries, several businesses and households. Subsequent chapters cover the following subjects: diverse economic thoughts about environmental qualities, estimates of environmental impacts and country performances, assessments of societal capabilities for sustainable development, and possibilities for changes of governances in this direction. Those findings end with a summary and conclusions about changes for sustainable development. All those assessments are supported by numerous tables and graphs, which are accessible to non-experts.

1.1 Objectives

The question is discussed on how economies can keep growing while maintaining availability of environmental qualities. Sound answer is needed, given that economic activities use land, minerals, fuels, organisms, and other natural resources, which cause pollution that degrades health and nature. In the words of the World Commission of Development Environment, such economy is "*to ensure that it meets the needs of the present without compromising the ability of future generations to meet their own needs*" (WCED, 1987, p. 43). Goal of this study is to assess if global changes do evolve toward sustainable development, measured by their economic, well-being, and environmental results in the past and possibilities for the future.

Economic growth is demanded as an instrument for consumption, health, safety, and other demands and aspirations for well-being and nature across generations, cultures, and gender, referred to as welfare (Sen, 2009). While economic activities are supposed to generate welfare growth in that broad sense, it does not per se imply the maximisation of income. A welfare growth is generated when activities create an additional value in terms of more desirable qualities. Good environment, one that

© The Author(s), under exclusive license to Springer Nature Switzerland AG 2025
Y. Krozer, *Economic Growth and the Environment*,
https://doi.org/10.1007/978-3-031-99181-3_1

foster all organisms, including humans, is a desirable quality, contrary to degradation of air, water, soil and other physical properties on earth, which threaten the health of people and nature. In this study, performances of economic activities are assessed, aiming to contribute to the welfare in than broad sense.

An economic value is obtained when the natural resources mentioned above are combined with the man-made resources of capital, labour, and knowledge. A higher value is generated when these combinations improve. While the uses of man-made resources for these combinations can partly be reversed, the uses of natural resources cause irreversible dissipations of energy and materials, which irrevocably cause impacts on environmental qualities, unless the dissipations are prevented. Two preventive possibilities are envisioned in the mainstream theorising about value creation across economies. These are the reduction of the usees of natural resources, and reduction of their dissipation during the uses (Leontief, 1973). First possibility is about the substitutions of natural resources for man-made capital, labour and knowledge. One option within this possibility is more use of capital instead of the natural resources, which can be equipment that uses less energy and materials for delivery of products. Another option could be the substitution of materials for labour. This one is about uses of labour in services rather than materials in products. Yet another option is larger uses of knowledge. More knowledge enables shifts from stocks to flows in energy and material; for example, the shifts from fossil fuels to renewable energy, and from minerals to bioresources. More knowledge can also replace harmful materials for less damaging ones, and it increases the value of used materials and energy; for instance, design in textiles. Second possibility is the prevention of harmful impacts caused by the dissipating energy and materials. One option is pollution prevention through reduction of noxious emissions. Another one is about compensations for harmful impacts. There are many actions that can be taken right now in each of these options. Many are already known, and there are still many to be discovered in the future. All those options are addressed in this book based on delivering performances across countries in time.

Initiating those actions is challenging. A widespread idea is that governments should initiate policies for environment protection, but experiences show that interests vested in the past prevailed in policymaking. Actually, environment protection is usually initiated by actions taken by the front-running entrepreneurs in businesses, and non-governmental organisations. Regarding that difference between 'should' and 'act,' this study refers to experiences across countries based on data. The data about these experiences covers several decades, with particular attention paid to the period from 1990 to 2015. Focus is on the annual average changes in performances during minimum one decade within that period, considered as trends. Trends in performances in time are assumed to be key factors as sustainable development is considered a process of change rather than a particular ideal to be attained in the future. This process of change is assessed with several indicators for economic activities, well-being of people, and environmental qualities, also called 'nature'. That period of twenty-five years encompasses low and high fuel prices, as well as a global political shift towards market transactions instead of policy making. While environmental policies are almost universally adopted during that period of time, the policy making is usually replaced by voluntary agreements with various interests, including agreements between rival interests with regard to the protection of environmental qualities. Herewith is focused on economic and environmental performances, whereas well-being is less detailed regarding other studies on the trends in health (Rosling, 2018), and in well-being (Pinker, 2018).

This study will underpin the changes in economic activities across countries during the last decades and opportunities in the near future based on these changes.

This Chap. 1 introduces the methods, economic terms, and assumptions, as well as a background of environmental policies. Subsequent chapters focus on four issues.

What are economists' ideas about economic growth and environmental quality? Chapter 2 shows several strings of economic thoughts ranging from neglect to adoration of the nature. The neo-Marxist, neo-Keynesian, and behavioural ideas, as well as mainstream, liberal and neo-liberal ideas about environmental impact in economic activities, are presented, along with a reality check on the neo-liberal aims. From the environmentalist viewpoint, the economic thoughts address environmental qualities in production, pollution sinks, in regulation, and in culture. Ideas about international fairness are presented and verified with data. Economic thoughts about avoiding environmental degradation in growing economies are linked to policies.

What were the environmental impacts during the last few decades? Chapter 3 shows estimates of environmental impacts across countries based on the mainstream environmentalist model, called IPAT (Ehrlich & Holdren, 1971). Changes in population and shifts in economic activities from agriculture and industry to services and knowledge work are assessed. The effects of consumption and technology on environmental performance are estimated on the global scale and across all countries. Best performing countries are assessed using indicators for the economy, well-being, and environmental impacts.

What changes in economic activities contribute to sustainable development? Chapter 4 is about innovations. This is comprehended in a broad sense of qualitative changes in entrepreneurial behaviour driven by competition, called "doing things differently" (Schumpeter, (1939) 1989). Global performances are assessed for agriculture, industry, and transportation. Also, the performances of consumers and of innovators in several countries are estimated. Innovations are also induced by environmental demands in policies driven by leisure time and knowledge workers. Policy and citizens' initiatives in sanitation, renewable energy, and protection of nature are presented.

How can changes for sustainable development be enhanced? Chapter 5 presents an answer. Governance is discussed, meaning execution of power through institutions, while institutions are comprehended in a broad sense of social and administrative organisations that enable uses of scarce resources. In line with the mainstream economic idea, it is assumed that continuity is prime interest of governances. This implies maintaining of the interests vested in the past (March & Olsen, 1984). So, pursuing changes causes tensions with the objective of continuity in governances. Factors that enabled shifts in the governances of a few dozen states following the decomposition of the Soviet Union in 1991 are assessed. These political transitions are used for assessing possibilities for the changes toward sustainable development.

Each chapter includes an introduction, methods, results, and conclusions, which can be read independently. Chapter 6 is a summary with final conclusions. Specialist expressions and mathematical modelling are avoided as much as possible, which allows non-experts to read.

1.2 Method

Experiences are assessed based on data from several sources with regard to the indicators for the natural resources and environmental impacts across all countries, with particular attention to the largest countries by population. Subsequently, the data sources, the indicators and the countries are covered in this section. The section ends with brief outline of the estimation method while details about the calculation methods are shown in Appendix 1. All formulas for the calculations are simple in line with the recommendation of Jan Blinowski, a Polish theoretical physicist (1939–2002), who insisted on the formulas not be longer than 5 cm.

Much data is used. These are interpreted by the author. Nearly all data refer to a few authoritative databases. Particularly, the World Bank database is important (World Bank, 2023). Additional data are obtained from databases of the OECD (2023), the Eurostat (2023), as well as by the IMF (2025), IEA (2025), and a few others. All databases are referred in the text when relevant. For data consistency, the World Bank database is mainly used. The study focuses on changes in time, calculated as annual average percentages throughout the period 1990–2015, unless otherwise mentioned. A long period of time is considered for assessments, a minimum of ten years. This is done in order to avoid the statistical bias that growing novelties usually have high growth rates. Maintaining high growth rates for a long time is challenging whether it is 'high tech' or 'low tech'. If time-series are incomplete for several years, the lack of data is interpolated or extrapolated. The accounting methods use simple formulas explained in words when relevant.

Indicators for economy, well-being, and environmental qualities are used. Most indicators of economic growth are based on the country's Gross Domestic Product (GDP) at constant prices, which means after inflation correction. In addition, indicators for income disparity are used. Indicators for well-being mainly address poverty, education and health, which are essential for assessments of fairness and capabilities in societies. Indicators for environmental qualities need some more explanation. They are composed of the uses of natural resources, and effects of these uses on environmental qualities as noxious pollution that causes impacts on organisms, including humans, and on materials, which also hinder economic activities. Table 1.1 shows these indicators. The focus is on diseases, climate change, toxic compounds, and biodiversity on the global scale. Environmental quality, the term often used in this study, refers to all use of mineral and biological natural resources that have impacts on the health of humans and nature. Many local impacts are untouched in the book as waste disposal, pollution of mining minerals, protecting particular species and others.

Table 1.1 Overview of main indicators in this study

Uses of natural resources	Effects of the uses	Environmental impacts
Freshwater withdrawal	Wastewater treatment	Water pollution
Fossil fuel uses	Carbon dioxide (CO_2)	Climate change
	Nitrous oxides (NOx)	Toxic chemicals
Extraction of forest	Nature protection areas	Biodiversity loss

Emerging issues of plastics spread, persistent compounds, deep-sea mining, biological warfare between species, pollution of space, and many other impacts remain uncovered in this book.

Three indicators of the natural resources are selected, which are the freshwater withdrawal, uses of fossil fuels and extraction of forests. These indicators are chosen because they are global in the sense of uses in all countries, and they cause major effects on environmental qualities, thereby important impacts. While they are considered as scarce resources, they are used as essential materials and energy in all economic activities. In addition, data on these natural resources can be found. Fourth generic indicator would be the material mass, but this indicator is unspecific because includes bulky materials and fine ones, and these data are deficient.

In the water use, global freshwater withdrawal was about 4100 km^3 in 2015, excluding water use by plants in agriculture and forestry incorporated in products. Agriculture used about 69% of it, which grew 2.5 times from 1950 to 1980 followed by saturation. All freshwater withdrawals cover about 2% of all freshwater stock on earth, which is about 0.0001% of 1338 million km^3 of all water in seas. In addition, water is desalinated, which increased from nil in the 1970s to more than 30 km^3 of desalinated seawater and 16 km^3 of desalinated wastewater in 2020 (Gleick & Cooley, 2021). Although water is assumed scarce, a significant amount of water available on Earth. Only a small fraction of all water is being utilized for economic activities. With respect to the energy uses, fossil fuels are scarce, but they are much used. These uses also cause various impacts. For example, an estimate of environmental impacts in life cycles of 498 commodities pinpointed the uses of fossil fuels as the most impactful resource uses (Huijbrechts et al., 2010). Contrary to the scarcity of fossil fuels, abundant renewable energy is not much used. The abundance of renewable energy is due to the 2.6 YJ (2.6×10^{15} MJ) of solar energy available on the Earth surface (Rogner, 2000). However, only 0.04% of it is used. For 2015, renewable energy accounted for only 18% of global energy consumption a year. In the World Bank data, even less in other estimates. This use could increase a few thousand times before approaching the available solar energy on earth. The use of land is a third indicator. Land is also scarce but available. Out of 130 million km^2 of land area, only 9.9% is used for agriculture and 2.8% for urban areas. Forests are apparently also abundant as they cover about 31% of the land area, but deforestation causes a decrease of the forest areas by −0.1% a year mainly caused by intensive logging for logs, pulp and paper. Remote sensing shows somewhat faster deforestation including the illegal log exports and shifting cultivation, mainly in tropical forests (Hoang & Kanemoto, 2021).

Generally, the natural resources are available on Earth. Salt water is abundant, as well as renewable energy, while scarce forest areas are extracted for low value products instead of replenishing for valuable forest services in education, tourism, and leisure. Scarcity of natural resources refers to the present squandering uses of fresh water, fossil fuels, and forests rather than their availability of the Earth. Better uses of natural resources improve economic performances, and reduce environmental impacts. Similar holds true for the material mass, which is displaced while remaining on Earth. A major issue is that these uses cause impacts that pose a threat to environmental qualities. Several indicators for environmental effects and impacts are used.

Wastewater can be indicated by biological, organic and inorganic pollutants, but this data across countries is not found. Instead of the pollutants, the number of people with access to wastewater treatment is indicated. This indicator is far from perfect because the treatment performances vary though treatment of wastewater is essential for public health and nature. Disposal of insufficiently treated wastewater into ambient water causes waterborne diseases as cholera, typhoid, hepatitis A, amoeba, and others. In addition, high concentrations of metals, organic chemical, bacteria, viruses and other compounds in wastewater threaten the health of all living organisms, including people. Leaks of wastewater into groundwater also threaten the quality of drinking water (Rathi et al., 2021).

Effects of resource uses on the air quality are indicated by emissions of CO_2 and NOx. Although CO_2 is often perceived not to be a pollutant, the increasing emission caused by combustion of fossil fuels is considered to be the main greenhouse gas, which causes climate change. Additional CO_2 emission, observed with remote sensing of the Earth surface, is caused by changing land uses. Particularly important are shifting cultivations with informal uses of bioresources (Houghton & Castanho, 2023), and impervious areas, which are areas covered with concrete, asphalt and other materials for infrastructural works (Qiu et al., 2024). While CO_2 emissions of shifting cultivation decline ones of infrastructure increase. In this study, solely CO_2 emission caused by combustion of fossil fuels and industrial processes is considered because it is observed in the statistical data. NOx is a toxic substance that also causes acidification of water in atmosphere, called acid rain, and respiratory diseases as asthma and COPD. This emission is used as an indicator of chemical releases into the environment though thousands of other chemicals are also dispersed.

Effect of the deforestation is not measured because sound data is not found. Instead, compensations are estimated with the land use dedicated to the protection of nature. The nature protection areas increase, and policies aim to increase these areas to 30% of all land and marine surfaces in 2030 year. These policies are based on the international agreement on biodiversity, known as the Kunming-Montreal deal (UNEP, 2023), and subsequent agreements about financing these areas.

The assumption is that larger use of water, fuels, and forests cause larger effects on environmental qualities, which are mitigated by wastewater treatment, emission reduction of CO_2 and NOx, and larger areas of nature protection. Environmental impacts are estimated by multiplication of the uses and mitigations. These impacts are: water pollution indicated by the freshwater withdrawal multiplied by wastewater treatment per m^3, climate change indicated by multiplying uses of fossil fuels and CO_2, in ton per fuel use, air pollution estimated by the fuel use multiplied by NOx in ton per fuel use, and the balance of forest area and multiplied by the nature protection area in m^2. All of those impacts are estimated in total and per capita in an indicative year and by annual average changes during a period of time. Aside water pollution, those impacts are assumed to surpass the hypothesised planetary boundaries of environmental qualities (Richardson et al., 2023). Meanwhile, water pollution is a major threat to public health.

Those indicators are assessed for 217 countries and institutional entities in the World Bank database; an example is the entity of Curacao that is part of the Netherlands. Those countries and entities are divided geographically in the European Union of 28 member countries (EU28), 24 other European countries, including the Russian Federation (Russia), Georgia and Armenia, 46 Asian countries including Turkey and Azerbaijan, 54 African ones, 5 North American ones, 41 South American ones, including Mexico and all countries in the Caribbean region, and 19 countries in Oceania, including colonies. Estimates are made of their changes in GDP per capita and environmental impacts. When the rates of changes are considered, it should be acknowledged that high rates indicate only changes in performances, not the performance levels. At low levels, performances improve usually faster than at high levels because it is easier to climb up from lower levels. The EU28 is considered as if one country though it is composed of 28 members: Belgium, Bulgaria, Czechia, Denmark, Germany, Estonia, Ireland, Greece, Spain, France, Croatia, Italy, Cyprus, Latvia, Lithuania, Luxembourg, Hungary, Malta, Netherlands, Austria, Poland, Portugal, Romania, Slovenia, Slovakia, Finland, Sweden, and the United Kingdom that was part of the EU until 2020. All of these are high-income countries by the World Bank standard mentioned below, except Bulgaria and Romania, which are considered as middle-income countries.

This assessment is focused on fifteen countries with populations larger than 100 million people in 2015, including Egypt that reached more than 100 million people one year later. These focus countries are mentioned below in ascending order of real GDP per capita in constant USD of 2015 year (USD_{2015}). Among the focus countries, the United States of America (USA), Japan, and the EU28 with the annual average of USD_{2015} 12,000 or more per capita are defined as high-income countries. Other high-income countries are: Iceland, Norway, Switzerland, the Gulf countries, Israel, Korea Republic, Canada, Australia, New Zealand, Singapore, and several smaller economies. All other countries are classified as middle-income and low-income countries. When these are considered together, they are called the lower income countries. Among the focus countries, middle-income countries include Mexico, the Russian Federation (Russia), Brazil, and the Republic of China (China), all of which have annual incomes between USD_{2015} 5000 and USD_{2015} 12,000 per capita. Egypt Arab Republic (Egypt), Indonesia, Philippines, Nigeria, India, Pakistan, Bangladesh, and Ethiopia are considered low-income countries where the income per capita is below USD_{2015} 4000 a year. Those thresholds for the incomes per capita are similar to the World Bank ones used for lending as defined in the World Bank helpdesk in 2023. That ranking of income is based on 2015 year, but the incomes changed thereafter as some economies grew faster than others. For example, the average annual income in China increased above the Mexican one, and the Bangladeshi averaged above Pakistan in 2021. These fifteen focus countries are decisive for the global economy and environment as they account for more than two-thirds of the global population, GDP, and environmental impacts measured with use of the indicators mentioned above.

For an overview, Table 1.2 shows vertically the focus countries and horizontally the main performance indicators used in this study. Population and GDP per capita for the economic performances. Life expectancy, infant mortality, enrolment in tertiary education, and gender parity indicate well-being. Sanitation, CO_2 emissions per capita, NOx emissions per capita, and nature protection show environmental indicators. Data for 2015 is presented based on the World Bank database.

Main economic indicators are population and income per capita, though business compositions, foreign investments, and other economic factors are also assessed when relevant. Within the global population of nearly 7.4 billion people in 2015, above 8 billion people in 2024, China and India cover more than one third. Meanwhile, the population of dozens of small countries was less than 0.1% of the India and China populations, which complicates coordination of transnational environmental impacts. The global average income per person was slightly above USD_{2015} 10,000 a year, but the incomes vary a lot across countries. Nearly USD_{2015} 57,000 a year in the USA was 90-fold of USD_{2015} 640 in Ethiopia. Meanwhile, the annual average income per person in Lichtenstein in Europe was three times higher than in the USA, while income in Burundi was half the Ethiopian average. International policies are hindered because economic interests diverge across countries with those large differences in the average income per person.

Social indicators in this study include life expectancy, infant mortality, and enrolment in education of all people, and specified for women. Several other indicators are also used, such as poverty, governmental expenditures on education and on health. The average life expectancy measured by years of lifespan indicates living conditions. The global average age of 70 years ranges from 50 years in Nigeria to 81 years in Japan. Infant mortality, measured by the number of deaths under 5 years per 1000 births, indicates the quality of health care. In the world, 43 of 1000 newborns die before 5 years old, while the spread between 3 deaths in Japan and 126 in Nigeria is observed. Education has achieved high enrolment rates for primary and secondary education in nearly all countries, but the enrolment rates for tertiary education differ between countries. Tertiary education encompasses colleges for the professional and academic studies. While globally 37% of all people in the educational age entered colleges, this enrolment was about 89% in the USA, but only 9% in Pakistan among the focus countries. Nearly everyone enrols in a college in the Republic of Korea, but almost nobody in Malawi does. Women are relatively successful in this enrolment as more women than men enter colleges, except in low-income countries. Income per capita is important for well-being, but it is not the only factor. For example, child

Table 1.2 Characteristics of the focus countries according to selected economic, social, and environmental indicators

Countries	Economic indicators		Social indicators				Environmental indicators			
	Million people	USD_{2015} per person	Life expectancy years of lifetime	Infant mortality death / 1000 birth	Enrolled in tertiary education percent	Gender parity women to men	Sanitation percent of population	CO_2 ton per capita	NOx ton per capita	Protected area % of total
World	7348	10,232	72	43	37	1.1	47	4.5	0.39	13
USA	321	56,763	79	7	89	1.3	98	15.6	0.81	26
Japan	127	34,961	84	3	–	–	79	9.3	0.15	2
EU28	445	30,485	81	4	67	1.2	89	6.5	0.49	22
Mexico	122	9617	75	16	32	1.0	45	3.9	0.32	7
Russia	144	9313	71	8	80	1.2	60	11.1	0.40	8
Brazil	204	8814	74	16	51	1.3	44	2.4	0.84	21
China	1380	8016	77	11	46	1.2	52	7.2	0.40	16
Egypt	92	3563	70	23	35	1.0	63	2.5	0.24	12
Indonesia	258	3332	70	28	33	1.1	–	1.9	0.34	5
Philippines	102	3001	71	30	38	1.2	55	1.1	0.12	3
Nigeria	181	2687	52	126	11	–	28	0.6	0.20	12
India	1310	1606	70	44	27	1.0	36	1.7	0.19	3
Pakistan	199	1357	66	76	9	0.9	–	0.8	0.29	10
Bangladesh	156	1248	70	38	14	0.7	34	0.5	0.18	5
Ethiopia	101	641	64	62	10	0.5	6	0.1	0.44	N.A

mortality is half lower in Russia than in richer Mexico, and half lower in China than in richer Brazil. Higher public expenditures on health reduce infant mortality.

Only a few environmental indicators are shown in this table. People access to sanitation is shown, which is important for public health. Sanitation was accessible to approximately 47% of the global population. Sanitation is almost universal in the USA, but only 6% of Ethiopians have access to it, while not many countries have higher and lower access levels. For healthy, clean ambient water and groundwater, wastewater treatment is needed at the end of sanitation pipes, but this access is far below one of sanitation. CO_2 emissions per capita indicate the impact on climate change. About 4.5 ton CO_2 per person was released globally in 2015, which ranged from 0.13 tons in Ethiopia to 120 times larger emission in the USA. Only oil and gas producers in the Gulf region released more per capita than in the USA, up to twice more in Qatar, while that emission below the Ethiopian level is rare. NOx emission that is toxic and cause respiratory diseases varies from 0.12 tons per capita on Philippines to 0.84 tons per capita in China, which are mid-income countries. Meanwhile, this emission was nearly twice as large per capita in high-income Singapore, and even higher in several low-income African countries. The percentage areas for protection of nature within all land and water areas reflects interests and efforts in maintaining biodiversity. Globally, 13% of land and water is protected, which varies from 2% in Japan to 26% in Brazil. In mountainous low-income Bhutan, 48% of all areas are protected while the nature areas were below 0.1% of all territories in high-income United Arab Emirates. These data illustrate that high income per capita sometimes enlarges environmental impacts, but it is not decisive for environmental qualities because higher income may reduce the uses of natural resource and increase prevention of environmental impacts. Systematic assessment will be elaborated in subsequent chapters in more detail.

Assessment of those indicators covers the period of twenty-five years from 1990 to 2015. Longer periods are considered if data is available, or shorter ones if reliable data is missing, but not shorter than ten years in order to assess trends. Those twenty-five years are divided into fifteen years of low fuel prices in constant dollars from 1990 to 2005, and ten years high fuel prices from 2005 to 2015. During the latter period, the annual average price of oil and gas per kg fuel tripled compared to the earlier period, along with sixfold price hikes during short periods of time. High prices of fossil fuels have triggered higher prices of all natural resources. Comparing those periods indicates the effects of high prices on uses of natural resources, which is useful for assessments of the effects of policies on fuel consumption, among other things. High prices of fossil fuels during the decade of 2005–2015 were mainly driven by growing global demands for fuels due to fast economic growth in China and India. It should be noted that the average price and the price hikes driven by the growing demand for energy from 2005 to 2015 were higher than the ones during the 'oil crisis' from 1974 to 1985, and during the Ukraine 'fuel crisis' shortly after the Russian invasion of Ukraine in the winter 2022. However, these price hikes of fuels during the period 2005–2015 did not catch much political attention because the global economy grew until 2008 when the bank crisis in 2008 attracted attention followed by the financial crises in high-income countries. High fuel prices and the financial crisis caused economic recessions in many countries, particularly in high-income ones. It illustrates the differences between perceptions and observation of the prices of natural resources. This assessment is about observations.

Developments in time are assessed rather than particular levels at points in time. These are measured by the annual average rate of changes during a period of time. A development is called a trend when similar changes are observed during a minimum of ten years in several countries. The similarity of changes is considered if small fluctuations across countries are observed. These fluctuations are measured by standard deviation of the changes in time. There are two reasons why it is important to point out trends. One reason is that even small annual changes that have been ongoing for decades generate major shifts. For example, a two percent annual average decrease in environmental impact over thirty years reduces the total impact by about half. In addition, trends in the past also indicate prospects for the future. For the forecasts, convergence or divergence of the past changes is important. When the changes converge across countries continuation of the particular development in the future can be expected, whereas the diverging changes across countries imply different development patterns in the future. In other words, a converging trend indicates a continuous pattern in the future, which implies a reasonably reliable forecast of development. Contrary to that, a diverging trend shows a discontinuity in the future, thereby uncertain forecast. These converging and diverging trends are measured by the declining, respectively enlarging standard deviation of the changes across countries in time. Another possible trend is fluctuation, which implies an uncertain assessment, particularly when fluctuations increases. The fluctuating trends are indicated by large, or increasing standard deviations in time. They also indicate discontinuities in the future. Forecasts are reasonable when the trends converge.

In addition to the (dis)continuities, acceleration and decelerations of the trends are estimated. A trend in a country can accelerate or decelerate throughout a period. This is measured by the rate of changes, it means annual average growth or decline, during the period 2005–2015 compared to the period 1990–2004. Unfortunately, these periods coincide with ones of high prices of natural resources, respectively, low prices, which cannot be disentangled, but the main factor is explained in the text insofar it is relevant. An acceleration will indicate continuation of the changes in the future. Continuation of a development is particularly plausible when the trends across countries converge and accelerate. When the rates of change decrease, called a deceleration, it is possible that the development slows down in the future. The decelerating trend shows stagnation in development, entailing a decline as a trend. The acceleration and deceleration are measured by the increasing, respectively decreasing growth rates in time. The increasing rates of change during ten years or longer, are considered as an acceleration. For example, global population grew until the early 2010s, but the growth rates declined and the trends across countries converged, which implies a stagnation and presumable decline of population in the future.

Linkages between the indicators are also assessed. All these assessments are done with Pearson correlations mainly because it is convenient to account in Excel. Most correlations are based on regressing of events across the focus countries in an indicative year, or on annual average changes of events over a period of time.

When the regressions are above 0.7 or below –0.7 ($R^2 > 0.7$, or $R^2 < -0.7$), events are assumed to be linked. No correlations, meaning no links, are assumed for the regressions between 0.3 and −0.3 ($R^2 > 0.3$, or < -0.3). Regressions in-between are considered to be moderately correlated, which means they are sometimes linked. The regressions of the social and environmental indicators with the average incomes per person across the focus countries shown in Table 1.2 are accounted. These regressions reveal that the incomes per capita are frequently relevant, but rarely decisive. The results of these regressions are somewhat positive for life expectancy ($R^2 = 0.60$). They are moderately negative for infant mortality ($R^2 = -0.5$), which means that lower mortality is sometimes linked to higher incomes. They are also moderately positive for enrolment in tertiary education ($R^2 = 0.6$), but not correlated with gender parity ($R^2 = 0.1$). The income per capita is highly correlated with sanitation ($R^2 = 0.8$), and CO_2 emissions ($R^2 = 0.8$), but moderately correlated with NOx emissions ($R^2 = 0.5$), and nature protection areas ($R^2 = 0.5$). Given that this study is focused on changes in time, a high correlation of the rates of change implies similar trends.

So far, all main methodological issues are covered. Several specific methods are introduced when directly relevant.

1.3 Economic Terms and Assumptions

Basic economic terms and normative assumptions in this study are briefly introduced in order to avoid misunderstandings. Readers who are acquainted with the economic and environmental vocabularies can skip this and the next section. Although it is aimed to use terms consistently, a few of them are used interchangeably. Economic growth and income growth are used in the sense of larger Gross Domestic Product after correction for inflation. Indicators of well-being are purposed for assessing livelihoods of people and social impacts. Environmental qualities and nature are used as synonyms of physical properties surrounding organisms, including humans. Below, the terms and assumptions are mentioned in the ascending order of integration in economic activities. These terms cover subsequently the production, entrepreneurs, price and quality, markets, national accounts, economic growth, and innovations. Conventional interpretations of the terms and assumption are presented next to heterodox opinions.

Production is defined as an output function of inputs, meaning that producing of goods (outputs) requires several resources (inputs). Mainstream economists consider values in the sense of willingness to pay for objects, focused on purchases of objects. In this study, goods are all objects valuable to people. This broad interpretation includes products which are largely based on materials, services delivered by labour, as well as affections considered valuable but immeasurable in money. Moreover, monetizing personal affections as love, friendship suchlike 'moral goods' is considered unethical (Tirole, 2017). Resources are natural and man-made. The natural resources refer to uses of environmental qualities for economic activities. Man-made resources include capital that is usually divided into assets and liabilities, labour that covers formal and informal work, and knowledge that includes comprehension as understanding, and know-how in the sense of skills to do work. Mainstream economists imagine that all resources are perfectly divisible, known, and utilized, which allow production to be changed instantly. In reality, minerals, machines, people, and expertise are poorly divisible objects. These imperfections cause wasteful outputs, time-lags in tuning production to demanded goods, deficient allocations of scarce resources, risky investments with regard to uncertain future, harmful pollution to be prevented and other losses. Those moral good and environmental qualities are considered common goods that are necessary for good functioning of any society. In the decision making, those moral goods can be considered as infrastructure for social relations. Environmental qualities enable operations with man-made resources. They can be comprehended as key infrastructure for economic activities. These social and environmental infrastructures are public goods that are used by many interests without specifying private ownership, which add to communication, roads, canals, and other physical infrastructure.

Entrepreneurs, which are individuals that create production, strive for better performance in the sense of personal profits and continuity. While the mainstream opinion is that entrepreneurs strive for the highest profits, the aim of continuing in profits, called profitability, can collide with it. As each entrepreneur pursues a private benefit competition is generated. Competition enables deliveries of valuable goods at minimal costs of resources, or maximum value, or both, known as efficiency. Goods and resources in competition are measured in monetary terms as prices. Mainstream economists focus on the lowest costs. Based on this idea, competition drives prices towards the lowest unit costs of supplies, also known as the lowest marginal costs, which are measured by the total costs divided by the volume of resources during a period of time. When non-monetary indicators are assessed, the unit costs per indicator are compared, called cost-effectiveness. For example, technology that reduces NOx emissions at the lowest unit cost is considered to be cost-effective. In this study, the monetary and non-monetary expressions are considered relevant for competition. Dispersed natural resources are often assumed to be costless though the interests that disperse them as pollution, the polluters, cause harm. Costs are induced when harmed interests render polluters liable for harms. These liabilities are prevented when license for activities is obtained from regulators that are supposed to balance the interests of polluters and harmed ones. Liabilities that are not covered by the licenses to operate pose risks in competition. As the polluter interests often prevail, individual environmentalists and environmental organisations act as entrepreneurs that represent harmed interests. Their interests collide.

Prices, social and physical terms are used in this study instead of putting prices on all values and resources. It is because prices do not reflect all demanded values and supplied resources. Mainstream economics focuses on achieving equilibrium between the producers' unit costs and the consumers' unit of benefits if all interested actors pursue their own interests, when consumers refer to the users of goods in businesses and households. Goods are generated in the value chains of several subsequent producers. As every subsequent supplier strives for incomes that cover all costs of resources and provide profits, consumer prices increase at every step of the supply chain. Income less purchase costs means a valuable addition, or value added. While producers add value in the chain at higher prices, consumers pursue the best quality at the lowest cost of purchases. Given that the qualities of purchases are known only after purchases during uses, uncertainties about qualities increase in value chain along with higher prices. In competition, the consumer demands for better quality at lower costs trigger producers to provide alternative, it is to innovate, In effect, supplies diversify unless innovations stagnate because of insufficient demands for qualities (Lancaster, 1966). When a producer compounds quality attributes into its goods, it is aware of the supplied qualities, but a purchasing consumer is unaware of these attributes. This asymmetric information increases uncertainties about qualities in value chains. As a result, consumers tend to purchase at the prices below fair prices for the deliveries, which causes that competition evolves towards lower prices rather than better product qualities at higher prices (Akerlof, 1970). In addition, producers can harm the interests uninvolved in transactions. These external effects refer to the deficiencies in moral goods and environmental qualities, such as greed and pollution. Unless producers are liable for supplying qualities, uncertainties about qualities cause deficient purchases and external effects, which impede innovations.

Markets involve exchanges of goods and services between producers and consumers. In mainstream economics, every consumer is supposed to define its individual preference for goods based on personal deliberations about losses and gains. This consumer utility is supposed to determine willingness to pay for goods, thereby the prices and quality of supplies in markets. Imbalances occur when the willingness to pay exceeds the purchase price, and vice versa, which provides a surplus to producers and consumers, respectively. The consumer surplus is rare in markets, given the producers' dominance. As observed by the founding father of modern economic theory, Adam Smith (1723–1790) in 1776: "*Consumption is the sole end and purpose of all production; and the interest of the producer ought to be attended to only so far as it may be necessary for promoting that of the consumer. The maxim is so perfectly self-evident that it would be absurd to attempt to prove it. But in the mercantile system, the interest of the consumer is almost constantly sacrificed to that of the producer; and it seems to consider production, and not consumption, as the ultimate end and object of all industry and commerce*" (Smith, (1776) 1986, page 719). It is observed that consumers emulate ceremonies of the leisure classes, which implies that purchases reflect social relations rather than deliberate losses and gains (Veblen, (1892) 2024). As a result, markets are not only transactions between producers and consumers that pursue their own interests, but also institutions that define social behaviour. Markets are developed in the course of the last two centuries into stock exchange, certifications, and other institutions that determine the qualities, prices, ownerships, permits, and other features in transactions (Polanyi, 1957). Transactions outside of these institutions are impeded and even persecuted; such as, informal labour and unregistered entrepreneurship.

When all monetary transactions in an area are added, their sum is labelled as Gross National Income (GDP). GDP plus exports minus imports equals the national income, or national expenditure. Monetary transactions that evolve independently of the production of goods, so called 'broad money', cover rents on loans and speculative exchanges among others. Relaxed financial regulations increase broad money. It is when the financial transactions are allowed to increase, given the transactions with goods. Given that the GDP accounts exclude informal, moral, and environmental goods deficiencies in GDPs are often pinpointed. To quote Robert Kennedy,murdered president-candidate in the USA about GDP "*it measures everything, in short, except that which makes life worthwhile*" (Kennedy, 1968). Mainstream economists argue that correcting for inflation resolves most shortcomings of GDP because deficiencies are accommodated in market prices after a while. This is indicated with GDP per capita after inflation corrections, called 'real' GDP (Aitken, 2019). Other economists recommend shadow pricing for the voluntary activities due to the divergence of household expenditures from their income. Many economists also suggest that the GDP accounts be corrected with the shadow prices for degradation of environmental qualities as demonstrated in so called Net National Income. Yet other ones recommend the use of parallel accounts for moral goods and environmental qualities because shadow prices are considered disputable and misleading in many cases. This study uses the parallel accounts.

Economic growth refers to changes in GDP, driven by higher value addition, given costs. Many economists, engineers, and environmentalists hold the view that only activities that convert the natural resources into products can add value. Agricultural cultivation of land is assumed productive, likewise the industrial processing of energy and materials into products. However, services are often considered as the distributive activities for the values added in agriculture and industry. Household work is seen as unproductive though studies on emancipation of genders show contributions to GDP (Chadeau, 1985). This study assumes that all human activities tend to add value, and that economies grow whenever value is added without undermining the values of other activities. When economies grow, business composition also changes. Presently, services grow faster than industries and agriculture in many countries. Services are labour-intensive meaning much labour resources are used per value added, while industry is material-intensive and agriculture is land-intensive, which are also energy-intensive. As the labour-intensive activities grow while the material-intensive and land-intensive activities saturate economies 'dematerialise' and reduce the environmental impacts quasi-autonomously, meaning without policy interventions.

Based on the mainstream idea, economic growth is generated by the scales of capital and labour, being sum of the domestic saving and foreign investment, respectively sum of the working population. Productivity of capital and labour in exponents of these scales are assumed decisive. Their productivity is measured by the monetary values of production (outputs) per resource use (inputs). According to many economists, their productivity is mainly attributed to production tools, meaning technologies. Uses of novel tools in transactions refer to innovations. Innovations that generate lower costs of resources and deliver higher value of sales increase productivity. The conventional idea is that investments in research and development (R&D) deliver novelties, it is inventions, that need to be protected from theft, copying, and other misuse with intellectual property rights (IPR). IPR cover patents for technology, trademarks for product, industrial design for models, and copyright for service. IPR is considered the indicator for successful R&D (Griliches, 1998). Having IPR enables to start a new firm, or new activities in a firm. Both are called startups in this study. They strive for profits that cover all costs. When startups successfully sell novelties, which are innovations, they capture a market share from competitors vested in the past, called incumbents. As innovators gain a market share while incumbents fail in competition, business compositions change. When the novelties disseminate through sales, the unit costs decrease and qualities improve in the process of 'learning by doing' in production of novelties and 'learning by using' in applications of them (Rosenberg, 1983). The practical knowledge, called know-how is considered a key entrepreneurial asset. Capturing opportunities for innovations is assumed to be key role of entrepreneurs while firm operations are driven by managers (Kirzner, 1997). It is observed that innovations accumulate over time, which causes fluctuations in business activities. Periodical upswings of value are followed by a downturn, which generates cycles in businesses and swings in economic growth and recession. Innovations also accumulate in space, referred to as the business clusters.

1.4 Background of Environmental Policies

Several terms linked to environmental policies are touched for comprehension of this study. These terms are: policies, environmental governance, sustainable development, performance indicators, and sustainable development goals.

Policies, strategies and suchlike plans of action are far from perfect. The issues perceived of low importance are delegated to lower hierarchy in organisations and postponed in favour of issues assumed urgent and assessed higher in hierarchies. Deficiencies evolve also within the organisations that implement actions, it is in governance. Given that organisations tend to act in line with ideas vested in the past the emerging issues are treated as if they are traditional unless sense of urgency pushes the issues towards higher hierarchies (Cyert and March, (1963), 1988). It is not different from the governments of states, being organisations with the monopoly power in enforcing norms and regulations. They are also bound to the administrative hierarchies and opinions of the past which operate largely independent of the social and economic interests that they are supposed to be governed. It implies that governances pursue continuity based on traditions, and that changes in governances evolve slowly. So, when private interests harm other ones, resolutions for tensions evolve within traditions, while societal tensions persist until decision makers higher in hierarchy sense of urgency to act. Shifts in governances emerge when political institutions collapse because cannot cope with the societal tensions (Cohen et al., 1972).

Environmental quality is considered by authorities when sense of urgency about harms is generated in societies. This is not a new issue. Environmental policies can look back on a long history of managing soil and floods, treatment of waste water, fire prevention, control of waste disposal, and other issues from ancient Mesopotamia, a few millennia BC, on to the present regulations on chemicals, climate change, biodiversity and so on. These policies enforced technologies for protection of environmental qualities as social goods despite opposition from private interests that had to pay for them. Growth of industries invoked more environmental protection. Environmental policies expanded over the course of the last century in response to citizen advocacy of environmental qualities and opposition to their degradation, called 'environmentalism'. Hazards to public health and safety are issued in the 1950s, followed by pollution prevention within firms, as well as environmental quality in water, air, and soil in the 1970s. Squandering of the natural resources by prevention and recycling of waste are addressed during the 1980s, followed by interventions in economic activities. International environmental policies also emerged. Examples are reduction of the particulate matter that causes respiratory diseases, prevention of dumping of garbage from ships to sea, protection areas for migratory birds and other species, reduction of chlorofluorocarbons that destroy ozone high in the atmosphere with risks of cancers, reduction of carbon dioxide emissions for mitigation of climate change, enlarging of areas for protection of nature, and others. The scope of demands posed by environmentalists expanded. Within environmental regulations, mainly standards for pollution controls are prescribed in permits. A permit allows economic activities and protects them from liabilities. This mainstream policy is enriched with the evolutionary idea about enforcing innovations that prevent environmental degradation, and with the behavioural ideas about voluntary agreements with support of pollution charges, subsidies and emission trading (Krozer and Nentjes, 2006). Over the course of decades, environmental policies have been disseminated to nearly all countries, and all of these instruments have been used (Hsu et al., 2016).

By the mid-1980s, the idea about economic development in balance with environmental qualities emerged within environmentalism, focused on prevention of squandering natural resources and noxious compounds (Reijnders, 1984). This idea is extended toward balancing of economic, social and environmental interests, called sustainable development. It is launched by the International Union for Conservation of Nature (IUCN) in its World Conservation Strategy aiming to match the interests for environmental qualities in high-income with the demands for better living in lower income countries (McCormick, 1986). This idea is enriched with ideas about innovations by the United Nations World Commission on Environment and Development. The tone in its report "Our Common Future" is optimistic: "*Humanity has the ability to make development sustainable to ensure that it meets the needs of the present without compromising the ability of future generations to meet their own needs. The concept of sustainable development does imply limits - not absolute limits but limitations imposed by the present state of technology and social organization on environmental resources and by the ability of the biosphere to absorb the effects of human activities. But technology and social organization can be both managed and improved to make way for a new era of economic growth*" (WCED, 1987, p. 43). Dissemination of this concept shifted attention from the impacts of economic activities on the environment towards the process of creating and implementing activities that improve economic, well-being and environmental performances in addition to each other. Although this idea is commented as solely a re-branding the mainstream economic concept of welfare (Beckerman, 1994), the idea about the need for generating innovations for sustainable development is widely adopted. This idea about sustainable innovations in the sense of qualitative improvements across the value chain is used in the book.

The envisaged improvements invoked a search for performance indicators that cover the economy, well-being, and the environment. Economy is generally indicated by GDP in constant prices per capita, as well as by indicators for the distribution of incomes and expenditures of resources. Well-being is often assessed with the indicators for health and education which are converted into the Human Development Index (UNDP, 2023). This index is supposed to indicate capabilities of people in generating economic growth in free societies (Sen, 1999). Other indicators of well-being are also popularised. An example is the satisfaction with the quality of life compounded in the Happiness Index (Helliwell et al., 2023). Indicating environmental performance is found challenging as various dimensions of environmental qualities need to be covered. Therefore, a framework with indicators for the societal pressures on environmental qualities, the state of the environment, and the societal responses to the pressures is developed by the Organisation for Economic Cooperation and Development, an institution of high-income countries as members (OECD, 1993). More indicators are introduced regarding various uses of nature, known as ecosystem services. For the inclusion of all these in policymaking, experts recommended economic accounts in parallel to the social and environmental accounts (Stiglitz et al., 2009). Parallel accounts are used in this study.

While those parallel accounts are science-based, a global political consensus about priorities for policies is reached by countries in the United Nations Organization (UNO) in mid-2015. This consensus defined the Sustainable Development Goals (SDG) with performance targets to be attained by 2030 (United Nations, 2019). Seventeen SDGs are defined for monitoring. They are: no poverty, zero hunger, good health and well-being, quality education, gender equality, clean water and sanitation, affordable and clean energy, decent work and economic growth, industry innovations and infrastructure, reduced inequalities, sustainable cities and communities, responsible consumption and production, climate action, life below water, life on land, peace, justice and strong institutions, and partnership for the goals. Each goal is monitored with the indicators for environment, society, and governance, called ESG indicators. Similar indicators are used in this study. There is reason for optimism if the SDGs are considered as an international cooperation on sustainable development. There is also concern about the SDG as a 'paper tiger' of unfulfilled pledges.

This study shows experiences and possibilities for sustainable development based on several indicators for economy, well-being, and the environment across all countries. Focus is on trends in societies of populous countries rather than policies.

References

Aitken, A. (2019). *Measuring welfare beyond GDP*. National Institute for Economic Review No. 249.

Akerlof, G. A. (1970). The market for “lemons”: quality uncertainty and market mechanism. *The Quarterly Journal of Economics, 84*(3), 488–500.

Beckerman, W. (1994). “Sustainable Development” is it a useful concept? *Environmental Values, 3*(3), 191–209.

Chadeau, A. (1985). Measuring household activities: Some international comparisons. *The Review of Income and Wealth, 31*(3), 237–253.

Cohen, M. D., March, J. G., & Olsen, J. G. (1972). A garbage can model of organizational choice. *Administrative Science Quarterly, 17*(1), 1–25.

Cyert, R. M., March, J. G. ((1963) 1988). A behavioural theory of organizational objectives. In: R. M. Cyert (ed.), *The economic theory of organization and the firm*(pp. 125–150). New York: New York University Press.

Ehrlich, P. R., & Holdren, J. P. (1971). Impact of population growth. *Science, 171*(3977), 1212–1217.

Eurostat. (2023). Retrieved April 18, 2025, from https://ec.europa.eu/eurostat/data/database.

Gleick, P. H., & Cooley, H. (2021). Freshwater scarcity. *Annual Review of Environment and Resources, 46*, 319–348.

Griliches, Z. (1996). The discovery of the residual: A historical note. *Journal of Economic Literature, XXXIV*, 1324–1330.

Helliwell, J. F., Layard, R., Sachs, J. D., de Neve, J.-E., Aknin, L. B., & Wang, S. (2023). *World happiness report*. Sustainable Development Solutions Network.

Hoang, N. T., & Kanemoto, K. (2021). Mapping the deforestation footprint of nations reveals growing threat to tropical forests, *Nature Ecology & Evolution*, 5, 845–853.

Houghton, R. A., & Castanho, A. (2023). Annual emissions of carbon from land use, land-use change, and forestry from 1850 to 2020. *Earth System Science Data Discussions, 15*(2025–2054), 2023.

Hsu, A. et al. (2016). *Environmental performance index*. New Haven, CT: Yale University. www.epi.yale.edu.

Huijbrechts, M. A. J., Hellweg, S., Frischknecht, R., Hendriks, H. M., Hungerbuthler, K., & Hendriks, A. J. (2010). Cumulative energy demand as predictor for the environmental burden of commodity production. *Environmental Science & Technology, 44*(6), 2169–2196.

IEA. (2025). Retrieved February 10, 2025, from https://www.iea.org/data-and-statistics/data-explorers.

IMF. (2025). Retrieved February 10, 2025, from https://data.imf.org/?sk=4c514d48-b6ba-49ed-8ab9-52b0c1a0179b&sid=1409151240976.

Kennedy, R. (1968). Remarks at the University of Kansas, March 18, 1968, John F. Kennedy Presidential Library and Museum. Retrieved September 4, 2023, from https://www.jfklibrary.org/learn/about-jfk/the-kennedy-family/robert-f-kennedy/robert-f-kennedy-speeches/remarks-at-the-university-of-kansas-march-18-1968.

Kirzner, I. (1997). Entrepreneurial discovery and the competitive market process: An Austrian approach. *Journal of Economic Literature, 35*(1), 60–85.

Krozer, Y., & Nentjes, A. (2006). An essay on innovations for sustainable development. *Environmental Science, 3*(3), 163–174.

Lancaster, K. J. (1966). A new approach to consumer theory. *Journal of Political Economy, 74*(2), 132–157.

Leontief, W. (1973). National income, economic structure, and environmental externalities. In M. Moss (Ed.), *The measurement of economic and social performance*. National Bureau of Economic Research, pp 565–576. Retrieved February 2, 2025, from https://www.nber.org/books-and-chapters/measurement-economic-and-social-performance.

March, J. G., & Olsen, J. P. (1984). The new institutionalism: Organizational factors in political life. *The American Political Science Review, 78*(3), 734–749.

McCormick, J., (1986). The origins of the world conservation strategy. *Environmental Review, 10*(3) (Autumn, 1986), 177–187.

OECD. (1993). *OECD Core set of indicators for environmental performance reviews.* Organisation for Economic Cooperation and Development, Paris, OCDE/GD(93)179.

OECD. Retrieved October 10, 2023, from https://stats.oecd.org/.

Pinker, S. (2018). Enlightment now, the case for reason. Science, humanism and progress. Penguin Books, Random House.

Polanyi, K. (1957). *The great transformation.* The Beacon Press, Boston.

Qiu, L., He, J., Yue, C., Ciais, P., & Zhen, C. (2024). Substantial terrestrial carbon emissions from global expansion of impervious surface area. *Nature Communications, 15*, 6456.

Rathi, B. S., Kumar, P. S., & Vo, D. N. (2021). Critical review on hazardous pollutants in water environment: Occurrence, monitoring, fate, removal technologies and risk assessment. *Science of The Total Environment*, *797*(149134).

Reijnders, L. (1984). *Pleidooi voor een duurzame relatie met het milieu.* Van Gennep.

Richardson, K., Steffen, W., Lucht, W., Bendtsen, J., Cornell, S. E., Donges, J. F., Druke, M., Fetzer, I., Bala, G., von Bloh, W., Feulner, G., Fiedler, S., Gerten, D., Gleeson, T., Hofmann, M., Huiskamp, W., Kummu, M., Mohan, Ch., Nogues-Bravo, D., Petri, S., Porkka, M., Rahmstorf, S., Schaphoff, S., Thonicke, K., Tobian, A., Virkki, V., Wang-Erlandsson, L., Weber, L., Rockstrom, J. (2023). Earth beyond six of nine planetary boundaries. *Science Advances 9*(eadh2458), 1–16.

Rogner, H. -H. (2000). *Energy resources in UNDP* (p. 167). New York: World Energy Assessment.

Rosenberg, N. (1983). Learning by using. In: N. Rosenberg (ed.), *Inside the black box.* Cambridge University Press, pp. 120–140.

Rosling, H. (2018). *Factfulness.* Hodder & Stoughton.

Schumpeter, J. A. ((1939) 1989). *Business cycles* (4th ed., p. 59). Philadelphia: Porcupine Press.

Sen, A. K. (1999). *Development as freedom.* Oxford University Press.

Sen, A. (2009). *The idea of justice* (1st ed.). Penguin Books.

Smith, A. (1776, 1986). *Inquiry into the nature and causes of the wealth of nations*, Book IV, Chapter 8.49. Edition 1986. London: Penguin Classics.

Stiglitz, J. E., Sen, A., Fitoussi, J. -P. (2009). *Report by the commission on the measurement of economic performance and social progress.* http://www.stiglitz-sen-fitoussi.fr/documents/rapportanglais.pdf (2–12–2013).

Tirole, J. (2017). *Economics for the common good.* Princeton University Press.

UNDP. (2023). Retrieved February 19, 2023, from https://hdr.undp.org/data-center/human-development-index#/indicies/HDI.

UNEP. (2023). Retrieved Decenber 7, 2023, from https://www.unep.org/news-and-stories/story/cop15-ends-landmark-biodiversity-agreement.

United Nations. (2019). *The sustainable development goals.*

Veblen, T. (1892). *The theory of the leisure class.* Retrieved June 4, 2014, from http://www.gutenberg.org/files/833/833-h/833-h.htm.

WCED, World Commission on Environment and Development. (1987). *Our common future* (1st ed.). Oxford University Press.

World Bank. (2023). Retrieved November 11, 2023, from https://data.worldbank.org/.

Chapter 2
Ideologies in Practices

Economic thoughts about environmental qualities are presented. Ones that underline human domination of nature, labelled 'economists', cover the neo-Marxist and liberal ideas about exploitation of the natural resources with help of technologies and their substitution of capital and labour. The radical neo-liberal idea of transactional societies is assessed as a failure in meeting its objectives. The ideas that perceive parity of human with nature, called 'environmentalist', are also covered. They address the shortages of natural resources, degradation of sinks by pollution, unsustainable uses of land, and unfair distribution of access to nature. Their radical idea for fairness is critically assessed based on experiences across countries. An alternative pattern, referred to as green growth, or broad welfare, is discussed.

2.1 Introduction

Is economic growth and environmental quality compatible with the economist's ideas? An answer is relevant for two practical reasons, aside curiosity. One reason is better comprehension of decisions taken in social organisations, businesses, and in policymaking because economists take prominent positions in many hierarchies. Another reason is the use of economics as a tool for assessing behaviour in societies, thereby assessing societal changes in the future. The former reason refers to the economist's role as moral guides, which has prevailed for centuries until the late 1700s. During subsequent centuries of industrialization, economists in Europe and the USA focused on assessing behaviour considered as if it is natural science (Sedláček, 2011). While sermons are largely replaced by engineering of behaviour, morality remains important in the environmentalist thinking. Generally, the role taken by economists can be described as 'instrumentation of policies'. Therefore, economists construct theories that are assumed to work if validated by observations. Projecting behaviour with the theoretical models evolved into the cornerstone of

© The Author(s), under exclusive license to Springer Nature Switzerland AG 2025
Y. Krozer, *Economic Growth and the Environment*,
https://doi.org/10.1007/978-3-031-99181-3_2

economic studies (Acemoğlu, 2009). This instrumentation also plays a role in the environmental debates.

Economic moralism about the nature is briefly mentioned below, followed by the instrumental ideas in subsequent sections. The economic moralism about the nature is rooted in religions, spiritualities, and ideologies. These roots are shortly covered solely for presentation of the diversity in ethical considerations about the nature in a global perspective (Ferkiss, 1993), with support of studies on the European tradition (Leiss, 1993; Grober, 2012; Wolloch, 2017). Two ethical viewpoints are at odds across religions, spiritualities, and ideologies. In the Anthropocentric viewpoint, humans are perceived as superior to other species. The nature is supposed to serve people. From the Ecocentric viewpoint, humans are a species among all others. Both approaches encompass various ideas, which cannot be related to the conventional political schemes of 'left' versus 'right', and cultural divisions between 'conservatives' versus 'progressives'.

The Anthropocentric ethics are prevalent in all religions. It is the foundation of world creation in the monotheistic religions of Judaism, Christianity, and Islam, as well as in the pantheistic religions of Hinduism and in the Confucian spirituality. These religions together covered nearly 70% of the global population in the late 1990s. Only 7% of the global population adheres to the Buddhist ethics of reciprocity between humans and nature. The anthropocentric approach prevails in secular ideas, as well. It is dominant in liberalism that is preoccupied with individual freedoms from the late 1700s onward, as well as in Marxism that is focused on social actions from the late 1800s on, and in populism that pursues to unite all societal interests under the banner of national leadership from the early 1900s onward. These ideologies are adopted by 16% of the global population. About fourteen percent of global population adhere other ideas and religions (Pow research, 2023). The idea that people are entitled to rule nature is adopted by most self-conscious people in the world, as well as by self-esteem of most economists. Inter alia, the biosemiotics research shows self-consciousness and self-esteem among other animals, as well (Despret, 2022).

The Ecocentric viewpoint underlines a respect for nature that is considered the common good of all species, including the mankind. This is expressed on fringes of most religions, spiritualities, and ideologies. The Ecocentric approach can be found in the Zen-Buddhism in Japan from the 1100s on, as well as in the Christian gospel by Francis of Assisi (1181–1226) in Europe, which recently revived under the headings of sustainability by the Catholic Church in "Laudato Si" (Pope Francis, 2025). This viewpoint is also important in the humanist ideas of Spinosa (1632–1677), as well as in the ideologies of scientific discoveries in the period of Romantism during the early 1800s, and among the neo-Marxists dedicated to the ecological principle in the land use. Within those Ecocentric strings, several thoughts consider humans as subordinated to nature. Among others, it can be found in the animistic religions, ancient Jainism, Taoism, as well as modern Bahai religion, and in Anthroposophical spirituality. Political ideologies that embrace the Ecocentric ethics also range from the left-wing ecological anarchism to the right-wing contenders by the libertarian 'New Age', as well as in the Völkisch nationalism of the 'blut und boden' (*blood and soil*) as symbols of nature.

The Anthropocentric and Ecocentric ethics are reflected in the instrumental uses of economics, which are called 'weak sustainability' and 'strong sustainability', respectively. These perspectives are used for the introduction of economic thinking linked to economic growth and environmental qualities. Section 2.2 addresses the way economists comprehend sustainable development from those ethical perspectives. Section 2.3 is about economists' strings of thought from the perspective of weak sustainability. The consistency of their radical expression in the 'neo-liberalism' is assessed in Sect. 2.4. Section 2.5 covers the perspective on strong sustainability, mostly based on opinions in the United Kingdom (UK) and United States of America (USA). Section 2.6 addresses assumptions about social fairness in the environmentalist thinking. Section 2.7 discusses the consistency of a radical idea about fairness, which advocates for a decline in income in high-income countries in favour of low-income ones, called degrowth. Section 2.8 addresses possibilities for linking economic growth and environmental qualities. Section 2.9 concludes about the ideas.

2.2 Weak and Strong Sustainability

In this section, main instrumental ideas from the perspectives of 'weak sustainability' and 'strong sustainability' are introduced (Pearce, 1990). In addition, uses of these ideas in policies are interpreted. These interpretations aim to illustrate consequences of ethical viewpoints for decisions about uses of resources for value addition, which generate economic growth and environmental impacts.

'Weak sustainability' focuses on substitutions of the natural resources for man-made ones. Materials and energy would be reduced through technologies, considered as substitutions of the natural resources for man-made capital fixed in machines. Other possibilities are replacements of natural resources by labour in services and more valuable uses of the natural resources due to crafts, designs and other know-how. Mainstream economists consider maintaining availability of environmental qualities as transactional processes similar to any other transactions. Prices are assumed to drive such transactions. Many mainstream economists downplay environmental degradation on the argument that market prices truly reflect scarcities of the natural resources. Low prices are assumed to indicate low demand for environmental qualities, and if this demand is low, there is no need for concerns. These economists, called 'cornucopias', worry about distortions of market prices by policies rather than about environmental impacts.

Other mainstream economists argue that imperfect distribution of ownership of environmental qualities causes deficient transaction prices. Nature is assumed to be a common good. In order to resolve this problem of the common good, policies should put higher prices on the activities that cause degradation of environmental qualities, or introduce instruments for the privatisation of nature. Price instruments resolve issues in this economic thinking. For example, the idea is that higher water prices would save water, CO_2 tax would invoke renewable energy, subsidies for environmental technologies would reduce air pollution and the pricing of species would foster biodiversity. Regarding deficient market prices, authorities enforce price instruments. For example, the lack of ownership for air and climate invoked the instrument of emission permits distributed among polluters, with trading of SO_2 and NO_x in the USA, respectively emission trading of CO_2 in the EU28, China and other countries. These price instruments would enhance sustainable development. Based on this argument, these mainstream economists advocate the shadow pricing of environmental degradation with taxation of specific impact, thereby correction of market deficiencies (Markandya & Pavan, 1999).

From this economic perspective, policy interventions are justified when they prevent losses related to natural resources, public health, and other common goods. When assessing damages to environmental quality, environmental impacts in physical terms are converted into economic losses in the monetary terms. Several valuation methods are employed for this purpose. They are usually divided into the revealed preferences through various assessment methods for harms, and the stated preferences using willingness to pay and willingness to accept. Given that the monetary values of damages and willingness are difficult to verify, if possible, all those methods are contentious. Despite these imperfections and disputable outcomes, such economic assessments of damages caused by environmental degradation provide insightful results for decision making, even though the results are disputable. For example, the value of environmental damages can be subtracted from the GDP for the assessments of countries performances taking into account these damages. The World Bank's correction of GDP refers to Net National Income (NNI). Comparison of GDP and NNI shows whether there has been progress towards sustainable development. In addition, 'Broad money' is estimated, which shows total monetary transfers of goods and the financial transfers without coverage by goods. These financial transfers cover rents from assets, liquidity operations, and accounts related to corruption. Illustrative estimates of the global 'Broad money', GDP, and Net National Income by the World Bank are shown in Graph 2.1. They are indexed from 1990 to 2015 (1990 = 100).

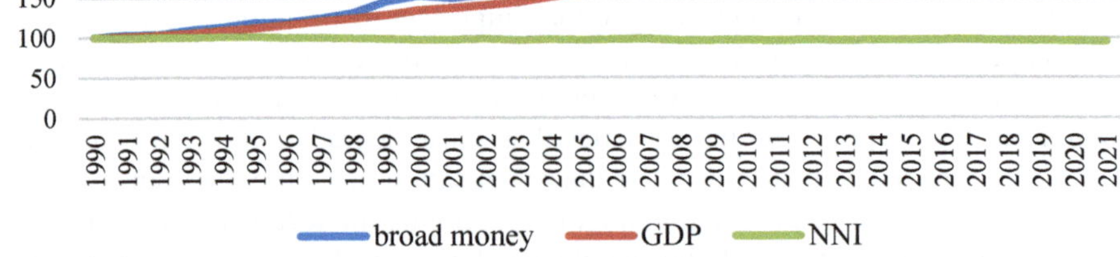

Graph 2.1 Indexed global GDP, Broad money and Net National Incomes in the World Bank accounts

These estimates show that the global GDP more than doubled from 1990 to 2015 while the Broad Money nearly quadrupled. The differences between GDP and Broad Money is equivalent to USD 14 trillion in 2015. For example, broad money increased 28 times during that period in China, which was mainly driven by rents from loans to other states, as well as domestic, regional governments and firms much allocated in construction. This way the financial business is boosted. It increased 11 times in Bangladesh, 8 times in Brazil, and 2 times in the USA. Although China is often perceived as the manufacturing hub, its financial and construction businesses enlarged.

Meanwhile, global Net National Income declined compared to GDP in 2015 by USD 13 trillion. Larger expenditures in the prevention of environmental damage would have been more efficient. That estimate of the Net National Income by the World Bank is based on corrections of the countries' GDP. These corrections cover depletion of energy, forests and minerals, damages caused by air pollutants and CO_2 emission prices at USD 40 per ton. Such estimates make the monetary consequences of environmental degradation tangible, which is useful for decisions about expenditures and regulations. However, these accounts underestimate the monetary losses of damages as polluting chemicals, loss of biodiversity and other environmental impacts are neglected. The shadow prices of assessments are also questionable. For example, the World Bank uses 40 USD per ton CO_2 as the unit costs of damage for NNI, while the International Monetary Fund (IMF) uses the range of USD 30–70 USD per ton CO_2 (Lagarde & Gaspar, 2019), and a comprehensive literature review shows the damage costs of USD 5 to 800 per ton CO_2 with the median costs of USD 104 per ton CO_2 (Tol, 2005). Moreover, it takes time to assess the monetary damages, which implies less opportunities for the damage prevention. Converting damages into money is also prone to mistakes and manipulation. An example is the declining global costs of damage to forestry despite ongoing deforestation, or negative damage costs of particulates in Brazil despite larger fuel use, and declining costs of damages in Nigeria and Egypt despite negligibly improved performances. When methods invoke discussions, attention is diverted from the damages. Such methods can improve in the future, but present uses cause biased decisions.

Economists that are considered advocates of the idea about 'strong sustainability' dispute if substitutions of the natural resource for man-made ones flexibly respond to prices. Even if high prices of natural resources encourage their substitution for man-made capital due to uses of technologies that reduce materials and energy per income, the results are usually disappointing. It is because the improvements saturate as the uses of materials and energy decline, and because the uses of natural resources increase in total as incomes grow due to material and energy savings, though the uses decrease per income. The latter is so called rebound effect of Jevon effect (Reijnders, 2021). In addition, the mainstream idea of substitution addresses changes in production, but consumption is largely based on the combinations of products with services. Consumption in growing economies usually adds product-services combinations rather than replace them. For example, it is observed that renewable energy is added to fossil fuels, whereas replacement of fossil fuels is rare. Many durable goods remain in place combined with new services, or purposed for new activities. Television in addition to radio is an example.

A more fundamental environmentalist opinions object the ideas about ownership of nature based on the argument that elements of nature are interlinked. For example, loss of a predator species destabilises an ecosystem by overgrazing entailing erosion of soils. In this argumentation, nature as a whole is a common good not only its elements, whereas substitutions of its elements hardly reduce impacts, and can accelerate degradation of nature. The elements of nature can be distinguished but not separated. Environmental qualities are considered a system to be maintained. Therefore, it is argued, human behaviour should adapt to the limits posed by carrying capacities of nature. For this adaptation, social and regulatory norms are advocated based on the precautionary approaches, meaning the norms purposed to prevent damages. Such norms can be targets for reducing environmental impacts. An example in climate change is the global policy target for reducing CO_2 emissions to achieve a maximum global temperature increase of 1.5 °C. Distance-to-target methods in environmental policies, invented by the National Environmental Bureau in the Netherlands in the mid-1980s (RIVM, 1987), became popular concepts in many policies.

Those targets alone can soothe conscience, but delay action. When costs are attached to the policy targets, this kind of target costing can support innovations. The costing can refer to hypothetical prices through fees and taxes. When the unit costs of environmental technologies are linked to the demanded targets, firms' cost-effective performance can be assessed in a way similar to the conventional target costing that is used in businesses and households (Krozer, 1990). Another possibility is putting limits on environmental impacts. Herewith, noxious compounds are converted into indexes for acidification, toxicity, and other environmental impacts, which can be used to assess performance in production and consumption. Such methods are popularised in life cycle assessments of products (UNEP, 2020a, 2020b). They improve understanding of the impacts in value chains, but deficient data and deliberations about various impacts can confuse decision making, which demotivates actions. Prices of environmental damages linked to those indexes do provide insightful results about the costs of environmental damages when consuming products (Steen, 1999). Advocates of 'strong sustainability' also pursue changes in individual and social behaviour that are tuned to the hypothesised limits of natural resources on Earth, known as the carrying capacity of the environment. These changes can be enhanced through certifications of consumption that are assumed to meet that carrying capacity. The certifications are insightful for the consumer purchases.

This study inclines towards strong sustainability, while the price instruments are considered essential for maintaining the availability of environmental qualities.

2.3 Economist Perspectives

Economists' ideas about environmental qualities, largely reflect changes in the business composition of economies. Uses of land were considered essential for economic activities until the late 1700s when most activities were based on agricultural production that depended on land. As industry expanded during the 1800s, economists turned their attention from the natural resources to the man-made resources of capital and labour. Next shift in economists' attention followed during the 1900s when man-made knowledge expanded for use in services. Present attention to the 'experience' economy reflects the importance of media. Communication through media would replace research and development of products by cheaper nudging with advertising (Pine and Gilmore, 1998). In effect, uses of the natural resources for value added declined in the course of last centuries as economies in most countries evolved from the material-intensive activities in agriculture and industry towards material-extensive services that use much labour for generating incomes. It does not mean that degradation of environmental qualities is resolved because the material-intensive activities keep growing though slower that the material-extensive ones. It does imply that many economists have lost interest in environmental issues. Insofar environmental qualities are considered, mainstream economists address the productive uses of natural resources for economic growth. It is mainly about cheap availability of fuels and minerals for economic activities.

A brief introduction to the main concepts in economic thinking presented in this section is purposed to help understand economic debates about environmental qualities, and for the comprehension and justification of objections to these debates from the environmentalist perspective. The introduction of physiocratic and mercantile principles aims to pinpoint different starting points in economic debates. Thereafter, the Marxist and liberal ideas about technology for the uses of natural resources during the 1800s are introduced. These ideas are diversified into several strings of thoughts during the last century. All those strings are also touched with regard to environmental qualities as an illustration of the diversity in economic thinking without exegesis of any specific string of thought. Mainly, the European and North American ideas are covered as they dominate economic science, though this dominance has declined during the 2000s.

Compared to many religions, economists thinking is on a recent date. Modern economic theory is rooted in agricultural activities that depend on land resources. After religious wars that decimated its population in Europe, agricultural production expanded in the early 1700s. The use of land was believed to be the foundation for economic circulation, which means the source of all value creation. According to Francois de Quesnay (1694–1774), who was a leading economist of the 1700s, farmers generated food, which was consumed by the craftsmen whose labour had delivered tools to farmers, while the craftsmen obtained capital from nobility in exchange for services. In this 'Physiocratic' model of economic circulation used for the national financial accounting, every transaction adds value to cover the costs of suppliers and own needs, while all transactions ultimately depend on the exhaustible land, which is synonymous with natural resources. This idea was disputed by the 'Mercantilist' economists, who argued that all value added is obtained through trade. In this idea, trade provides benefits to all parties involved in transactions because products can be supplied at lower prices due to specializations in production. In turn, the specialisations enable to generate various prices and qualities, thereby, provide ample opportunities for trade (Rothbard, 1995). Economic theories in subsequent three centuries evolved along those lines. Economists were preoccupied with uses of resources, not necessarily the natural ones, or with the traded commodities on the stock exchange founded in the USA in the 1790s, and trades with communication technologies on the Nasdaq from the 1970s onward.

In the wake of industrialization, attention to nature declined during the 1800s. Adam Smith, an adept of the Physiocratic viewpoint, remorsefully expressed the loss of rural life in the following words. "*The beauty of the country besides, the pleasure of a country life, the tranquillity of mind which it promises, and wherever the injustice of human laws does not disturb it, the independency which it really affords, have charms that more or less attract everybody; and as to cultivate the ground was the original destination of man, so in every stage of his existence he seems to retain a predilection for this primitive employment*" (Smith, 1986). In his view, industrialization was driven by the self-interest of entrepreneurs. Their self-interest drove competition for profits. This competition has generated better agricultural methods, division of tasks in manufacturing, specialisation in financing, and other changes that have enabled to decrease cost per unit of product. The unit cost is reduced by buying raw materials extracted from natural resources in colonies abroad. Lower unit costs enable to decrease prices in domestic markets and increase profits. In that idea, larger profits enable the accumulation of man-made capital for economic growth. Meanwhile, the mercantile thinking addressed the purchasers' demands. These demands are assumed to express a rational selection of qualities based on individual preferences, called utilities. The capital-based economy in the USA and England in the 1800s provoked rival sets of ideas that persisted throughout the last century until present. They are often branded as the socialist ideas, which oppose capitalism, and the liberal ones, which embrace capitalism, while many nuances within each of them can be found. Below, these thoughts are briefly discussed, mainly with respect to environmental qualities. Those ideas are linked to practices.

The socialist ideas that oppose the capitalist mode of production usually refer to the Marx theory on extraction of value from labour for accumulation of capital. The natural resources were considered free gifts of nature to be used through technologies consolidated in machines. Technologies are perceived as pinnacles of human creativity. In opposition to the capitalist competition, the states are supposed to determine prices and qualities of resources. As the natural resources played a minor role in the Marx theory, these socialist states hardly cared about environmental qualities. In effect, these states generated material-intensive, polluting economies (Zacharova, 2017). Their high material-intensity persisted in Russia, China and other former socialist states into the twenty first century. The importance of technologies for processing of natural resources in economies is acknowledged in theorising about competition linked to the neo-Marxist tradition. Attention to innovations, understood as sales and uses of novel technologies for profits, triggered a string of thoughts labelled as 'evolutionary' or 'modern' economic theory. Innovations are considered drivers of higher productivity as they replace incumbent, less productive activities. New firms, the innovators, would be more productive due to better resource utilization through development and use of the practical knowledge (know-how) in businesses. Know-how would create technology for larger scale production, which would reduce unit costs of products. It is argued that economies of scale would increase productivity, but eventually lock businesses into a costly fixation of obsolete technologies, followed by economic stagnation (Arthur, 1989). Changes in fixed patterns of technologies would require state interventions through regulations and financing of innovations (Romer, 1994). This idea is popularised as the 'mission-oriented policy' (Mazzucato, 2017). Therefore, economic growth would require skilled populations with abundant know-how, along with state interventions aimed at replacing incumbents by innovators.

These ideas are also applied in environmental policies. An argument has gained popularity that these policies would lead to technological lock-in through the enforcement of rigid regulations driven by policy objectives on short term. This would lead to end-of-pipe technologies for pollution control instead of encouraging process-integrated technologies for pollution prevention (Driel and Krozer, 1988); an example is incinerating waste instead of recycling. Resolving this lock-in would need policies dedicated to the'technology forcing' in favour of process-integrated, so called 'cleaner technologies' (Kemp, 1995). An array of policy instruments for interventions is purposed to enhance cleaner technologies for various environmental issues. Deliberated uses of these instruments are labelled as the transition management (Arentsen, 2001). Successful policies for cleaner technologies are support of wind and solar power technologies for decreases of the carbon-intensive resources, which prevent costly end-of-pipe technologies for CO_2-capture.

Liberal economists, meanwhile, have addressed price competition. Their focus is on capital and labour resources, whereas natural resources are usually ignored because assumed hardly relevant in economic activities. Low relevance is justified by low and declining share of the costs of natural in value addition. As John Stuart Mill, a leading liberal economist and philosopher of the early 1800s, observed: "*But the crude material generally forms so small a portion of the total cost, that any tendency which may exist to a progressive increase in that single item, is much over-balanced by the diminution continually taking place in all the other elements; to which diminution it is impossible at present to assign any limit*" (Mill, (1848), 1985:64). Liberal economists were concerned about the overexploitation of the natural resources because of the declining prices. This would hinder the economy. As wood was costly, the use of coal expanded during the economic boom in the mid-1800s in England. It invoked predictions about the exhaustion of coal. Among leading experts and politicians, William Stanley Jevons asserted that more efficient production and uses of coal were annulled by larger uses (Sorrell, 2009). This idea, called a rebound effect or Jevons effect, is widely observed. For example, an increasing efficiency of car engines can reduce fuel use and costs per travel distance, but this reduction also enhances driving, which results in larger fuel use in total.

In the mainstream economic thinking, the natural resources remain available for economic growth as long as they are replaced for man-made resources at a faster rate than economic growth (Solow, 1973). This replacement is observed as the 'dematerialization' of economies. Pollution is also addressed. Insufficient liability for pollution would cause harm to the interests unrelated to the pollution source because these polluters would have no interest in costly prevention of these external effects. Therefore, taxes on polluters and liabilities for damage with compensations for victims are recommended. These instruments would accommodate the impacts of harms in the prices of transactions, which would prevent damages (Pigou, 1920). This argument is extended to all common good that cannot be distributed as property rights. Given that the deficient distribution of property rights cause low market prices of environmental qualities, authorities would need to enforce that distribution, or payments for these qualities (Baumol and Oates, 1975). The latter idea is vested in environmental policies as the 'polluter pays principle'. With regard to this principle, economists usually recommend taxes that reflect the costs and the benefits of preventing environmental degradation. However, authorities usually enforce permits because polluters oppose these price instruments.

Another string of liberal economic ideas emerged during economic crisis of the 1930s. While the mainstream liberal economists recommended austerity other economists pinpointed at deficient demands. The deficient demands could be countered by the investments in public works on roads, sanitation and other infrastructure driven by the states. Such investments would not undermine competition because those public goods are used by many interests for generation of private incomes. Incomes from capital, called rents, due to larger demands, and more payments to employees due to employment would increase circulation of money, thereby outweigh the costs of those investments (Keynes, 1936). Application of this theory in the USA before the World War II from 1939 to 1945 (WW2)) cushioned the economic crisis, indeed. This idea is embraced by so called neo-Keynesian and post-Keynesian scholars and policies in many countries after WW2. Public investments in social securities, literacy, and other attributes of well-being created welfare states while investments in roads, power grid, sanitation, waste management, environment protection, and other means of using natural resources generated economic infrastructure.

In that train of thoughts, continuous public investments would be needed. Investments in innovations would generate economic expansion followed by crises. When innovations disseminate business activities would boom, followed by a decline of business when the dissemination would saturate. It is when policies need to invoke innovations through tougher demands along with support of research and development (R&D). These effects of innovations on economies are indicated by the income growth above productivity of labour (Solow, 1957). It is also argued that the supplies of high-value goods generate economic growth, not per se the cost reduction as assumed in the mainstream economics. For high-value goods, higher social capabilities in innovating are needed, which require larger public expenditures in education, care, culture and other social interests (Helpman, 2004). Those productivity swings are reflected in demands for environmental qualities. The environmentalist demands are loud during economic booms and weaken during slumps when the economic arguments gain attention.

That focus on the demand side of economic activities invoked attentions for behaviour of individuals, groups and institutions. Behavioural, groups arrangements and policy incentives influence consumer behaviour, which implies that policy instruments invoke behavioural changes (Thaler & Susskind, 2008). It is also underpinned that individuals and groups follow patterns and group interests vested in the past rather than pursue risky changes unless perceived unavoidable (Kahneman, 2011). With respect to environmental qualities, it is argued that the common goods of nature are overused when private interest is allowed to act at the cost of social interests, so called free riding. This 'tragedy of commons' would persist as long as free-riding of private interests is not corrected by an authority (Hardin, 1968). Other behavioural economists argued that collective arrangements that enshrine cultural norms in the communities prevent the overuse of common goods. These collective agreements usher moral codes for restriction of free riding, and social agreements for protection of environmental qualities (Ostrom, 1998), but such arrangements can impede changes in economies and often turn into bureaucratic regulations (Barbier, 2011).

That advocacy for policy interventions during the second half of the 1900s invoked a counter-reaction, labelled as neo-classical economics. These neo-classical opponents of the state interventions referred to the theorizing during the late 1800s about resources as divisible and replaceable if prices reflect scarcities in markets. This idea of perfect competition presents economies as auctions, where all entrepreneurs instantly match prices and quantities of purchases. When capital and labour flexibly respond to prices, the lowest unit costs of all resources are achieved, called the Pareto optimum. In order to achieve optimal results, the neo-classic economists recommend flexible substitutions of capital and labour through deregulations of collective ownerships and securities in labour, along with securing incomes from capital through the monetary policies of low inflation. That idea evolved into the neo-liberal advocacy of negotiations between individuals about the individual preferences instead of the state interventions. By the 1950s, the neo-liberal ideal of a transactional society was launched as the political ideal (Hayek, 2005). Price substitution became the basis for models of economic growth. Economic growth would be driven by the replacement of labour by capital, while capital would grow when people could gain access to capital transactions through lower interest rates. By the early 2000s, the idea of transactional societies instead of regulations by authorities has gained popularity across countries.

In this neo-classic theorising, environmental issue would be resolved if free transactions between all interests would be allowed. Such policies would enable individual polluters and harmed interests to reach agreements about payments for pollution prevention at maximum mutual benefit. Whether polluters pay or obtain payments for pollution reduction is assumed negotiateable as the agreements are supposed to deliver optimal social benefit (Coase, 1963). In line with this ideal, environmental policies based on the ‘polluters pay’ principle are turned into ‘self-regulation’ with gentlemen’s agreements between businesses and environmental policies about goals and means. Self-regulation would enable polluters to avoid regulatory payments for environmental harms. However, self-regulation usually fails when public and private interests collide because private negotiations about the common good of environmental qualities are laborious and results cause uncertainties. Scarce successes in the self-regulations were achieved when a few dominant private interests could convince and force other interests to adopt their solution. A few examples are substitution of chlorofluorohydrocarbons (CFC’s) that breaks down ozone layers high in atmosphere for hydrofluorohydrocarbons (HFC), replacement of phosphate in washing powder, and polycarbonate plastic bottles for glass bottles.

The neo-classic economists also argued that scarcities of the natural resources would trigger higher market prices which would invoke innovations that substitute incumbent interests in technologies. From this perspective, transactions between interests that are free in pursuing self-interest would establish prices for technologies that generate socially optimal allocation of natural resources (Nordhaus, 1973). This idea of a ‘market pull’ in innovations for optimal allocation of resources remains popular, although experiences show that innovations are usually driven by entrepreneurs that generate know-how (Mowery & Rosenberg, 1979). The market-pull idea of the neo-classic economists implies that innovations can be served on demand if the particular demand is sufficiently strong to alter prices. In this train of thought, technologies change toward low-impact on the environment if sufficient demands are generated. This implies that polluting technologies emerge because demands for environmental qualities are low. In this idea, scarcities of natural resources and impacts on environmental qualities can be resolved when new technologies are demanded, referred to as eco-modernism. Examples of such eco-modern technological proposal are mineral exploitation in deep sea and cosmos because of costly exploitation of available reserves, and geoengineering of climate when the demands for mitigation of climate change are sufficiently strong. While this idea of technological solution to environmental problems is embraced in policies, it is also criticised as a pathway to the totalitarian rule by a class of wealthy technocrats that earn on innovations without ethical considerations (Riemens, 2024).

Economic theories pay little attention to environmental qualities and evolve toward a denial of environmental degradation in the neo-liberal train of thoughts. Regarding this idea, animosity of environmentalists towards economic theories is not surprising.

2.4 Neo-Liberal Economics Assessed

It is assessed if the neo-liberal idea delivered results in line with its expectations. If the objectives of neo-liberal ideas about the transactional societies were successfully applied, it is reasonable to expect that the eco-modernist ideas about transactions with technologies also work toward optimal allocation of scarce resources. However, if the applications of neo-liberal ideas failed, transactions in technological change based on prices should be rejected. The expected results of the neo-liberal policies and achieved ones are being compared.

Main objectives of the neo-liberal policies were enhancing the economic growth of the countries that adopted these ideas. This would evolve along with faster income generation in lower income countries due to their low costs of labour. Low-cost labour would attract foreign investments for growth, known as a 'trickle-down effect'. In addition, lower public spendings and larger income disparities within countries would motivate people to work harder, which would increase labour productivity (Springer et al., 2016). Main means to achieve these objectives were the abolishment of the social securities, privatisation of public goods, along with transactions between citizens instead of regulations, and law and order with regard to deviant behaviour (Deeming, 2017). The 1980s saw the rise of neo-liberal policies in the USA, UK, and a few other Anglo-Saxon nations. During the subsequent decades, the neo-liberal policies pursued transactional societies worldwide while the policies aiming at the collective interests were tempered, being assumed inefficient. Various political parties, including conservatives and social-democrats of the 'New Left', adopted the idea that the transactions between individuals through markets should be prioritised because state interventions would cause inefficient allocation of scarce resources. In the 1990s, these policies were also adopted by most states whose economies were rooted in the state directives, called socialist and communist countries as the Soviet Union, China and India, among others. The neo-liberal policies prevailed during the 2000s in most countries and in several institutions of the United Nations (UN) until the financial crisis in 2008. This is followed by an economic recession in most high-income countries, and shifts to the populist leaderships in Italy, Hungary, Turkey, and other countries during the 2010s. Regarding the dissemination of the neo-liberal policies across the world for nearly three decades, several objectives could have been achieved. This question if the neoliberal policies deliver in line with their objective is answered with regards to higher economic growth, 'trickle down' of income across and within countries, the shift from public transactions to private ones, and the uses of capital by the middle class. Therefore, statistical data on the global scale and in the focus countries in the period 1990–2015 are used. All monetary data are in constant USD of 2015.

Global economic growth was not boosted by the neo-liberal policies. On the contrary, the growth rate decreased from 2.2% annual average between 1960 and 1989 to 1.7% between 1990 and 2015. That decrease is observed despite booming businesses in information and communication technologies from the 1980s onwards. While global income growth slowed down, growth rates diverged across countries, but not in favour of the champions of neo-liberal ideas. The growth rates decreased in high-income countries such as the USA, Japan, and the EU, which were the main promoters of the neoliberal idea, and they increased in mid-income and low-income countries. Particularly, high growth rates are experienced in the lower income countries that turned their economies from the state directives to market transactions as in China and Ethiopia. Faster economic growth is also observed in the mixed state-market economies that encouraged entrepreneurship as in India and Vietnam. Azerbaijan, Equatorial Guinea and a few other oil producing economies also grew fast due to fuel exports during high fuel prices after 2004. However, economic stability decreased because the growth rates fluctuated more across the focus countries, measured by the increasing standard deviations of growth rates from 1990 to 2015. Particularly, strong fluctuations are observed in high-income fuel exporting countries as Qatar and United Arab Emirates (UAE), in lower income countries that shifted from the state-planning to market-economies after the collapse of Soviet Union, as well as in low-income Haiti, Zimbabwe and other countries that abolished, or released dictatorships. Economic growth accelerated when governance turned away from dictatorships toward more freedom in businesses, press, and political organisations. It confirms the finding that dictatorships impede economic growth (Papaioannou and Luiten van Zanten, 2005). Economic growth is boosted in the countries that overturned the dictatorships, but not in the countries that championed the neo-liberal policies.

A 'trickle down' effect between high-income countries and lower income ones is observed. From 1990 to 2020, high-income countries saw the most significant decline in their economic share compared to previous decades. This can be attributed to the neo-liberal policies. As a result, high-income countries lost nearly 20% of their share in global income, while mid-income countries gained nearly the same amount, and low-income ones gained a bit. Graph 2.2 shows the total GDP of all high-, mid-, and low-income countries from 1990 to 2015. The higher share of lower income countries in the global income was mainly generated through the domestic efforts, whereas the importance attached by the neo-liberal policies to foreign investments is overstated. A modest role of foreign investments in economic growth is observed though relevant in several knowledge-intensive businesses as electronics. Firstly, the growth of global foreign investments was limited and their share in all countries' investments was small. The annual global average of foreign investments in focus countries has been rarely above 4% of all investments throughout that period, while the investments measured by global savings that resemble investments varied from 20 to 40% of GDP. Second, foreign investments rarely enhanced GDP directly as their growth rates did not evolve synchronic with the GDP growth rates. Only a few low-income countries could have benefited from larger foreign investments, as Ethiopia and Botswana. Foreign investments were significant for international operating businesses and could have offset declines in domestic businesses, but they were not the drivers of GDP growth. The importance of shifting from state-driven governances to market-based ones was greater. Deep recessions after these shifts in governance preceded the elevation of about billion people from poverty to moderate income.

The privatization of public activities would foster entrepreneurship and would discipline labour. Tax shifts from the capital incomes to labour incomes would support this. This privatisation idea is partially realised measured by the global expenditures, products, and income. They are equivalents by definition on the global scale and reasonably balanced annually by individual countries. Graph 2.3 shows the share of public and private expenditures in the global GDP. Global public expenditures are presented in total. Global private expenditures are divided into three categories: capital income from rents on the natural resources, all other capital incomes, and labour incomes. Yearly averages from 1990–1995 and 2010–2015 are shown, which

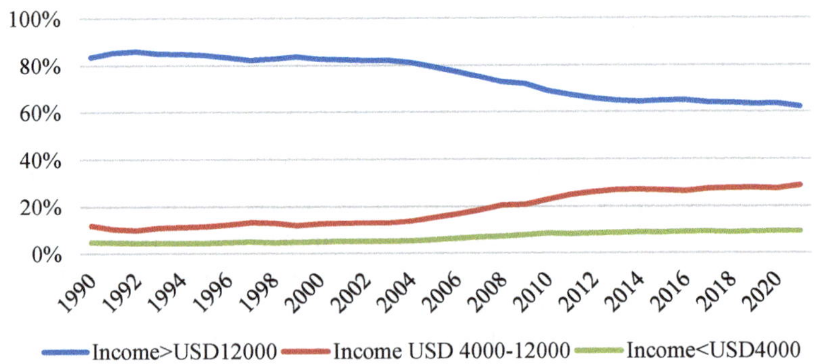

Graph 2.2 Shares high, mid and low income countries in global GDP

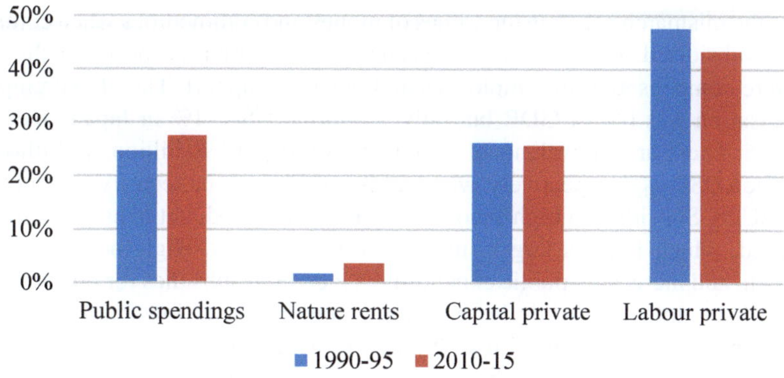

Graph 2.3 Share of public and private expenditures in the global GDP (5 years averages)

show the periods of initial neo-liberal policies, respectively the saturation period. All calculations are made using data from the World Bank.

Public expenditures have increased globally, contrary to the privatization objective of the neo-liberal policies. Their shares in the global GDP increased from an average of 25% in the early 1990s to 27% in the mid-2010s, which means that private expenditure declined from 75 to 73% of the global GDP. Public expenditures increased despite the shifts from state-driven economies to market-based ones in Russia, China, and many other countries. They increased in most countries, even in the USA and the UK which initiated and promoted the neo-liberal policies. During the early 1990s, high-income countries promoted privatisation while their public expenditures in GDP were nearly twice higher and increased faster than the shares in lower income countries with the public expenditures usually below 20% of GDP. These differences remained unchanged two decades later. For example, public expenditures in the UK in 2015 were 38% of GDP, growing by 0.8% annual average during 1990–2015 compared to India with 15% and 0.04%, respectively. The privatization was successful in countries that shifted from state-driven to market-based economies where the shares of private expenditures decline from more than 90% of GDP to about one third of that. Otherwise, the privatisation ideal failed.

The purpose of the largest public expenditures is assessed for the period 2005–2015 because earlier data is deficient. The main purpose were subsidies for businesses. With the exception of missing data on China and Nigeria, global subsidies in total covered about 40% of global public expenditures in 2015 while 60% were investments. Subsidies were particularly high in high-income countries. In 2015, subsidies in the USA covered 61% of public expenditures, in Japan 67%, and 48% in the EU28, and they increased annually from 2005 to 2015. Moreover, these subsidies increased during the neo-liberal policies despite a popularised phrase that 'bad money drives out good money', meaning that subsidies undermine entrepreneurial earnings (Mellor, 2019). This phrase against subsidies refers to the nineteenth century warning against the mismatch between the values of money and commodities when commodities are subsidised, known as the Gresham law. The main purposes of the subsidies were compensation for employees and business support. The global employee compensation was 6% of GDP, but only 2% in the USA, 1% in Japan, and 6% in the EU28. These are equivalents of an annual average of 390 billion, 45 billion, and 740 billion USD_{2015}, respectively, which illustrate high social security for employees in the EU28. Subsidies in high-income countries increased, but ones for employees decreased, which implies larger subsidies for businesses. High-income countries with high, and increasing public expenditures increased subsidies for businesses and reduced for employees, while lower income countries with low, hardly increasing public expenditures subsidised mainly employees. Higher subsidies for businesses and lower for employees in high-income countries did not increase their economic growth, but inflamed social discontent about declining welfare, and ultimately about democracy.

Private expenditures in global GDP remained similar in total, but their composition has changed. Private expenditures on natural resources, which are equivalents of the rents on natural resources, have gone up. They were only a few percent of GDP in the early 1990s, and doubled in the mid-2010s when average prices of oil and gas tripled while fuel consumption hardly declined. As a result of these price hikes, the rents on natural resources converged across countries to 4–5% of GDP during the 2000s, while they were twice higher in Kuwait, Iraq, Oman, and other oil-exporting countries. The share of global capital expenditures, equivalent of the capital income, in global GDP somewhat increase. It was about 26% of all private expenditures during the period of low fuel prices from 1990 to 2004 and high fuel prices from 2005 to 2015. This illustrates that high prices of natural resources do not hinder growth of capital, which implies that the mimicking high market prices through high taxes on natural resources does not hinder business. Contrary to larger capital expenditures, private expenditures on labour, equivalent to labour income, decreased globally from 48% in the early 1990s to 43% in the mid-2010s. This share declined mainly in high-income countries after the financial crisis in 2008. It is when social discontent about the income loss invoked political changes for the populist rulings. Contrary to high-income countries, the share of private expenditures dedicated to labour slowly increased in lower income countries.

An objective of neo-liberal policies was to motivate workers through larger income disparities. Insofar data is available and reliable, the disparities of incomes decreased in most focus countries, but increase in the USA and China, which were the two largest economies by 2025. This is measured by the Gini coefficients which show the share of the ascending ten percent income in total income of a country from 0 for completely equal incomes to 1 for completely unequal ones. Meanwhile, the middle incomes declined while the highest and lowest ones increased, if measured by 10% higher income compared to 40% mid-income and 50% lowest income in GDP (Chancel, 2020a). Across all countries and income classes, fastest income growth is reached by the highest income classes, whereas declines are experienced by the middle classes in high-income countries, and slow growth of the middle class and low-income class in low-income ones (Milanovic, 2011). In effect, poverty globally has declined, measured by the percentage of people living under USD 6.85 a day, which is a yardstick provided by the World Bank. While poverty increased in many high-income countries where the percentage of poverty rarely exceeded 5% of the population, poverty decreased in lower income countries where the percentages of poverty were several times higher. Mitigating poverty through social security is also improved in most countries, when measured by the increasing contributions of employers and employees to social security, and growing receipts of remittance in low-income countries. However, differences in social security across high-income countries increased. For example, social security is aggravated in the USA and the UK, while it is improved in France and Germany. Apparently, policies in many countries protected the lowest incomes against deprivation pursued by the neo-liberal policies in order to foster labour discipline.

As the neo-liberal economics failed to fulfil its promises, the idea of strong leadership that unifies all societal interests for resolving issues gained popularity. Present dissemination of populism could be hypothesised as a political reaction to that neo-liberal failure. This populism seeks leadership of wealthy individuals in businesses rather than the military leadership as in Italy, Spain, Germany,and other countries during the first half of the 1900s. Indeed, global concentration of capital within and across countries increased as more incomes are generated from the ownership of assets than from labour (Piketty, 2014). That concentration of wealth is observed as 1% top incomes within GDP grew fast in the USA, France, China and South Africa between mid-1980s to mid-2000s (Roser, 2023). These top incomes accrued more assets, which is observed across countries. An illustration of it is that 410 billionaires with assets above USD 5 billion possessed nearly USD 7.5 trillion in 2021, which represents 2% of all global wealth. Most multi-billionaires are found in the USA, China, India, and Russia. Meanwhile, the EU28 with larger GDP than China has fewer multi-billionaires. Concentration of wealth above 3% of all country's wealth is found in high-income Sweden, mid-income Mexico, as well as low-income India, Nigeria, and South Africa. This estimate based on the Bloomberg data for private wealth (Bloomberg, 2023), and on the Credit Suisse data for the countries' wealth (Credit Suisse, 2022) shows the concentration of capital irrespective of countries income per capita. The neoliberal policies have driven the concentration of wealth, and political power into the hands of oligarchs. It reminds us of the wealth and power of the nobility shortly before World War I (1914–1918).

Given those failures, the neo-liberal ideas about transactional societies do not work in practice. Similar holds true for the eco-modernist ideas. As the interactions between decision makers in businesses and politics intensify, risky technologies are not expressed in higher market prices of insurances, neither in regulations. Instead, public costs of damage control increase. Given deficient incentives for the prevention of damages caused by technologies, the eco-modernist proposals for explorations of new natural resources and mitigations of environmental impacts need precaution before allowances for implementation. This precautionary approach can be enforced with liabilities for damages caused by developers and users of technologies. Liabilities for harms to people and nature do work as experiences in aviation, oil spills and other disasters. However, policies prevent liabilities of the interests that are confronted with high payments for damages. For instance, operators of the nuclear power plants are not liable, neither insured for heavy accidents in operations because the costs of damages exceed the insurance cost coverage. In effect, public societies pay the costs of accidents.

Regarding slow-down of economic growth and shifting public expenditures to wealthy oligarchs, the neo-liberal idea about transnational societies failed in practices and so, the eco-modernist ideas about market transactions in technological change. Precaution for damages caused by eco-modernist technologies should be linked to liabilities for damages.

2.5 Environmentalist Perspectives

After that review of the economists' thinking about natural resources and assessment of their radical expression in the neoliberal ideology and policy, attention is drawn to the environmentalist perspective. This viewpoint encompasses ideas expressed in economics of natural resources, environmental economics, ecological economics, biobased economics, and other disciplines. A common feature in the environmentalist view is that all economic activities depend on the use of nature. The environmentalist ideas are presented in four categories known as the ecosystem services. The first category is about the provisioning services, which are services that enable the uses of natural resources for value addition. Herewith, the environmentalist arguments focus on the scarcity of natural resources. This study addresses the withdrawal of water, which is essential for all organisms, as well as the use of fuels and forests, which cover nearly all rents from natural resources. The second category is about the regulatory services. This one addresses the natural sinks that absorb noxious residues from economic activities. Degraded absorption of the natural sinks causes pollution that threatens the life of all organisms and degrades materials. This study covers wastewater that is a cause of waterborne diseases, CO_2 emissions than influence climate, toxic NOx emissions. The third category is about the supporting services, in particular the nature use. Loss of biodiversity and amenities of nature are pinpointed in the environmentalist thinking. In this study, loss of forests and protection of nature are assessed. Finally, fourth category of ecosystem services, is about the cultural services. From the environmentalist perspective, they encompass various issues related to well-being. The scarcity of natural resources, pollution, and land uses are covered in this section, followed by the cultural services related to fairness in the next section.

Natural resources are considered to be scarce, as opposed to abundant man-made labour due to population growth. This economic theorising from the late 1700s is at the core of the environmentalist thinking until present days. In this theorising, human population is assumed to grow exponentially, and their demands for the natural resources even faster due to higher income per capita, whereas the availability of natural resources for population would grow linearly. This assumption refers to the idea of population dynamics in closed systems, which means growth of living organisms without inflow of the natural resources from outside. Based on this theory, it is argued that human populations are trapped in recurring cycles of growing demands for food at faster rates than the recovery rate of natural resources, which cause scarcity of food. This scarcity would increase prices, making the purchases unaffordable, and causing mass starvation. This theory by Thomas Robert Malthus, an Anglican pastor in the late 1700s, was based on historical works and travellers' observations (Malthus, 1798). His idea constitutes the cornerstone of environmentalist thinking even today. Inter alia, similar idea has been expressed by Giovanni Botero, an Italian Jesuit, two centuries earlier than Malthus. That assumption about the collapsing populations, labelled as the Malthusian trap, was widely accepted as the natural order, a synonym for God's will. In particular, the English elite of the 1800s promoted this idea as an economic expression of Darwinian evolution theory. For example, Herbert Spencer, a leading liberal philosopher and politician of that time used the Malthusian trap as the interpretation of the Darwinian idea about survival of the fittest. He also used this idea in policies as a moral justification for his opposition against the laws in support of poor people. He had many supporters within the English elite. For example, John Stuart Mill envisioned a stationary state of economy when population grows because land would not be able to feed all people. In order to contain population growth, their followers, called neo-Malthusians, opposed the eradication of poverty, and promoted forced birth controls with selections of the best human breeds (Desrochers and Hoffbauer, 2009).

Those neo-Malthusian ideas about limitation for reproduction were adopted by the environmentalists during the 1900s with various interpretations. A popular environmentalist interpretation advocates voluntary reduction of birth with regard to limitation of the natural resources (Matrtinez-Alier and Mansjuan, 2025). On the extreme of political spectrum, the neo-Malthusian organisations that press on governments for birth controls and selection of breeds generated a string of authoritarian environmentalism, called 'eco-fascism' (Zamurs, 2023). The neo-Malthusian ideas in modern environmentalism are tangible. During economic boom driven by chemical industries after World War II (1939–1945), the idea of the Malthusian trap caused by closed environmental system on earth was rephrased as the 'spaceship earth' (Boulding, 1966). The threat of population growth for the natural resources was also popularised by trailblazers of modern environmentalism as the "Population Bomb" (Ehrlich, 1976). Collapse of the global civilization within a few decades caused by the increasing use of natural resources and pollution was forecasted by Meadows and colleagues with computer simulations (Meadows et al., 1972). These doomsday forecasts were propagated by a global think tank called the Club of Rome though their predictions were also criticized for neglect of innovations in economic development (Albertone, 2025).

Time and again, shortages of minerals, climate change, dispersion of chemicals, biodiversity loss, and other environmental problems would be signs of collapsing civilizations unless population and economic growth could be stopped. The ideal of the 'steady state' economy on the global scale is rephrased as nil-growth with distribution of all resources across countries (Daly and Cobb, 1994). Scarcity of natural resources within a hypothesized closed system of earth was also embraced by the governmental institutions and non-governmental organisations in environmental assessments. For example, the OECD launched measurements of material flows as 'material footprints' (OECD, 2008), but measuring waste streams is deficient. The Global Footprint Network, which is an environmentalist organisation, argued about absolute limits for uses of the natural resources based on the biological absorption of solar energy, called 'Ecological footprint' (Global Footprint Network, 2023). So far, those neo-Malthusian predictions proved to be false, which could hold true in the future as well .

No doubt that the scarcity of natural resources is a relevant issue in economies as agriculture and industries rely on them, but the idea of the Malthusian trap has two major flaws. The first weakness is the assumption that the Earth is a closed system. Annual inflow of solar energy on the earth's surface is a few thousand times larger than present global energy consumption, and annual volcanic eruptions from within earth add huge amounts of materials on the earth's surface. These primary resources are almost unlimited as the materials do not disappear after consumption, but they are dislocated and decomposed. Also, recycling and reuse of products and materials are possible and needed to avoid mineral shortages and prevent waste disposal. They do need additional resources in collecting and processing dispersed materials into secondary materials. The second flaw is that scarcity of particular natural resources can be prevented through innovation in material-efficiency, meaning material use per value, and in substitutions for more abundant materials though material-efficiency is subject to the rebound effect as mentioned in Sect. 2.2. Replacement of scarce natural by better available ones is also possible. This was observed in the past. For example, coal was exploited in deeper mines due to steam machines in the 1800s, followed by the growing exploitation of oil and gas in the 1900s as the exploitation of coal became costly (Rosenberg, 1975). Since then, the availability of fossil fuels has increased due to better exploration and exploitation technologies while prices of natural resources declined (Shafiee and Topal, 2009). Economist ideas about scarcities of natural resources are confusing. Mainstream economists argue that declining prices of natural resources due to technological change falsely indicate availability of minerals as they can cover up excessive exploitations (Nordhaus, 2010). Other economists argue that scarcities of natural resources arise when policies protect the monopolies of incumbent interests against innovators. For example, the entitlements for gas monopolies in street lights obstructed uses of electric lights despite frequent gas explosions that caused city fires (DiLorenzo, 1996). Meanwhile, evolutionary economists argue that particular businesses need monopoly position for capital accumulation and public funding in order to finance large investments. However, this idea of 'natural monopolies' in economies proved is used to establish the state firms in the 1960s and turn them into private ones in the 1990s. A realistic assumption is that the Malthusian trap emerges in the specific conditions when innovations for better uses of natural resources stagnate because incumbent interests are protected by the monopoly power of authorities. Well-performing economies in competition generate innovations that prevent this trap.

Pollution is another environmental issue. Mounting pollution caused by emission of noxious compounds is indisputable. It is a result of unavoidable dissipation of energy and minerals during processing of natural resources. It threatens economic activities, public health and environmental qualities unless they are absorbed and neutralised by environmental sinks (Georgescu-Roegen, 1971). Although pollution and its prevention are issued throughout civilisation, it expanded during industrialisation from the early 1800s onward. In particular, the expansion of polluting production of electric power is issued in the early 1900s, but economic depression in 1929 drew attention to unemployment and income. The growth of chemical industries in the second half of the 1900s triggered the rise of environmentalism. It also invoked policies with regulations that prescribed technologies in production facilities aimed at preventing pollution. In the 1970s, these environmental policies introduced the 'precautionary principle', using the best available technologies based on the 'polluter pays principle'. Preventing harms caused by pollution is pursued with the help of environmental technologies paid by polluters. These principles are enforced in licenses for production. During subsequent decades, these principles disseminate to nearly all countries and extended to cover emissions, waste, safety, and a few dozen other issues (Spash, 2021). By 1990s, these regulations are relaxed and and the growth of investments in environmental technologies stagnated with the arguments that they hinder profitable investments and enhance migration to unregulated areas, although minor effects of environmental policies on the profits and migration are observed. The disseminating neo-liberal ideas about transactional societies pushed forward voluntary agreements between authorities and firms, which replaced the precautionary principle. The use of best available technologies in licenses is also abandoned, while the polluter pays principle is largely replaced by subsidies for pollution controls. Environmental policy turned into a source of subsidies for businesses through cash transfers and relaxation of tax. This source can be exemplified by policies on climate change. From the 1990s on, large firms had to pay for CO_2 emission within framework of the international agreement on mitigation of climate change sealed in 1997 in Kyoto, but the average payment remained below USD_{2000} 2 per ton CO_2 until the 2010s (O'Mahony, 2020). Meanwhile, the subsidies for energy exceeded USD_{2000} 1900 billion a year, equivalent of average USD_{2000} 51 per ton CO_2 as estimated by the International Monetary Fund (Clements et al., 2013). These subsidies exclude the costs of damages caused by the effects of CO_2 emissions on climate change, which are paid by societies, being implicit subsidies to emission sources of CO_2. The International Monetary Fund estimated environmental damages at about 5700 billion USD_{2010}, equivalent of about 8% of the global GDP (Coady et al., 2015). As these subsidies mainly support the interests in fossil fuels, while they hinder innovations in renewable energy technologies that prevent pollution. These relaxations undermine the sinks for absorption of CO_2 and other emissions, which cause climate change and pollution.

Growth of pollution is tempered by economic changes towards labour-intensive activities, meaning much labour per product value. Meanwhile, the material-intensive activities continued but at slower growth rates. In addition, environmental technologies for pollution prevention are implemented. In result, the increase of pollution slowed down, or even decreased in total while incomes grew. With regard to lower pollution per income, it is hypothesised that higher income automatically reduces pollution. Pollution would increase at low income, but decrease above USD 30,000 per person a year due to shifts away from agriculture and industries toward services and larger expenditures on environmental technologies (Grossman & Krueger, 1991). The idea is called the 'Environmental Kuznets Curve' after Simon Kuznets' hypothesis about an inverse U-like income disparity function of income growth, which proved to be false. This idea is extensively tested. Those tests show variation across countries (Bruijn et al., 1999), and pollutants (Stern, 2004) dependent on the stringency of policies (Dasgupta et al., 2006), urgency about reduction of pollutants (Galeotti, 2007), investments in environmental technologies (Bertinelli et al., 2012), education in countries with high income disparity (Maranzano, 2022), and other factors. Regarding the variety of factors that influence pollution, the hypothesis is usually dismissed. Pollution largely depends on the enforcement of regulations that invoke environmental technologies in pollution prevention because pollution sources have no interest in paying these technologies.

Land use is about consequences of economic activities on nature and biodiversity. A deplorable state of biodiversity is widely acknowledged (IPBES, 2025). This is observed despite growing areas dedicated to nature, as well as policies purposed for the land uses with protection of ecosystems, and organisations in the protection of nature with several millions of members in many countries. Moreover, the importance of nature for economic activities, in particular for the land use, has been widely acknowledged.

Land use with respect to nature is advocated in the 1800s by Henry George (1839–1897). He pursued the collective use of land within the carrying capacity of local ecosystems, and promoted communities for self-sufficient production and modest consumption as an alternative to the commodification of agricultural production. This idea is revived in the modern environmentalist thinking hundred years later as a phrase 'small is beautiful' and in the advocacy of taxation on land instead of on labour and capital. Shift to small scale agricultural production invoked by high taxes on land would foster sustainable uses of land. Similar ideas are expressed in studies on the communities' adaptations to local ecosystems in order to prevent overuse of common lands. It is observed that the communities acting on subsistence levels tune their population and consumption to the constraints posed by local ecosystems through a range of actions which enlarge care, leisure, culture and personal relations for well-being instead of consumption of commodities (Sahlin, 2011). Such 'natural economies', it is theorized, can grow infinitely within closed ecosystems if they continuously improve extractions of the natural resources for value adding services (Perrings, 1985). These ideas are also expressed in the diversifications of land use for balance with nature, conversion of biomaterials into durable products with recycling of residues. Substitutions of the natural resources for the man-made labour and capital could maintain local ecosystems and enlarge economic activities in local communities, as well as in modern forestry. Free riding in the uses of natural resources would be prevented through moral codes and cultural traditions enforced in social regulations, which define behaviour and technology tuned to the carrying capacity of nature (Ostrom, 1990). However, rigid social regulations also impede innovations as observed in the land use based on spiritual and ideological directives.

Nature is also considered to be inspirational and supportive for arts, crafts, and knowledge while commodification of nature by industries is assumed to undermine the diversity of nature and skills of people (Ruskin, 2023). This thinking, which has gone into oblivion for half a century, is revived in the late 1900s. Economists of the 1960s pinpointed at the bequest and intrinsic values of nature, which considered the nature as an essential asset for well-being of present and future generations (Krutilla, 1967). The value of nature in itself triggered advocacy of entitlements for the rights of nature (Mishan, 1993). These ideas invoked economic thinking about the supportive values of nature. The concept of 'total value assessment' is introduced. It encompasses the direct and indirect 'user values' in the uses of nature, as well as the non-user' values as options for present consumers, bequest for the future consumers, and the intrinsic values of nature (McNeely, 1988). This idea about the supportive roles of nature also inspired the development of know-how about mimicking of organisms in ecosystems for production, called Biomimicry (Benyus, 2002), and the development of crafts tuned to interactions in ecosystems, called 'Flourishing' in product design (Ehrenfeld, 2008).

Those idealised relations to the land uses in balance with biodiversity are also commented as the nostalgia of remnants in rural nobility, and the interests of urban elites aiming to protect land ownership (Enzensberger, 1982). Disputing such critiques is beyond the scope of this book, but it can be noted that the advocacy of the supportive services of nature encompasses various interests in high-income countries. Along with land owners trying to protect properties from intruders, one finds investors and activists in nature organizations who hike, watch birds, hug trees, and exploit natural amenities in various ways. With 30 million registered members of environmental organisations in the EU (EEB, 2020), and 10 million in the USA (Statista, 2020), excluding the scouting and similar organisations indirectly involved in the protection of nature, the amenities of nature attract various societal interests. Nearly one in ten citizens in high-income countries are dedicated to pay for these amenities. Their paying members exceed the membership of political parties. Apparently, amenities of nature appeal to all social classes.

Environmentalist perspectives evolved from the image of doomsday towards maintaining natural resources, preventing degradation of environmental sinks, and protecting qualities of nature.

2.6 Fairness in Using Nature

The cultural services of ecosystems include various ethical relations in economic activities, for convenience labelled as fairness. This inclusions broadened the scope of environmentalism toward the moral goods in relations to social and environmental issues. That broadening of the environmentalist scope can be comprehended as a side-effect of promoting sustainable development. When the idea of sustainable development was embraced by the United Nations in the late 1980s, most environmentalists took a critical stand. Their concern was that the interest for environmental quality would be diluted by the pursuit of economic growth and well-being, but within a few decades they diluted this interest by embracing demands for social fairness under the banner of environmentalism. These demands are only touched for illustration of the diversity in present environmentalist thinking about economic development. Although several demands are mentioned, more can be found. While that diversity of demands inspires many inventive activities in business and social organisations, it also adds complexities to decisions about investments and policies because justifications of objections for activities pile up. Below, these demands are related to the fairness with respect to nature, social relations, and economic relations.

Fairness in nature refers to the broader uses of environmental qualities than the natural resources. Attention is given to the rights of non-humans. Animal rights are successfully pursued in regards to deplored animal integrity in intensive husbandry, animal experiments, as well as shows, sports, and other uses of animals for human interests without consideration of their well-being. Meanwhile, the rights of animals for their well-being are widely adopted (Chavez, 2023). This advocacy evolved from societal fringes of activism towards broader lifestyles as vegetarian and vegan diets, which disseminated from the dedicated shops to supermarkets in high-income countries. While the consumption of meat in lower income countries has increased, the number of people dedicated to vegetarian diets has grown in high-income countries. In addition to animal rights, the rights of nature in a broad sense are advocated. The rights of nature are used as a tool for protecting vulnerable ecosystems and for utilisation of the indigenous knowledge about local species and uses of nature for survival within closed system of the environment. These uses expand from the protection of threatened species toward management of nature at large (Gilbert et al., 2023). By the early 2020s, more than 400 rights for rivers, forests, and other elements of nature are formalized in 39 countries. These nature rights support individuals and organisations, often local indigenous communities, in opposition against constructions that damage local ecosystems and polluting extractions of the natural resources (Kahui et al., 2024). The nature rights help the environmentalists to keep stance in conflicts between wildlife and human settlements, but they also reinforce the position of human superiority with respect to nature given that people decide about the nature rights.

Fairness in social relations is an umbrella for the advocacy of non-monetised moral goods in economic activities. Ethical consumption is pursued, which means the purchase and use of goods with respect to environmental qualities and well-being in value chains. These considerations include fair payments for work, healthy food, environmental impacts, and other demands that express the quality of supplies. Although the ethical purchases cover not more than a few percent of total consumer expenditures, these fringes grow faster than all consumption in high-income countries (Devinney et al., 2010). Unfortunately, insufficient empirical information for a reliable assessment is found about the ethical consumption in lower income countries though a lot is conceptualised (Kutaula et al., 2024). It is also argued that fairness in social relations would be attained if economic activities are shifted towards communities because local interactions generate checks and balances of interests (Schumacher, 1973). These ideas inspired community initiatives in energy, land uses, designs, education dedicated to local economic development. Yet, another issue is about care and education. As these activities are often done by women without payment, they are also considered to be moral goods. Therefore, the environmentalist thinking embraced emancipation of gender. The idea is popularised that environmental qualities provide the foundation for all human activities, while the non-monetary care enables monetary activities on top of them (Henderson, 1989). Such ideas inspired gender groups aiming at environmental performances tuned to care. Also, the ideas of basic income are advocated as a tool for encouraging services that prevent environmental degradation. Furthermore, the integrity of indigenous communities is addressed with respect to the rights of local population for the exploitation of local natural resources. These ownership rights are advocated with regard to dispossession of millions of people defined as indigenous population (Hitchcock, 1994). Parity in the rights for indigenous communities for economic activities and in uses of indigenous knowledge for managing ecosystems is advocated through decision making in panels of indigenous communities (Lertzman & Vredenburg, 2005). The environmental interests can also collide with the indigenous property rights, illustrated by conflicts about carbon storage and protection of species in the areas for protection of nature. Finding solutions for these trade-offs is challenging.

Fairness in economic relations across countries focuses on the international distribution of environmental qualities taking into consideration inequalities in power, income and well-being. Linking fair economic relations to environmental impacts triggered much dispute in the environmentalist theorising and in practice. In theory, an environmentalist argument is that income inequalities aggravate environmental impacts. This argument assumes that wealthy people spend more on luxury goods which cause large environmental impacts and they accrue power for maintaining these impacts (Boyce, 1994). However, this argument is scrutinized with data about the declining environmental impacts per income of those who obtain higher incomes though the total impact of a person with high income is larger than one with low income (Scruggs, 1998). It is also hypothesised that more egalitarian societies by income per capita spend more on environmental technologies, which would deliver better environmental performances (Vona and Patrizio, 2011). However, the opposite is also observed. Low CO_2 emissions in lower income countries with large income-inequalities are observed, which is driven by activities that absorb CO_2 emissions. These activities are the uses of biofuels in subsistence economies and larger spendings on food per income (Grunewald et al., 2017). Moreover, people in lower income countries spend a larger share of their incomes on the material-intensive products than people in high-income countries who spend a large part of the incomes on labour-intensive services, which implies lower environmental impacts per income (Wu et al., 2019). Fair distribution of incomes and environmental quality across countries is even more difficult to define. Fair distribution is pursued in the division of expenditures for mitigating climate change, biodiversity loss, and other global environmental problems, known as 'burden sharing'. Possibilities of burden sharing are assessed with regard to allocations of funding based on population size, countries impact, or impact reduction, welfare, or costs and benefits (Ringius et al., 2000). Funding is also pledged by high-income countries, but the fund raising for burden sharing is slow, and implementation by the beneficiaries is also sluggish (Songwe et al., 2022). Fairness in international policies is out of sight when the national interests prevail.

Fairness in economic relations within a country addresses environmental effects of income transfers from higher incomes to lower incomes within a country. Assessments show that reducing income-inequality has little environmental impact because consumption in lower income classes is rather material-intensive. People with lower income spend a larger part of income on food, shelter, and suchlike material-intensive basic goods compared to people with higher incomes who spend more on labour-intensive services (Baffes, 2018). Changes in the use of natural resources per income, are indicated with income-elasticities, meaning a unit of change in that use per unit of change in income. If alternatives are available, changes in the uses tend to be low for basic goods (0 to 1), high for luxuries (above 1), and negative for inferior goods (below 0). The income-elasticities vary across the indicators of natural resources. The income-elasticities of freshwater uses are estimated below 0.6 in one review (Dalhuijsen et al., 2003), slightly higher in another review (Arbués et al., 2003), and low negative to low positive in still another review (Havranek et al., 2017). Low positive income-elasticities of fuel use are observed during high fuel prices in low-income countries (Choe, 1981), as well as in residential energy uses in the USA (Burke & Csereklyei, 2016), and in a review of several high-income countries (Pottier, 2021). Forest uses increase during economic contractions, but these uses increase less than proportional to economic growth because wooden materials are replaced by other materials. Low positive income-elasticities are estimated for lumber, paper and other forest products, as well as for the forests of bordering low-income countries (Cuaresma and Heger, 2019), and in several low-income countries (Assa, 2020). Low income elasticities imply that the income growth increases environmental impacts less than proportionally to the incomes, and vice versa, a decline of incomes does not reduce as much of the impact.

By issuing fairness, environmentalism embraced distribution of incomes, well-being, cultural diversity, and environmental qualities across and within countries. This inspired many activities but also confused decision making because of non-linear links of incomes and environmental impacts.

2.7 A Degrowth Assessed

As the neo-Malthusian ideas about the decay of population within the closed system of environmental qualities are linked to the demands for fairness, the environmentalist thinking radicalised. Conventional focus on protection of environmental qualities is considered insufficient with regard to inequalities in income and well-being while economic growth assumed colliding with the constraints posed by carrying capacity of the earth. Ideas about the consumption reduction in high-income countries by factor 4, or even factor 10 are launched in the early 2000s. It is argued that 2 to 4 earths would be needed to maintain their consumption. From this viewpoint, the advocacy of far reaching reduction of incomes is a logic step. In result, the hypothesised boundaries of the ecological carrying capacity are linked with the reduction and distribution of the global income into the idea 'degrowth'.

In the idea of degrowth, incomes reduction in high-income countries would voluntarily align to those environmental boundaries along with the income shifts to lower incomes within and across countries (Jackson, 2011). In addition, fair relations in societies are envisaged through keeping economic activities within a narrow path of limitations for the consumption, which are posed by that carrying capacity, and necessary increase in well-being (Raworth, 2017). That voluntary reduction of the highest incomes in support of lower incomes within and across countries would be attained through agreements about well-being, cooperation instead of competition, flourishing design, emancipation of minorities and other actions for the global fairness (Cosme et al., 2017). This way, the degrowth would address main attributes of welfare, thereby generate a renewal of the environmentalism (Fitzpatric et al., 2022). These ideas about degrowth are often associated with the left-wing ideology of fairness in the sense of distribution of income and power, being scrutinised by the conservative political streams as 'woke'. However, this is a misconception. Vocal advocates of changes in incomes and consumption are also found on the extreme right-wing of the political spectrum, when fairness is considered as a political power of rural local communities and so called 'common people' are opposed to the urban elites (Broder, 2025). Regarding the popularity of degrowth within modern environmentalism, its practical consequences are assessed before presentation of the ideas about bridging the economist and environmentalist viewpoints in the next section.

In this assessment, the idea of degrowth refers to an authoritative definition as reduction of the global annual average income toward USD 11,000 per person across countries. This level of income would allow activities within a hypothesized global ecological footprint (Hickel, 2019). That income is similar to the global average in 2015. For high-income countries, this degrowth implies the income reduction down to one-fifth of the average income in the USA, to one-third in Japan, and to half in the EU28, Gulf countries, and other high-income countries, along with voluntary transfer to people with lower incomes. Such an idea is disputable for three different reasons. It is unethical. Given that most people pursue higher income, not many voluntarily reduce incomes by half, or more. Even the spokesman of the 'Effective Altruism', an organisation whose members are dedicated to invest in 'the doing good', is not ready to spend more than a quarter, or third of his income on charity (Beukers, 2024). So, there are reasons for enforcement. Indeed, radical tinkerers propagate disruption of economic activities by force (Malm, 2025). Suchlike enforcement is experienced in several communist countries as mass murder of middle class and opponents. Second issue is that the degrowth idea refers to a fictitious boundary of environmental carrying capacity without considering substitutions of the natural resources for the man-made ones. In this an interpretation of 'strong sustainability', the uses of solar energy, bioresources, recycled materials, and other sustainable innovations are non-existing. The major, third, issue is if the degrowth reduces environmental impacts, or aggravates them. A gradual reduction of incomes could be imagined in the case of global economic crisis caused by ongoing political conflicts, or epidemics. For example, 5% annual decline would reduce incomes by half within two decades. The issue is whether this crisis can deliver the envisioned results. An answer is given for indicators of well-being and environmental qualities with the use of statistical data on economic recession during the last decades as an approximation of that degrowth.

Consequences of the recessions in present high-income countries are estimated. This estimate excludes the recessions after the shifts from the state-directed economies to market-based ones because these are rather specific cases presented in Chap. 5. The estimate is focused on the economic recessions mainly caused by the financial crises after collapse of banks in 2008. A minimum of 3 consecutive years of declining GDP from 2005 to 2015 is considered, which avoids temporary economic fluctuations. These declines are observed in Cyprus, Spain, Greece, Finland, and Italy in the EU, which are net consumers of fossil fuels, as well as in the United Arab Emirates (UAE), Brunei-Darusalam, Bahrain, Oman, and Qatar in Asia, which are net fuel producers. Contractions of fuel producing economies during high fuel prices indicate that higher turnovers of particular businesses do not necessarily improve the countries performances. Antigua and Barbuda, Barbados, and Puerto Rico in Latin America could also be considered if good data would be found. Annual average changes in indicators per capita are considered. Income impacts are indicated by real GDP. Well-being is indicated by the percentage poverty in populations, defined by the World Bank as the income below 6.85 USD_{2010} per person a day, as well as by the annual government expenditures on education, and ones on health. The environmental impacts are indicated by coverage of wastewater treatment per m^3 water use, CO_2 in ton in climate change, NOx in ton of air pollution, as well as m^2 nature restoration defined by deforestation minus nature protection areas. The annual average changes per capita are estimated. Firstly, the baselines for indicators and countries are defined, which are changes throughout the period 2005–2015. The changes during the recession are subtracted from the changes defined by the baselines. So, the calculation per indicator per country is: the annual average change during the recessions minus the annual average change during that decade. Results are shown in the fuel-consuming and fuel-producing countries, sequentially.

Graph 2.4 shows the economic, social, and environmental impacts of recessions in the EU countries. The horizontal axis presents the countries' GDP, poverty, education, health, water pollution, climate change, air pollution, and nature areas. Cyprus, Spain, Greece, Finland and Italy are shown next to each other. The vertical axis shows percent changes during the recessions in addition to the baseline throughout the period 2005–2015. Positive percentages mean increases, and negative ones mean decreases. Several data sets are missing due to insufficient reliability.

Income loss has been observed in those EU countries. Particularly, Cyprus and Greece experienced deep economic crises as they lost an average of about 3% of GDP per year, in addition to lower GDP during 2005–2015 compared to 1990–2004. A cumulative decline of about 20% in real income is experienced in these two countries, which is still far from the envisioned 50% degrowth in the EU28. Poverty has increased in all those EU countries. These increases were larger than the decline in GDP. A relative high increase was experienced in Finland, where poverty did not exist before 2005, but the largest increase in total was in Greece, where nearly 750,000

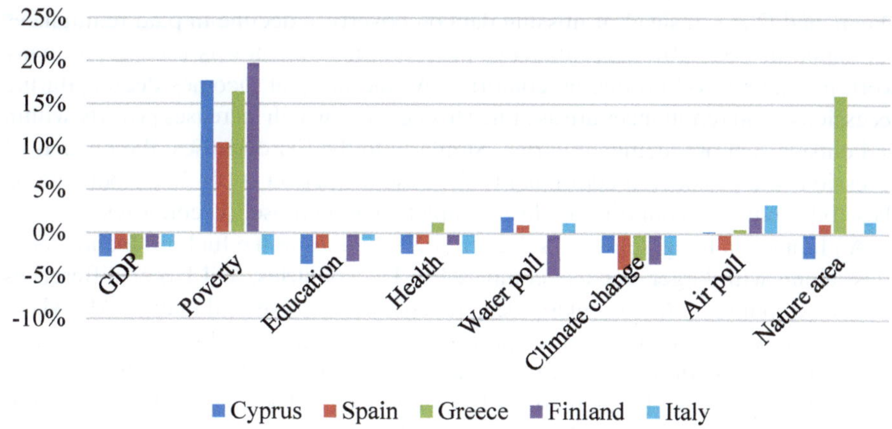

Graph 2.4 Impacts of economic recessions on well-being and environmental qualities in a few EU countries

people fell into poverty. Educational expenditures of the governments in Cyprus and Finland declined significantly, while they increased in Greece. The impact on health expenditures varied. While the Greek government increased expenditures, the Italian government decreased them. Those differences can be attributed to the specific countries' policies. The environmental impacts of recessions also vary across indicators and countries depending on resource use and environmental technologies. Those recessions increased water pollution in Cyprus, Spain, and Italy as more water was used while wastewater treatment stagnated. Finland saw a decrease in water pollution due to lower water use. In all of those EU countries, the impact of climate change decreased in line with the recession rates due to lower fuel use and the shift to less CO_2-intensive fuels. In Spain and Finland, the impact of climate change, declined faster than GDP declines. Apparently, high fuel prices and lower incomes led to energy savings and larger use of renewable energy in these countries. Despite lower fuel use, air pollution by NOx has hardly declined in Spain. Air pollution even increased in other EU countries. Presumably, the use of environmental technologies for de-NOxing has stagnated. Nature restoration has improved in Greece where additional 600 km^2 nature areas have been established, compared to Cyprus where larger deforestation is not compensated by additional nature areas. Based on the economic contractions in the EU, a degrowth by a few percent annual decrease of incomes would dramatically aggravate poverty and cause stagnation in education and health. Water pollution would exacerbate. Climate change would slow down, while air pollution and degradation of nature would vary across countries. The countries' policies are presumably decisive factors for the variety of impacts across the countries. Only climate change slowed down across countries.

Those fuel-producing countries experienced a deeper economic recession than the EU countries. The consequences can be seen in Graph 2.5. On the horizontal axis, the impacts are shown for the United Arab Emirates (UAE), Bahrain, Brunei-Darusalam,

Oman, and Qatar. Instead of missing data on poverty, a decline in paid remittances per capita in USD 2015 approximates poverty. This indicator is used given many work migrants in oil producing countries. As the migrant incomes decline during recessions, paid remittances are assumed to decrease, which increases poverty within and outside fuel producing countries. Similarly to the EU countries, the impacts of recessions are considered additional to the baseline period 2005–2015, but data on these oil producing countries are less complete than in those EU countries.

A glimpse on the graph shows deeper GDP declines in the fuel producing countries, along with larger impacts compared to EU countries, and larger differences across the countries. A particularly deep recession is experienced in the UAE, where the cumulative decline in income approaches 50% degrowth. Poverty increased in Brunei-Darusalam during its mild recession, but declined in the aftermath of it. This is presumably due to the increase in foreign workers. Their government expenditures on education and health have significantly decreased, except in Brunei Darussalam where they have increased. Countries' performances in water pollution vary. Water pollution increased in the UAE despite lower water use because wastewater treatment stagnated, whereas it decreased in Oman and Qatar due to more wastewater treatment. Furthermore, water use decreased in Oman but increased in Qatar. Brunei-Darusalam lacks information. The impact on climate change decreased in

Graph 2.5 Impacts of economic recessions on well-being and environmental qualities in a few oil producing countries

all countries except Qatar, where it increased due to larger fuel use. Air pollution decreased in UAE, Bahrein and Oman, but increased in Brunei-Darusalam despite lower fuel use, while more fuel is used in Qatar. Nature restoration declined, except an increase in Brunei-Darusalam. Data for Qatar is missing. Recessions worsened well-being, while environmental impacts vary from aggravation to improvement across fuel producers. Similar to the EU countries, policies were decisive in determining the impact of recessions on well-being and the environment. Climate change slowed down in most fuel producing countries.

Challenging the dogma of economic growth is courageous, but the envisioned degrowth would aggravate well-being without much improvement of environmental qualities, aside some mitigation of climate change, and even aggravate water pollution and nature protection.

2.8 Policies for Sustainable Development

Integration of the environmentalist ideas with the ideas about economic growth is also pursued. Regarding the common good property of environmental qualities, it is assumed that authorities would define policies that demand higher performances in using natural resources and pollution prevention. Main justification for the state interventions in market transactions and voluntary actions was that higher performances would cause costs and benefits to societies, but provide little benefit to the private interests. So, spontaneous improvements could not be expected. In this train of thought, policies would generate public investments in environmental qualities and invoke larger private investments through regulations, which would reduce the social costs of environmental degradation, thereby increase productivity (Kuipers & Nentjes, 1973). This idea was widely approved in the 1980s. In the Netherlands, as an example, the environmentalist organisation cooperated with the trade unions on joined plans for investments (FNV, 1987), and attracted the attention of the employers organisation with plans for cleaner technologies (LMO, 1988). Public investments were hardly disputed, but regulations were debated. Regulations included a variety of instruments divided into the direct regulation with licences, economic regulation with charges, and social regulation through moral suasion. Licenses for private activities were the main instrument, but charges were usually opposed by businesses. Subsidies were also used in the economic regulation, and public agreements (covenants) in the social regulation, while emission trading combined the direct and economic regulation (Opschoor & Vos, 1989). Although economists emphatically advocated charges because they could increase performances at lowest unit costs, licenses and covenants with subsidies prevailed in policies. While the demands for environmental performances varied across countries and liabilities for environmental degradation were usually opposed, the idea of sustainable development was widely approved as it envisioned a released dependency on the natural resources due higher value activities.

From the 1990s onward, environmental policies began to shift from regulation toward voluntary agreements with supportive subsidies. The emerging neo-liberal idea was the driving force. The World Business Council on Sustainable Development (WBCSD) advocated a balance between profitability, social equity, and environmental quality, known as the Triple Bottom Line of profit, people, and planet (Elkington, 1999). Background of this advocacy was a widespread business complain that environmental regulations posed constrains for profitable investments. Policies in many countries shifted away from regulations towards voluntary agreements with businesses. Such co-operative stand became the cornerstone of environmental policies in many countries despite failures to comply with modest performance in agreements (Ashford, 1996). This shift away from the policy demands to 'fail soft' transactions was intended to protect the laggards in environmental performances, which were usually processors of natural resources, but hindered the front runners, innovative businesses in producing consumer products and services. Furthermore, fail soft policies transferred the financial burden of environmental regulations from businesses to public. For example, the share of businesses in the environmental expenditures in the USA decreased from about 70% to 40% between 1985 and 1995 (Pearce & Palmer, 2001).

Responsibilities for environmental qualities are also changed. Based on the 'polluter pays principle', polluting producers are liable for damages while licences in the production permits allow pollution below the level set in the permits, which enables polluters to avoid liabilities. In result, liabilities for environmental impacts are rare despite a few positive experiences compared to other policy instruments. An example is the liability of house owners for soil pollution in the Netherlands, but exempted agriculture. This liability resolved problems with soil pollution in housing, while pollution of agricultural soil remained. Other countries erected costly public funds based on taxes for this purpose as the Superfund in the USA. Liabilities for packaging, electronics and other waste streams in Germany with take-back obligation invoked redesign of products for waste prevention, but this instrument was obstructed by the EU regulation in favour of controlled disposal.

As businesses advocated the shared responsibility for environmental quality between the state, business, and citizen, policies shifted focus from regulations of production in industries toward consumption. Consumers are pinpointed as polluters that should pay. This is justified by the idea that sovereign consumer can change purchases, and influence the decisions of producers in value chains. Consumers' choices in purchases with respect to prices, as well as social and environmental issues are promoted as consumer social responsibility. By the late 1990s, liabilities of producers based on the polluter pays principle are turned towards the consumer responsibilities for purchases. Meanwhile, policies turned from mining and basic industry, which are usually most material-consuming and polluting businesses, toward processing materials into products downstream in value chains. Attention shifted from regulations toward consumer demands. Life cycle assessment of environmental impacts boomed. They aimed to cover the impacts throughout the value chain starting from the winning natural resources, through processing of materials, consumption, and disposal, but deficient assessments of products caused confusion. Moreover, firms introduced various labels and certifications which obscured consumer decisions. While citizen organisations advocated liabilities for harmful qualities, producers effectively oppose them. Laggards in material-intensive basic industry could reduce performances while front-runners invented eco-design, ecosystem services, circular economy, life cycle management and other business models which enabled profitable renewable energy, biobased products, and other innovations for economic growth, well-being and environmental qualities, called sustainable innovations.

Regarding sustainable innovations, reducing environmental impacts along with economic growth is envisioned. Experts argued that far reaching regulatory demands for environmental qualities induce innovations (Porter & van de Linde, 1995), that pollution prevention provides social benefits (Jaffe et al., 2001), that demands trigger cost-reducing innovations (Krozer, 2008), and private benefits of pollution prevention (Ambec & Lanoie, 2008). An idea of the impacts reducing economic growth emerged, known as 'green growth'. Such ideas are embraced by many governments and the United Nations (UNEP, 2011a). It is observed that economic growth coincides with lower uses of natural resources. Observations across countries confirmed that the uses of natural increased were slower than incomes in most countries, and decreased in total in several countries. These improvements in economic and environmental performance are referred to as 'relative' and 'absolute' decoupling, respectively (UNEP, 2011b).

Enhancing sustainable development is envisioned through the decreasing costs of labour along with the increasing costs of natural resources. Therefore, shift of the taxes on labour into taxes on the natural resources is advocated. This would facilitate labour-intensive activities and temper material-intensive ones. This idea about the tax shift is widely embraced by international institutions as ILO, 2015; Laubinger et al., 2020; UNEP, EEB, 2022, and others. However, such tax reform was successfully opposed by the material-intensive industries on the argument that it would undermine their activities, which could be realistic and on purpose. In addition, fiscal authorities argued that the shift in taxation away from labour into natural resources would increase imbalances in public incomes. Although this issue could be mitigated by clustering of natural resources into a general basis for taxation, such tax reforms move slowly.

Those ideas about 'green growth', and decoupling income from environmental impacts paved the way for the introduction of Sustainable Development Goals (SDG's). Therefore, monitoring and reporting about the countries performances with use of indicators for environment, society and governance (ESG's) are approved by the UN in the 2015. They are implemented in 2016. Progress is illustrated in Appendix B based on the reporting by the World Bank. This Appendix shows ESG indicators, the availability of data in the World Bank database, and the assessments of annual average changes during the period 1990–2004, 2005–2015, and 2016–2020. Comparing the changes during those periods indicates improvements of performances. Comparison of that last period with the periods before the agreement about SDGs, indicates whether the improvements can be attributed to the policies related to the SDGs. Of the 71 ESG indicators in the database, sufficient data is available for assessment of the shifts for 37 indicators, which are mainly indicators for environmental qualities. Insofar data is available, improvements are found for 11 indicators. These are: lower forest depletion, decline of CO_2 emission per capita, lower fertility rate of people, less methane emission per capita, lower exposure to particulate matter (PM2.5), lower percentage population above 65 years, increasing ratio female to male in labour force, larger uses of renewable energy, larger research and development, and strengthened legal rights. Compared to the SDG objectives, more progress is needed.

Proposals for generating income growth along with well-being and environmental qualities are launched and approved in various countries policies. An example is the proposal for 'Broad Welfare' in the Netherlands (SER, 2024). Faster progress is achievable when citizens' organizations are able to express urgency and convince interests to act. Political decisions are sensitive to such pressures as observed for climate change (Escher and Walter-Rogg, 2018), and SDG's (Kroll and Zipperer, 2020). So far, 'green growth' remained policy without tangible policy instruments. A step forward could be the elimination of implicit and explicit, harmful subsidies from environmental perspective as advocated by institutions as the International Monetary Fund. Elimination of such subsidies for the production and uses of fossil fuels, agricultural production, mining and wasteful infrastructure would accelerate change towards sustainable development.

During the last half century, policies shifted from the regulations of pollution sources towards consumer demands for performance in value chains, and fostering economic changes through subsidies.

2.9 Conclusions

It is discussed whether the economists' ideas about economic growth are compatible with environmental qualities, which is relevant given prominent positions of many economists in politics, business, and social organisations. This is discussed with regard to the ethical views on human relations to nature found in religions, spiritual streams and philosophies, followed by a brief review of the economic and environmentalist thinking. While the mainstream, Anthropocentric viewpoint perceives nature as a service for human activities, the Ecocentric one considers people to be shepherds, or servants of nature. In economics, comprehended as an instrument for decision making of authorities, businesses, and citizens' organizations, as well as of individuals, those ethical perspectives are expressed in the scholarly ideas about 'weak' sustainability for the Anthropocentric views and 'strong' sustainability for the Ecocentric ones. These opinions refer to the assumptions about possibilities of substitutions of the natural resources for man-made one. Herewith, the advocacy of weak sustainability assumes that flexible substitutions prevent environmental degradation contrary to the ideas about strong sustainability that assume limited or impossible substitutions. While both perspectives are reflected in decisions about policies, many opinions radicalised into collisions between interests. The moderate opinions can find a common perspective on progress to sustainable development.

Economic theorising encompasses various strings of thoughts based on the Anthropocentric perspective. Within that perspective, one string of thoughts considers land as the foundation of value additions, land being equivalent to natural resources, whereas another string focuses on trade. These strings of thought evolved during the last two centuries into several theories that partly support, or object each other. While the conversions of natural resources into goods through technologies are considered essential human assets in the neo-Marxist theorising, the liberal economic focus on trade largely disregards environmental qualities given their low prices. The liberal idea about flexible substitutions of the natural resources for man-made ones through market prices became the mainstream in economics, largely due to the disastrous track records of neo-Marxist economies in practice. As the idea of flexible substitutions gained popularity, the ideal of frictionless transactions between individuals that pursue own interests became the cornerstone in economic thinking. The political interpretation of that ideal disseminated across countries, labelled as neo-liberalism.

Reflections on nearly three decades of neo-liberal policies show that this idea has largely failed with regard to its promises. Instead of faster economic growth, the rates declined globally and in all high-income countries that promoted this policy. Meanwhile, economic growth accelerated in lower income countries that turned away from state directives towards market transactions. In the result, high-income countries lost their share in the global economy to mid-income ones, while population in low-income countries remained poor. The neo-liberal privatization aiming at efficient allocations of capital and labour also failed given higher shares of public expenditures in GDP across countries with several exceptions. Public expenditures hardly declined in high-income countries that promoted neo-liberal policies, mainly due to larger subsidies for businesses. Private expenditures on the natural resources increased and private man-made capital grew, while the labour incomes decreased. Main result of the neo-liberal policies is the accumulation of wealth in the hands of several hundreds multi-billionaires across countries. After three decades of neo-liberalism, a global oligarchy controls markets and policies, similar to nobility before World War I followed by World Wars.

Meanwhile, advocacy of the Ecocentric perspective deliberates various environmental issues, labelled as environmentalism. Scarcity of natural resources is issued. Based on the assumption that the Earth is a closed system and the resource substitutions are impossible, an irrevocable collapse of the growing global economy is predicted time and again throughout the last centuries. However, the earth's surface is an open system that receives energy and materials, and innovations did invoke substitutions. As of now, the collapse has turned out to be a false prophecy. Another issue is pollution. It is worrying because noxious compounds degrade environmental sinks and threaten all organisms and materials. Several threats are prevented with environmental technologies induced by stringent demands, but policies tend to protect laggards with 'fail-soft' agreements, which hinder innovators. Another issue is the degradation of ecosystems. Deploring biodiversity is issued with regard to the land use in the agricultural communities and amenities of nature in urban networks. The environmentalism also pursues the cultural uses of nature for well-being. These aspirations encompass the rights of animals and ecosystems, emancipation in non-monetary work, indigenous rights for uses of land, fair distribution of income and natural resources, and other issues. With regard to fairness, radical environmentalists envision a degrowth. A radical reduction and distribution of global incomes is envisaged in order to align to the debatable carrying capacity of the environment on Earth. However, experiences with economic recessions in high-income EU28 and in oil exporting countries during the last decades show more unfairness with modest improvements, or aggravations in environmental performance. Poverty multiplied, education and health worsened, water pollution increased because less wastewater is treated. While impact on climate change was somewhat reduced, air pollution hardly improved or worsened because less environmental technology was used. Nature protection, improved in a few countries, but deteriorated when more forests are exploited, or less nature areas are protected. A degrowth would cause disasters for well-being, and minor improvements, or aggravation of environmental performances. Changes in economic activities are decisive for sustainable development.

Improving environmental performance can be achieved by altering production and consumption through forceful demands for sustainable innovations. In the past, authorities enforced such demands. Stringent policies with freedoms in development and use of innovations reduced environmental impacts without obstructing economies, and enhancing them in many cases. However, these policies were objected by polluters who had to pay. In result, 'fail soft' agreements are pursued along with public funding through subsidies for polluters. Liabilities of polluters for damages are also turned into voluntary responsibilities of consumers. While the regulations are relaxed, consumer demands also invoke innovations for responsible production and consumption. As policies protect laggards, sustainable innovations emerge mainly due to consumers and citizens pressures. These pressures enable a global agreement on Sustainable Development Goals that still needs a proper compliance. Strengthening policy demands would improve environmental performance, thereby compliance with the goals.

When reflecting on those strings of thoughts, it is observed that the transactional societies and the degrowth are utopias with ingredients for tragedies in practices. The idea of sustainable development in the sense of economic growth along with even better performances in well-being and environmental qualities provides a realistic correction for the transactional hossana and the environmentalists doomsday. Meanwhile, moderate economist and environmentalist thinking converged toward the stream of thoughts that sustainable innovations in the sense of qualitative changes in businesses reduce environmental impacts and enable value added. This possibility can be enhanced through the demanding policies along with making labour cheaper and natural resources costlier in taxation and financing. Shift of the tax burden from labour onto natural resources would accelerate economic growth with higher social and environmental performances.

References

Acemoğlu, D. (2009). *Introduction to modern economic growth*. Princeton University Press.

Albertone, B. (2025). Lost principles of a 'sustainable developmentalism.' *Review of International Political Economy*. https://doi.org/10.1080/09692290.2024.2447735

Ambec, S., & Lanoie, P. (2008). Does it pay to be *green*? A systematic overview. *Academy of Management Perspectives, 22*(4), 45–62. (Nov., 2008).

Arbués, F., Garcia-Valiñas, M. Á., & Martinez-Espiñeira, R. (2003). Estimation of residential water demand: A state-of-the-art review. *Journal of Socio-Economics, 32*, 81–102.

Arentsen, M. J., Dinica, V., & Marquart E. (2001). Innovating innovation policy. Rethinking green innovation policy in evolutionary perspective. *Économies et Sociétés*, Série Dynamique technologique et organization 4(4), 563–583

Arthur, W. B. (1989). Competing technologies, increasing returns and lock–in by historical events. *The Economic Journal, 99*, 116–131.

Ashford, N. A. (1996). The influence of information–based initiatives and negotiated environmental agreements on technological changes. In C. Carraro & F. Lévêque (Eds.), *Voluntary approaches in environmental policy* (1e ed., pp. 137–150). Kluwer Academic Publishers.

Assa, B. S. K. (2020). The deforestation-income relationship: Evidence of deforestation convergence across developing countries. *Environment and Development Economics, 2020*, 1–20.

Baffes, J., Kabundi, A., Nagle, P., & Ohnsorge, F. (2018). *The role of major emerging markets in global commodity demand*. World Bank, Policy Research Working Paper 8595.

Barbier, E. B. (2011). Transaction costs and the transition XE "transition" to environmentally sustainable development XE "sustainable development." *Environmental Innovation and Societal Transitions, 1*, 58–69.

Baumol, W. J., & Oates, W. F. (1975). *The theory of environmental policy* (1st ed., pp. 14–55). Prentice-Hall.

Benyus, J.M. (2002). *Biomimicry* (1st ed.). HarperCollins, New York.

Bertinelli, L., Strobl, E., & Zou, B. (2012). Sustainable economic development: Theory and Evidence. *Energy Economics, 34*, 1105–1114.

Beukers, G. (2024). Interview met William Macaskill. *Volkskrant*, 12–8–2024, p. 12.

Boulding, K. E. (1966). *The economics of the coming spaceship earth*. John Hopkins University Press. Retrieved May 6, 2020, from https://www.semanticscholar.org/paper/The-Economics-of-the-Coming-Spaceship-Earth-Boulding/88cb333c9c7ebb5d852c037372eccc39c12ca691.

Boyce, J. K. (1994). Inequality as a cause of environmental degradation. *Ecological Economics, 11*(3), 169–178.

Broder, D. (2025). The Rise of the Degrowther Right, Jacobine 3–5–2025. Retrieved March 11, 2025, from https://jacobin.com/2025/03/right-wing-ecology-degrowth-nationalism?__s=9pdefy2dic9hkmzk8v7i&__s=0659fl17s4xbswnach2m&utm_campaign=Your+Syllabus+This+Week&utm_medium=email&utm_source=drip

Burke, P. J., & Csereklyei, Z. (2016). Understanding the energy-GDP elasticity: A sectoral approach. *Energy Economics, 58*, 199–210.

Chancel, L. (2020b). *Unsustainable inequalities*. Harvard University Press.

Chancel, L. (2020). *Unsustainable Inequalities*. Harvard University Press, Cambridge Massachusetts. Appendix with data figure 2.1 and 2.2, accessed 9–11–2023.

Chavez, C. (2023). Peter Singer's fresh take on Animal Liberation – a book that changed the world, but not enough. *Conversation*, 12–6–2023, Retrieved June 24, 2024, from https://theconversation.com/peter-singers-fresh-take-on-animal-liberation-a-book-that-changed-the-world-but-not-enough-205830.

Choe, B. J. (1981). *Energy demand elasticities: Concept evidence and implications, World Bank, DWC-8102*.

Clements, B., Coady, D., Fabrizio, S., Gupta, S., Alleyne, T., & Sdralevich, C. (2013). *Energy subsidies reform: Lessons and implications*. Mimeo: International Monetary Fund.

Coady, D., Parry, I., Sears, L., & Shang, B. (2015). *How large are global energy subsidies?*, International Monetary Fund, New York, report. WP/15/105.

Coase, R. ((1963) 1972). The problem of Social Cost. reprint in R. Dorfman en, & N. S. Dorfman (Eds.), *Economics of the environment, selected readings*, 1st Edition. New York: W.W. Norton & Company, pp. 142–171

Cosme, I., Santos, R., & O'Neill, D. W. (2017). Assessing the degrowth discourse: A review and analysis of academic degrowth policy proposals. *Journal of Cleaner Production, 149*, 321–334.

Cuaresma, J. C., & Heger, M. (2019). Deforestation and economic development: Evidence fromnational borders. *Land Use Policy, 84*, e347–e353.

Dalhuisen, J. M., Florax, R. J. G. M., de Groot, H. L. F., & Nijkamp, P. (2003). Price and income elasticities of residential water demand: A meta-analysis. *Land Economics, 79*(2), 292–308.

Daly, H. E., & Cobb, J. B. (1994). *For the common good* (2nd ed.). Boston: Beacon Press.

Dasgupta, S., Hamilton, K., Pandey, K. D., & Wheeler, D. (2006). Environment during growth: Accounting for governance and vulnerability. *World Development, 34*(9), 1597–1611.

de Bruijn, S. M., & Heintz, R. J. (1999). The environmental Kuznets curve hypothesis. In J. C. J. M. van den Bergh (Ed.), *Handbook of environmental and resource economics* (1st ed., pp. 656–677). Edward Elgar.

Despret, V. (2022). *Wat zouden dieren zeggen als wij ze de juiste vragen stellen, Noordboek, Gorredijk; original Que diraient lex animaux, si...on leux possait les bonnes questions?* (p. 2012). Le Découverte.

Desrochers, P., & Hoffbauer, C. (2009). The post war intellectual roots of the population bomb. Fairfield Osborn's 'Our Plundered Planet' and William Vogt's 'Road to Survival' in Retrospect. *The Electronic Journal of Sustainable Development, 1*(3), 37–61.

Devinney, T. M., Auger, P., & Eckhardt, G. M. (2010). *The myth of the ethical consumer, 1st Edition Cambridge University Press*. United Kingdom.

DiLorenzo, T. J. (1996). The myth of natural monopoly. *The Review of Austrian Economics, 9*(2), 43–58.

EEB. (2020). Retrieved December 22, 2020, from https://eeb.org/membership/about-membership/.

EEB. (2022). European Environmental Bureau. *The role of (environmental) taxation in supporting sustainable transition*. Retrieved September 27, 2024, from https://www.eea.europa.eu/publications/the-role-of-environmental-taxation.

Ehrenfeld, J. (2008). *Sustainability by design* (1st ed.). Yale University Press.

Ehrlich, P. R. (1976). *The population bomb*. Rivercity Press.

Elkington, J. (1999). *Cannibals with Forks, The Triple Bottom Line of Businesses in 21st Century*. Gabriola BC, Canada: New Society Publishers.

Enzensberger, H. M. (1982). *A critique of political* ecology. In R. Grimm, & B. Armstrong (Eds.), *Critical essays*. Continuum, New York.

Escher, R., & Walter-Rogg, M. (2018). Does the conceptualization and measurement of democracy quality matter in comparative climate policy research? *Politics and Governance, 6*(1), 117–144.

Ferkiss, V. (1993). *Nature*. Technology & Society.

Fitzpatric, N., Parrique, T., & Comse, I. (2022). Exploring degrowth policy proposals: A systematic mapping with thematic synthesis. *Journal of Cleaner Production, 365*, 1327, 64. Retrieved July 20, 2023, from https://www.sciencedirect.com/science/article/pii/S0959652622023629#bib33.

FNV. (1987). *Investeren in milieu*, Amsterdam. Retrieved January 3, 2025, from https://books.google.nl/books/about/Investeren_in_het_milieu.html?id=iyfJzwEACAAJ&redir_esc=y.

Pope Franciscus (2025). Retrieved April 19, 2025, from https://www.vatican.va/content/francesco/en/encyclicals/documents/papa-francesco_20150524_enciclica-laudato-si.html.

Galeotti, M. (2007). Economic growth and the quality of the environment: Taking stock. *Environment, Development and Sustainability, 9*, 427–454.

Georgescu-Roegen, N. (1971). *The entropy law and the economic process*. A Harvard Paperback. Retrieved May 3, 2020, from https://www.scribd.com/document/267519123/The-Entropy-Law-and-the-Economic-Process-by-Nicholas-Georgescu-Roegen-pdf.

Gilbert, J., Macpherson, E., Jones, E., & Dehm, J. (2023). The rights of nature as a legal response to the global environmental crisis? A critical review of international law's 'greening' agenda. *Netherlands Yearbook of International Law, 2021*, 47–74.
Grober, U. (2012). *Sustainability*. Green Books, Totnes, UK.
Grossman, G. M., & Krueger, A. B. (1991). *Environmental impacts of a north american free trade agreement*. NBER, Working Paper Series, 3914, mimeo.
Grunewald, N., Klasen, S., Martínez-Zarzoso, I., & Muris, C. (2017). The trade-off between income inequality and carbon dioxide emissions. *Ecological Economics, 142*(C), 249–256.
Hardin, G. (1968). The Tragedy of the Commons. *Science, 162*(3859), 1243–1248.
Havranek, T., Irsova, Z., & Vlach, T. (2017). *Measuring the income elasticity of water demand: The importance of publication and endogeneity bias*. IES Working Paper 2/2017, IES FSV, Charles University, Prague.
Hayek, F. A. (1945, 2005). *The Road to Serfdom*. London: The Institute of Economic Affairs (approved condensed version)
Helpman, E. (2004). *The mystery of economic growth* (1st ed.). The Belknap press of the Harvard University Press.
Henderson. H. (1989). *Development beyond economism; local path to sustainable development*, 5th annual E.F. Schumacher Lecture. Great Barrington, MA: John Dewey Academy. Retrieved June 24, 2024, from, https://centerforneweconomics.org/publications/development-beyond-economism-local-paths-to-sustainable-development/.
Hickel, J. (2019). The contradiction of the sustainable development goals: Growth versus ecology on a finite planet. *Sustainable Development, 1–2*, 1–12. https://doi.org/10.1002/sd.1947
Hitchcock, R. K. (1994). International human rights, environment, and indigenous people. *Colorado Journal of International Environmental Law and Policy, 5*(1), 1–21.
Retrieved November 9, 2023, from https://www.bloomberg.com/billionaires/.
ILO. (2015). *Guidelines for a just transition towards environmentally sustainable economies and societies for all*. Geneva.
IPBES. (2025). *Global assessment report on biodiversity and ecosystem services*. Retrieved February 11, 2025, from https://www.ipbes.net/global-assessment.
Jackson, T. (2011). *Prosperity without growth* (2nd ed.). New York: Earthscan.
Jaffe, A. B., Newell, R. G., Stavins, R. N. (2001). Technology policy for energy and the environment. In A B Jaffe, J Lerner, S Stern (Eds.), *Innovation Policy and the Economy*. Cambridge: MIT Press.
Kahneman, D. (2011). *Thinking, fast and slow* (1st ed.). Penguin.
Kahui, V., Armstrong, C. W., & Aanesen, M. (2024). Comparative analysis of Rights of Nature (RoN) case studies worldwide: Features of emergence and design. *Ecological Economics, 221*. Retrieved June 24, 2024, from https://www.sciencedirect.com/science/article/pii/S0921800924000909.
Kemp, R. (1995). *Environmental policy and technical change*. MERIT, Universiteit van Maastricht, PhD thesis.
Keynes, J. M. (1936). *The general theory of employment, interest, and money*. Retrieved April 19, 2025, from chrome-extension://efaidnbmnnnibpcajpcglclefindmkaj/https://www.files.ethz.ch/isn/125515/1366_keynestheoryofemployment.pdf.
Kroll, Ch., & Zipperer, V. (2020). The political economy of the sustainable development goals (SDGs): Does performance on the SDGs affect re-election? *Sustainability, 12*(6445), 1–14.
Krozer, Y. (2008). *Innovations and the environment*. Springer.
Krozer, Y. (1990). Decision model for environmental strategies of corporations. In: O.-J. Van Gerwen (Ed.) *Financiering van het milieubeleid*, Raad voor Milieu- en Natuuronderzoek, Den Haag, pp. 101–105.
Krutilla, J. V. (1967). Conservation reconsidered. *The American Economic Review, 57*(4), 777–786.
Kuipers, S. K., & Nentjes, A. (1973). Pollution in a neo-classical world: The classics rehabilitated? *The Economist, 121*(1), 52–67.

Kutaula, S., Gillani, A., Gregory-Smith, D., & Bartikowski, B. (2024). Ethical consumerism in emerging markets: opportunities and challenges. *Journal of Business Ethics, 191*, 651–673.
Lagarde, C., & Gaspar, V. (2019). *Getting real on meeting paris climate change commitments*. IMF. Retrieved December 14, 2020, from https://blogs.imf.org/2019/05/03/getting-real-on-meeting-paris-climate-change-commitments/?utm_medium=email&utm_source=govdelivery.
Laubinger, F., Lanzi, E., & Chateau, J. (2020). *Labour market consequences of a transition to a circular economy: A review paper*. OECD.
Leiss, W. (1993). *The domination of nature*. McGill Queens University Press.
Lertzman, D. A., & Vredenburg, H. (2005). Indigenous peoples, resource extraction and sustainable development: An ethical approach. *Journal of Business Ethics, 56*, 239–254.
LMO, Landelijk Milieu Overleg. (1988). *Op zoek naar Goede Daden, nota Milieu en Technologische Ontwikkeling*, Utrecht.
Malm, A. (2025). Retrieved April 19, 2025, from https://jacobin.com/author/andreas-malm.
Malthus, T. R. ((1798) 1826). *An essay on the principle of population*, vol. 1 [1826, 6th ed]. Retrieved May 2, 2020, from https://oll.libertyfund.org/titles/malthus-an-essay-on-the-principle-of-population-vol-1-1826-6th-ed.
Maranzano, P., Cerdeira Bento, J. P., & Manera, M. (2022). The role of education and income inequality on environmental quality: A panel data analysis of the EKC hypothesis on OECD countries. *Sustainability, 14*, 1622. https://doi.org/10.3390/su14031622
Markandya, A., & Pavan, M. (1999). *Green accounting in Europe–four case studies*. Springer Science + Business Media B.V.
Martinez-Alier, J., & Masjuan, E. (2025). Neo-Malthusianism in the Early 20th Century, Universidad Autonoma de Barcelona. Retrieved February 27, 2025, from chrome-extension://efaidnbmnnnibpcajpcglclefindmkaj/https://www.isecoeco.org/pdf/Neo-malthusianism.pdf
Mazzucato, M. (2017). Mission-oriented innovation policies: challenges and opportunities. *Industrial and Corporate Change, 27*(5), 803–815.
McNeely, J. (1988). Economics and biological diversity (1st ed.). International Union for Conservation of Nature, Glad.
Meadows, D..H., Meadows, D. L., Randers, J., & Behrens III, W. W. (1972). *Limits to growth*. A Potomac Associates Book, Washington D.C. Retrieved May 2, 2020, from http://donellameadows.org/the-limits-to-growth-now-available-to-read-online/.
Mellor, M., (2019). Neoliberalism has tricked us into believing a fairytale about where money comes from. *The Conversation*, 22–6–2019.
Milanovic, B. (2012). *Global Income Inequalities by Numbers: in History and Now*. Policy Research Working Paper, number 6259, World Bank, Washington.
Mill, J. S. ((1884) 1985). *The principles of political economy*, Book IV, Chapter VI, Penguin Classics, New York.
Mishan, E. J. ((1968) 1993). *The cost of economic growth* (1st ed). London: Weidenfeld and Nicholson, pp. 30–46.
Mowery F., & Rosenberg, N. (1979). The influence of market demand on innovation: a critical review of some recent empirical studies, *Research Policy* 8, 102–153.
Ecological Footprint Network. Retrieved September 29, 2023, from https://www.footprintnetwork.org/our-work/ecological-footprint/.
Nordhaus, W. (1973). The allocation of energy resources. *Brookings Papers on Economic Activity, 3*, 1973.
Nordhaus, W. D. (2010). *The perils of learning model for modelling endogenous technical change*. Retrieved May 25, 2020, from https://www.nap.edu/read/13023/chapter/15.
O'Mahony, T. (2020). State of the art in carbon taxes: A review of the global conclusions. *Green Finance, 2*(4), 409–423.
OECD. (2008). *Measuring material flows and resource productivity*. Paris.
Opschoor, J. B., & Vos, H. B. (1989). *Economic instruments for environmental protection, Organisation for economic co–operation and development.*

Ostrom, E. (1990). *Governing the commons: The evolution of institutions for collective action.* Cambridge University Press.

Ostrom, E. (1998). A behavioural approach to the rational choice theory of collective action. *American Political Science Review, 92*(1), 1–22.

Papaioannou, K. J., & Luiten van Zanten, J. (2015). The dictator effect: How long years in office affect economic development. *Journal of Institutional Economics, 11*(1), 111–139.

Pearce, D., & Kerry Turner, R. (1990). *Economics of natural resources and the environment.* Pearson Education, Essex.

Pearce, D., & Palmer, C. (2001). Public and private spending on environmental protection: A cross-countries policy analysis. *Fiscal Studies, 22*(4), 403–456.

Perrings, C. (1985). The natural economy revisited. *Economic Development and Cultural Change, 33*(4), 827–850.

Pigou, A. C. (1920). *The economics of welfare* (1st ed., pp. 115–117). MacMillan.

Piketty, T. (2014). *Capital in the twenty-first century* (1st ed.). The Belknap Press the Harvard University Press.

Pine I, B. J., & Gilmore, J. H. (1998). Welcome to the experience economy. *Harvard Business Review*, July-August.

Porter, M. E., & van der Linde, C. (1995). Green and competitive: Ending the stalemate. *Harvard Business Review, September/october, 1995*, 119–134.

Pottier, A. (2021). *Expenditure-elasticity and income-elasticity of GHG emissions–a survey of literature on household carbon footprint.* FAERE Working Paper, 2021.01.

Retrieved January 31, 2023, from https://www.pewresearch.org/religion/2015/04/02/religious-projection-table/.

Raworth, K. (2017). Donut Economie. *Nieuw Amsterdam*, Amsterdam (Dutch translation).

Reijnders, L. (2021). Substitution, natural capital and sustainability. *Journal of Integrative Environmental Sciences, 18*(1), 115–142.

Riemens, R. (2024). Fixing the earth: Whole-systems thinking in Silicon Valley's environmental ideology. *Digital Technology, Culture and Society, 8*(4), 294–311.

Ringius, L., Torvanger, A., & Underdal, A. (2000). *Burden differentiation: Fairness principles and proposals.* Oslo, Norway: Center for International Climate, and Environmental Research.

RIVM, Rijksinstituut voor Volksgezondheid en Milieuhygiëne. (1989). *Zorgen voor Morgen*, Samson H.D. Tjeenk Willink BV, Alphen aan den Rijn.

Romer, P. M. (1994). The origin of endogenous growth. *Journal of Economic Perspectives, 8*(1), 3–22.

Rosenberg, N. (1975). Technological innovation and natural resources: The niggardliness of nature reconsidered. In N. Rosenberg (Ed.), *Perspectives on technology* (pp. 229–259). Cambridge University Press.

Roser, M. (2023). *Our world in data.* Retrieved November 9, 2023, from https://ourworldindata.org/grapher/income-share-top-1-before-tax-wid?tab=chart.

Rothbard, M. N. (1995). *Economic thought before adam smith.* Edward Elgar.

Ruskin, J. (1904, 2023). *The science of political economy*, Books III to V. Retrieved February 4, 2023, from littp://www.arcli ive.org/details/completeworksofli07georiala.

Sahlin, M. ((1971) 2011). *Stone age economics.* 1st Paperback Edition. New York: Routledge.

Schumacher, E. F. (1973). *Small is beautiful.* Blond & Biggs.

Scruggs, L. A. (1998). Political and economic inequality and the environment. *Ecological Economics, 26*, 259–275.

Sedláček, T. (2011). *Economics of good and evil; The quest for economic meaning from gilgamesh to wall street.* Oxford University Press.

SER. (2024). *Perspective on broad prosperity in 2040: Building the economy of the future.* Retrieved February 27, 2025, from https://www.ser.nl/en/publications/perspective-broad-prosperity-2040.

Shafiee, S., & Topal, E. (2009). When will fossil fuel reserves be diminished. *Energy Policy, 37*, 181–189.

Smith, A., (1776, 1986). On the natural progress of opulence, reprint in A. Smith, *The wealth of nations*, Book III, Chapter I, Penguin Classics, London, p. 481.
Solow, R. M. (1957). Technical change and the aggregate production function. *Review of Economics and Statistics, 39*(3), 312–320.
Solow, R. M. ((1973) 1977), The economics of resources or the resources of economics, reprint in R. Dofman, N.S. Dorfman (Eds.) *Economics of the environment*, 1st ed. W.W. Norton & Company Inc, New York, pp. 354–370.
Songwe, V., Stern, N., & Bhattacharya, A. (2022). *Finance for climate action: Scaling up investment for climate and development*. London: Grantham Research Institute on Climate Change and the Environment, London School of Economics and Political Science.
Sorrell, S. (2009). Jevons' Paradox revisited: The evidence for backfire from improved energy efficiency. *Energy Policy, 37*, 1456–1469.
Spash, C. L. (2021). *The history of pollution 'externalities' in economic thought*. WU Vienna University of Economics and Business. SRE-Discussion Papers No. 01/2021 https://doi.org/10.57938/c61ad395-7a3d-425a-9969-203de844de22.
Springer, S., Birch, K., & MacLeavy, J. (2016). *Introduction to neoliberalism, the handbook of neoliberalism*. Routledge, New York, pp 1–14. Deeming, C. (2017). The lost and the new 'liberal world' of welfare capitalism: a critical assessment of Gøsta Esping-Andersen's. *The Three Worlds of Welfare Capitalism* a Quarter Century Later, *Social Policy & Society, 16*(3), 405–422
Statista. (2020). Retrieved December 22, 2020, from https://www.statista.com/statistics/190934/membership-of-national-environmental-and-conservation-organizations-2005-2006/.
Steen, B. (1999). *A systematic approach to environmental priority strategies in product development (EPS)*. Version 2000-Models and Data" CPM-report 1999:5. http://eps.esa.chalmers.se
Stern, D. I. (2004). Rise and fall of the environmental kuznets curve. *World Development, 32*(8), 1419–1439.
Credit Suisse. (2022). *Global Wealth Report and data book*. Credit Suisse Group AG.
Thaler, R. H., & Sustein, C. R. (2008). *Nudge, improving decisions about health, wealth and happiness*, 1st Edition. New Heaven & London: Yale University Press.
Tol, R. S. J. (2005). Marginal damage costs of carbon dioxide emissions. *Energy Policy, 33*, 2064–2074.
UNEP. (2011). *Green Economy Report*. New York.
UNEP. (2011). *Decoupling natural resource use and environmental impacts from economic growth*. A Report of the Working Group on Decoupling to the International Resource Panel. In: M. Fischer-Kowalski, M. Swilling, E. U. von Weizsäcker, Y. Ren, Y. Yoriguchi, W. Crane, F. Krausmann, N. Eisenmenger, S. Giljum, P. Hennicke, P. Romero Lankao, A. Siriban Manalang, S. Sewerin, United Nations Environment Program, Nairobi.
UNEP. (2020). *Guidelines for social life cycle assessment of products and organizations*. Nairobi.
UNEP. (2020). *Financing circularity*. Nairobi
van Driel, P., & Krozer, Y. (1988). Innovation and preventive environmental policy. In F. Dietz (Ed.), *Environmental policy in a market economy* (pp. 78–92). Pudoc.
Vona, F., & Fabrizio, P. (2011). Income inequality and the development of environmental technologies. *Ecological Economics, 70*(11), 2201–2213.
Wolloch, N. (2017). *Nature in the history of economic thought: How natural resources became an economic concept*. Routledge.
Wu, Z., Schaffartzik, A., Shao, Q., Wang, D., Li, G., Su, Y., & Rao, L. (2019). Does economic recession reduce material use? Empirical evidence based on 157 economies worldwide. *Journal of Cleaner Production, 167*, 120–132.
Zacharova, O. (2017). State environmental ideology, from tsarist empire to sustainable Russia. *Brics Law Journal, 4*(4), 39–64.
Zamurs, A. (2023). Climate change, reproductive justice and existential politics: Examining histories and implications of neo-malthusianism in the U.S. environmental movement. Yale University. Retrieved February 27, 2025, from https://elischolar.library.yale.edu/.

Chapter 3
Environmental Performance of Economies

It is shown that many growing economies improved environmental performances during the last decades when environmental regulations were pulled back in favour of market negotiations. Based on the environmentalist model for assessing impacts, it is shown that the resource-intensity of economies declined mainly due to changing economic activities towards services, and that environmental efficiency improved through more uses of environmental technologies. Economic growth at lower environmental impacts is achieved in a larger number of high-, mid-, and low-income countries while a few dozen economies grew along with more well-being and better environmental qualities. Factors that generate high performances are underpinned.

3.1 Introduction

Have growing economies reduced environmental impact? This question addresses the debate about the link between economic growth and environmental impacts. The usual opinion of environmentalists is that growing economies have negative impacts on environmental qualities because additional natural resources are needed for conversions into material products, which irrevocably dissipate as emissions. The emphasis is placed on the irreversible trade-offs between economic growth and environmental qualities. With reference to the rebound effect, it is argued that more efficient uses of particular natural resources, which reduce some environmental impacts per income, cause larger total impacts as the uses of natural resources increases when economies grow (Ward et al., 2016). This environmentalist idea about the rebound effects became a *bon ton* in the scientific communication (Wiedemann et al., 2020). Those ideas popularise the assumption that economic growth undermines the environment. However, these scholarly forecasts differ from observation of environmental impacts in hindsight. Insightful is a comparison of the forecasted well-being and environmental impacts in the early 1980s with the revealed results in the early 2000s. The results show better health and less poverty, along with smaller

© The Author(s), under exclusive license to Springer Nature Switzerland AG 2025
Y. Krozer, *Economic Growth and the Environment*,
https://doi.org/10.1007/978-3-031-99181-3_3

ozone gap, better water quality, and other improvements compared to the forecast, but global impacts on climate and biodiversity worsened compared to the forecasts (Chenoweth & Feitelson, 2005).

What were the impacts of economic growth, what were the drivers of the improvements and aggravations, and what economies grew along with better environmental performances? Assessing these impacts, factors, and countries performances contributes to the debate about whether sustainable development is in progress, or it is obstructed. Those questions are answered in this chapter based on authoritative statistical data across all countries with particular attention to the changes globally and in the focus countries. Next to environmental impacts, changes in well-being are indicated. Whether economic growth has increased or reduced environmental impacts is assessed for the period 1990–2015 when neo-liberal politics are adopted in many countries. While environmental policies disseminated to nearly all countries, the policy demands are often relaxed in favour of voluntary agreements during that period of time. Statistical data are used for estimates with the mainstream environmentalist model of environmental impacts caused by economic activities. This model refers to the neo-Malthusian thinking about the population dynamic within closed system. In this model, environmental impacts, denoted as I, are supposed to be the result of population, denoted as P. It is based on the assumption that every person consumes environmental qualities throughout lifetime denoted, k. An environmental impact with this fixed consumption is function of P and k (Ehrlich & Holdren, 1971). This is formalised:

$$I = \mathrm{k} \cdot P \tag{3.1}$$

For example, P number of people that use, k ton of oil per person causes, I impact because CO_2 emissions caused by combustions generate greenhouse effects high in atmosphere, which change climate on the earth. As it is acknowledged that income and technology also influence environmental impacts that neo-Malthusian model is adapted to these factors. It is also observed that consumption patterns are relevant, given income. Therefore, consumption of products is considered throughout life cycles of extracting, producing, distributing, consuming, and disposing of materials during the lifespan of a person, which is called affluence. In addition, it is found that technologies influence consumption of natural resources and reduce environmental impacts of using these resources. In result, environmental impacts, I, would depend on population, P, as well as consumption related to income, A, and application of technologies, T, that can increase or reduce the impacts given the population and affluence. This is formalised as:

$$I = P \cdot A \cdot T. \tag{3.2}$$

This IPAT model gained much popularity within environmentalist thinking though the factors that determine environmental impacts are considered as independent of each other while they are linked in reality (Alcott, 2010).

In order to determine the effects of consumption and technologies on environmental qualities, given population and its income, the IPAT model is converted into so called 'Kaya identity' (Chertow, 2001). In this model, environmental impacts, I, are the results of the number of people, P, and expenditures per person a/p. When multiplied, they equal GDP. In addition, technology, T, is divided into two factors. One factor is the material consumption per income, m/a. It shows changes in consumption patterns when income per person changes. Material consumption per income is called the 'resource intensity'. Higher resource intensity means more uses of the natural resources per income. Second factor is the effect of material uses on environmental qualities, i/m. This addresses applications of technologies. Environmental impacts of material use are referred to as 'environmental efficiency'. Higher environmental efficiency implies lower impacts per the uses of natural resources. Multiplications of the resource intensity and environmental efficiency indicate environmental impacts of GDP. Formal model is:

$$I = P \cdot a/p \cdot m/a \cdot i/m \tag{3.3}$$

This model, labelled as ImPAT, enables to specify changes in the resource-intensity of consumption and improving environmental-efficiency in production (Waggoner & Ausubel, 2002). The ImPAT model is used for estimating environmental impacts of countries' GDP. The resource-intensities are estimated for fresh-water use in m^3, ton fuel uses and m^2 forest areas, each one per USD_{2015}. The estimates of environmental efficiency cover: access to wastewater treatment in m^3 per m^3 of water use, ton CO_2 emissions per ton fuel, ton NOx emissions per ton fuel, and m^2 nature protection areas for compensation of m^2 deforestation. Multiplications of those resource-intensities and environmental efficiencies show total water pollution, climate change, air pollution, and nature restoration. Water pollution and nature restoration do not specify pollutants, but better data on all countries is not found.

It is expected that the use of natural resources is reduced in time due to more uses of man-made capital, labour, and knowledge resources per income, and that environmental technologies reduce impacts per resources in time. If the resource-intensity and environmental-efficiency of GDP decrease, it means a decoupling of economic growth from environmental impacts. Their rates of change are relevant. If the rates of changes are low the impacts per income decline, meaning a relative decoupling, and if these rates of change exceed the rates of economic growth, environmental impacts decrease in total, called absolute decoupling. These estimates are calculated with ImPAT model for all 217 countries and entities in the World Bank database. The results are tabulated and discussed mainly with regard to the global level and fifteen focus countries with populations exceeding 100 million people as mentioned in the general introduction. Many results are also shown for other countries.

Countries populations are assessed in Sect. 3.2. Changes of incomes and economic activities are presented in Sect. 3.3. The consumption of services during the last decades and their consequences for the use of natural resources are addressed in Sect. 3.4. Section 3.5 presents the resource-intensities across countries. Section 3.6

presents environmental efficiency. Section 3.7 illustrates how they are integrated into environmental impacts. Based on these results, high environmental performers are identified in Sect. 3.8, and conclusions are drawn in Sect. 3.9.

3.2 Population Scales and Skills

Is there an overshoot of global population? An answer to this question depends on the specific perspectives and interests. While larger population is considered a threat from the environmentalist perspective, it is perceived as a blessing by the mainstream economists advocating growth. Environmentalists argued in the early 1800s that the earth cannot carry all 1 billion people on earth that time, as well as in 1960s with 3 billion people, and in 2022 with 8 billion people. Meanwhile, the mainstream economists complained about a shortage of people to work. Presently, the decline of populations is considered a global risk for economic growth (IMF, 2024). However, a smaller, more skilled global populations could bridge these opposing economic and environmental perspectives as a pathway for sustainable development. This possibility is assessed based on trends in the scale of population, labour forces, education, and gender participation in it.

A brief introduction to the assessment methods is useful. The population scale was assessed based on the number of people and growth in the past. This growth in the past may not continue in the future if the birth rate declines faster than the death rate. The growth and birth-to-death ratio in the past are used to assess expectations about future population. In addition, the use of resources depends on people who do the job, called labour force. The labour force excludes people in education, retired people, and those who are not able or willing to do it for many reasons. By definition of the World Bank, people who are employed constitute the labour force, while the unemployed, and not registered as an employee are excluded. Self-employed are included in the labour force. This is particularly relevant in lower income countries where many people work in small enterprises, which are usually craft shops, called 'micro-enterprises'. From the mainstream economic viewpoint, a growing labour force is needed. In many jobs it is not just about the number of people, but their skills are needed. These skills depend on levels of education, which are indicated by the percentage of educated people in the population and the enrolment into those levels. Compared to maximum literacy by 100%, meaning that all people in the world know to read and write, the literacy rate in 2015 exceeded 80% in most countries. This is only a statistical figure based on obligatory primary education for children in most countries though several countries exclude females from education. However, not all children participated in education, and many young people who did participate remained illiterate. Despite this deficiency, usual statistical data is used. According to this data education increased in most countries. Enrolments of children into the primary education and young people into the secondary education in low-income countries are approximately half of the maximum. High-income areas have much higher rates of those enrolments, but the increases of those enrolments are faster in low-income countries than in high-income countries and mid-income ones where the enrolments saturated as they approach the maximum possible. Regarding that saturation of the primary and secondary education in many countries and demands for skilled labour, the assessment of skills requires more ambitious criteria. Therefore, the enrolment rates in the tertiary education and their gender parity are considered, which means the participation in technical, professional, and academic colleges, respectively the female participation in them compared to the male participation. The female participation in the tertiary education is considered important not only because it is fair to women but also because women's education is essential for the societal well-being and for qualified labour that enables economic growth.

Based on those assumptions, changes in populations and labour force across countries are assessed with regard to population growth in the past, aging rates, labour forces, as well as enrolment in tertiary education and participation of women in it. All these indicators for the focus countries are shown in Table 3.1. It covers the number of people in 2015 and their growth rates, the growth rates of births minus deaths and labour force, as well as the enrolment rates and growth in tertiary education and gender parity in 2015.

The global population is growing, but its growth rates declined as a trend, from 2.1% during the 1960s to less than 0.8% in the 2010s. Nevertheless, it does not

Table 3.1 Selected indicators for populations and their capabilities in the focus countries

Growth period 1991–2015 * 2005–2015	Population million people		Death-birth	Labour force	Enrol tertiary education %		Gender parity enrolled
	2015	Growth (%)	Growth (%)	Growth (%)	2015	Growth (%)	2015
World	7,348	1.3	0.5	1.4	37	4	1.1
USA	321	1.0	1.1	0.9	89	1*	1.3
Japan	127	0.1	2.6	0.1	–	–	–
EU	445	0.2	0.9	0.4	67	3	1.2
Mexico	122	1.5	2.0	2.4	32	3	1.0
Russia	144	−0.1	0.6	0.02	80	2	1.2
Brazil	204	1.3	1.7	2.1	51	7	1.3
China	1,380	0.8	2.3	0.9	46	12	1.2
Egypt	92	2.0	−0.7	2.5	35	2	1.0
Indonesia	258	1.4	0.1	2.0	33	6	1.1
Philippines	102	2.0	1.2	2.6	38	3	1.2
Nigeria	181	2.6	−1.0	2.3	11	1	–
India	1,310	1.6	0.4	1.6	27	9	1.0
Pakistan	199	2.5	−0.3	3.2	9	10	0.9
Bangladesh	156	1.7	−0.1	2.3	14	8	0.7
Ethiopia	101	3.0	−2.4	3.5	10	14	0.5

automatically imply a slow-down of the economic growth. As the population growth is only indirectly linked to economic growth, their correlation across focus countries is low. This link varies across countries. For example, the population growth in mid-income China was slow while income growth was fast, contrary to fast population growth with slow economic growth in mid-incomes Mexico and Brazil, and low-income Indonesia. Also, the population growth in low-income Ethiopia was nearly twice faster than in low-income India while both economies grew fast. Migration also drives the scale and growth of population and economy in several countries with small local population. Migrants constituted the largest part of the population in high-income Gulf countries as Bahrain, Oman, Qatar, Saudi Arabia, and UAE and their high, 7% annual growth of population and fast economic growth are largely driven by net immigration, defined as immigration minus emigration. Vice versa, high net emigration caused only 1% population growth and economic stagnation in Eritrea, Zimbabwe, and several other low-income countries.

A larger population in the future is often assumed, but it is uncertain. An authoritative assessment of the global population in 2050 shows a broad band of outcomes ranging from less than present 8 billion people to more than 10 billion people in the 2030s (UN DESA, 2022). A slower global population growth can be expected given the decelerating trend in population growth, but the forecasts are uncertain regarding the diverging trends of population growth across the focus countries. A lower band is plausible if the past trend continues. If the trend of growth rates during the 2010s is linearly extrapolated into the next decades, the global population will turn around from growth into decline within a decade after 2030. The downward trend in the global balance of births minus deaths in the past also supports the lower band of population forecasts. While the birth rates and the death rates decelerated and converged across countries from 1990 to 2015, the birth rates declined faster than death rates in nearly all countries. Exceptions are Kazakhstan and Russia, which have high death rates and low birth rates. Instead of the neo-Malthusian doomsday, many countries face the decline of population due to slow birth rates. This motivates promotion of births in several countries, justified by the economic growth, labour supply, military forces, and other policy objectives.

The balance of birth-minus-deaths determines the composition of populations in the future, which is important for the future labour force. Low-income countries have higher rates of population growth than high-income countries and mid-income ones due to their higher birth rates. The birth rates in low-income countries are usually above 30 per 1000 persons, compared to less than 10 per 1000 persons in high-income and mid-income ones. High-income countries and most mid-income ones have low birth rates and low infant mortality at birth, but their infant mortaility hardly decreases. Meanwhile, the birth rates decrease fast in low-income countries, as well as the infant mortality at birth. The latter decreased in low-income countries by half during the last few decades, though 60 deaths per 1000 births in the Western and Southern Africa is still high compared to less than 10 dead infants per 1000 births in high income countries. Exceptions are countries with religions rulings as Afghanistan, and Westbank and Gaza where the birth rates increase. Apparently, most women all over the world choose to take fewer children when the survival of children at birth increases, if they have this choice. In effect, populations are young in low-income countries but the growth rates of youth saturate. These changes are mirrored by the death rates. Populations in high-income and mid-income countries is aging as their death rates slowly decrease, thereby the average lifetime slowly increases. Their maximum lifetime approaches an asymptote of about 95 years on average if the trends of the last decade are extrapolated. The death rates decrease faster in low-income countries, but their lifespan is only 60 years on average. Their average lifespan elongates faster than in mid-income and high-income countries, except in Eswatini, Namibia, and Syria. This implies aging populations in lower income countries within a few decades. Regarding the growth trend in the past, as well as the decreasing birth-minus-death rates, it is plausible that the global population starts to decrease within a few decades.

A smaller global population can be as productive by value as a larger one, or even more productive, when there are more jobs to do the demanded work and better education for development of necessary skills is accessible. The global labour force covered 45% of the global population in 2015. It also grows as more people got a job in most focus countries, except in the USA and Nigeria. Apparently, there is no problem on the global scale and in most countries, but there are imbalances in the demands and supplies of labour as some countries seek labour while others seek businesses that provide jobs. For example, the labour force in many African countries is below 30% of the population with many young people without skills that are demanded in labour markets. It is not surprising that many of them want to emigrate, among others to the Gulf countries whose migrant labour force constitutes more than 70% of the population. Mismatch between demand and supply across countries can be resolved by policies that encourage acquisition of skills, investments in low-income countries and regulated migration of the labour force.

More worrying is the trend of declining balance of birth minus death. This trend reduces the labour force in the future. This is worrying because difficult to resolve as the trend converges across countries. As a result, percentage of elderly people in populations increases in nearly all countries. These aging societies could somewhat reduce environmental impacts. This expectation is based on observations that elderly people use less income for durable products, less transport, leisure, culture, and other services in so called 'complex consumption' compared to young consumers. Per income, elderly people use more food, cloths and suchlike 'simple consumption'. Nevertheless, the consumption patterns of old and young people increasingly align to each other over time which implies that the differences in environmental impacts decline (Gilleard & Higgs, 2011). More important are the economic consequences given larger expenditures on care, retirement, and social securities. Moreover, elderly people could be more skilled and experienced, but they are usually less productive when these expenditures are considered. This hinders economic growth that is needed to cover these expenditures (Harper, 2014). As larger parts of the countries' population get older environmental impacts can be somewhat reduced, but it becomes more expensive to maintain the income per person. It is an urgent issue in high-income countries with long-living populations and low birth rates, and it becomes an issue in lower income countries as their lifetime elongates and birth rates decline.

Higher skills of the labour force and technologies that replace labour can mitigate that impact of aging on economic growth. An increase of the enrolments in education in nearly all countries is feasible, and it is plausible regarding the convergence cross-countries trend of higher enrolment into the tertiary education. A higher enrolment enhances skills which presumably generate economic growth regarding high correlation of the tertiary education and birth of firms (startups) across the focus countries. Another encouraging trend across nearly all countries is the increasing female enrolment into the tertiary education. It is fair, and expands skilled labour, which contributes to economic growth. The increasing female enrolment in the tertiary education on the global scale could continue in the future as the enrolment is presently low in many low-income countries, even negligible in Malawi and Afghanistan. Another factor is the use of technologies that enable to replace the workforce, for convenience called robotisation. A lot is speculated about substitution of labour for capital through robots with artificial intelligence. Estimates suggest that the demands for labour hardly decline while demands for skill change (Fang et al., 2024). So, economic impacts of the aging societies along with declining global population in the future will need social policies. Rather than pushing for higher birth rates, those policies could pursue more skills for jobs and regulated migration opportunities, better health and labour conditions, flexible transitions from jobs to retirement, and other actions that improve execution of jobs.

The global population presumably declines and ages within the next few decades. To meet this challenge, enrolment in higher education should increase, particularly for women, along with investing in jobs and the skills of labour in low-income countries, and in the regulation of job migration.

3.3 Affluence

Does affluent consumption drive larger uses of the natural resources? A lot depends on social norms. Rigid social norms that cause environmental degradation and poverty are illustrated with a few historical examples in Europe. This is followed by an assessment of changes in income in the last century and their effect on population and energy uses.

A few examples in the European history after the fall of Roman Empire in 500 AC illustrate the detrimental effects of rigid social norms on environmental qualities, well-being and economic development. An illustrative impact on environmental qualities is the degradation of soil and overexploitation of forests despite the declining population and income during nearly thousand years after the 500s AC, which means after the fall of Ancient Roman Empire. This environmental degradation is caused by the agricultural practices with 'slash and burn' of forests. This practice was cheaper and more convenient than the fertilisation of soil, which was used in the Roman agriculture for centuries but abandoned in large parts of Europe (Hoffmann, 2015). Rigid social norms in Europe were also disastrous for well-being. For example, the rigour of promiscuity impeded the use of soap for bathing in Europe during nearly millennium after the fall of Roman Empire, while soap was widely available and used in the neighbouring Arab countries (Ridner, 2020). Rigid social norms obstructed economies in Europe while economies flourished in Asia. A major constraint to economic development in Europe was the religious ban on usury, though usury enabled the accumulation of capital and financing of risky entrepreneurial initiatives in the development of agricultural practices. In effect, main sources of the European capital were robbery and conquest used for rude exploitation of slaves, serfs, and women with mass starvation (Koyama, 2010). Rigour of norms still has suchlike dark sides when they constrain deviant opinions and behaviour.

Then, how the global economic growth emerged? Experiences in Europe provide an answer. Economies grew in Europe when rigid norms were lifted after religious wars that decimated the European population during about hundred years until the late-1600s. During the subsequent century, called the Enlightenment, entrepreneurs could undertake risky activities due to the capital accumulation and scientific discoveries with guaranteed ownership with help of emerging intellectual property rights. Explorative travels could be made and machines could be developed and purchased, which enhanced industries in England and France, followed by the industrial expansion during the next two centuries. From the early 1800s onward, the global economy has continuously grown, largely driven by innovations in industries. As peoples' incomes increased, conditions for living improved, which reduced mortality of children and prolonged lifespan of people. In effect, the global population grew (Rosenberg and Birdzell, 1986).

Though the annual average global economic growth has been rarely above 2% and the population growth has been usually below 1.5% throughout the last two centuries, the long-term results were impressive. Along with about tenfold increase of the global population, the global yearly average income per capita in constant US Dollars of the year 2000 (USD_{2000}) grew about seven times, which is estimated with the Maddison data (Maddison, 2023). Globally, the yearly average income per person was a few hundred USD_{2000} during the early 1800s and reached more than ten thousand USD_{2000} in 2000. Nearly all countries became richer measured by the average income per capita, but disparities in the richness also increased. On average, a typical European had less income than an Asian and a North African in the early 1800s, but became nearly three times richer by the early 2000s. Meanwhile, a typical colonist in the USA was even poorer than a European, and nearly twice as rich two centuries later. The Russian colonists of Siberia and the Australian ones in the Oceania also became richer, but their incomes fluctuated greatly over time. Although the incomes per capita in Africa, Asia, and Latin America also grew their average growth rates were below the global average and fluctuated. Nowadays, economies in North America, Europe, and the Oceania are often labelled as the 'West' are richer per capita than the countries of Confederation of Independent States (CIS), often considered as Russia, which are usually richer per capita than most African, Asia, and Latin American countries, called the 'South'. These labels have a political meaning rather than a geographical one.

A lot is debated about the reason for industrial expansion in the 'West' during the 1800s, instead of in the 'South' where most people lived and incomes per capita were higher before the 1800s. A few viewpoints are mentioned, purposed solely to illustrate the diversity of ideas about this subject. A popular explanation is the colonialism. In this idea, the military superiority of the 'West' enforced the colonial exploitation of labour and natural resources in the 'South', which generated cheap materials and labour for the Western industries (Wallerstein, 1974). Another idea is that elites in the 'South' opposed innovations because they could force women, slaves, and serfs to work at negligible costs instead of paying for development and purchases of machines (Pommerantz, 2000). Environmental qualities are also considered. Warm climates would be supportive of the agricultural activities in the South, whereas the temperate climates would suit the industrial ones in the West (Lander, 1998). Importance of energy for economic growth in the West is also underlined. Particularly, the discoveries and exploitations of energy-dense fossil fuels for industrial production are considered important (Smil, 2019). Although all these ideas have weak points, they can partially be valid in addition to each other as these ideas do not contradict each other. Continuity of economic growth is explained by increasing productivity, it is the increasing value of produced goods per purchased resources, driven by larger demands for goods and cheaper resources. As mortality declined due to more food, heat, light, and other goods for private consumption, as well as sanitation, city lights, care, and other public services, demand for products and services grew. Meanwhile, costs of supplies for agriculture and industrial declined due to larger production scale, exploitation of labour in the South, cheap imports of the natural resources, and better technologies. In result, the productivity increases in agriculture and industries rendered economic growth in the 'West' throughout two centuries (Kremer, 1993).

How the Western economic growth relates to the uses of natural resources is far from clear given that fossil fuels and other minerals were known and used in Asia well-before the industrialisation in Europe. Numerous studies theorised about the relation of economic growth to the use of natural resources. It is often focused on energy uses, with particular attention to fossil fuels. A meta-review of 686 studies shows four models: no direct relation, incomes generate energy, energy growth generates incomes, and feedback loops (Kalimeris et al., 2014). From the environmentalist viewpoint, larger energy consumption would drive higher income. Growing uses of fossil fuels would explain the income growth during the 1900s because higher energy densities of fossil fuels compared to renewable energy of biomass and labour could generate larger power. This viewpoint is underpinned with the historic correlations between income, consumed energy, and fossil fuels for several countries in time (Ayres & Voudouris, 2014) and the correlations across several countries (Beaudreau & Lightfoot, 2015). Both studies focused on high-income countries. However, high correlations are not observed when the growth of energy uses and income are correlated and the scale of continents is considered because these growth rates across countries vary a lot.

Despite those models, causalities are disputable given that population grew slower than the energy use that grew slower than income throughout last centuries, and that those growth rates diverged as trends across countries insofar data is available. The growth rates of population, energy use, and income decouple in time. This decoupling is illustrated in Graph 3.1 as indexes of the global population by the number of people,

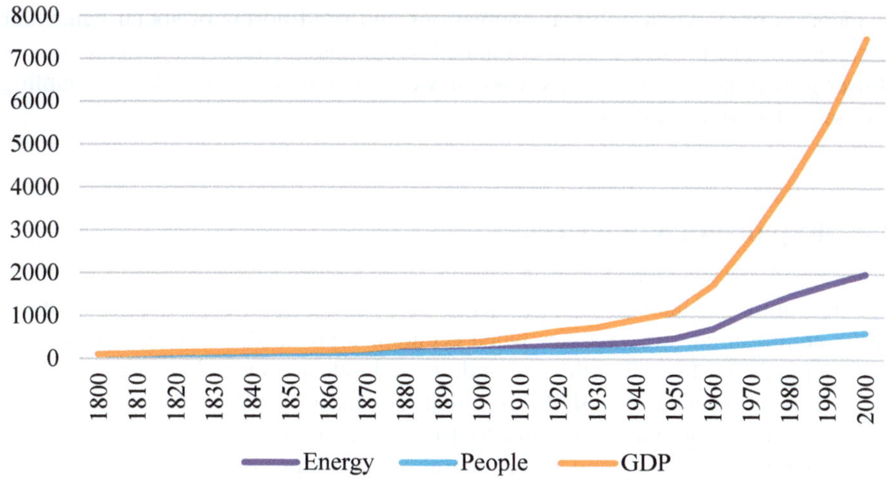

Graph 3.1 Indexes total population, income and energy

energy use in power units (PWh), and income in USD_{2011} from 1800 to 2000 year (1800 = 100). These data refer to Maddison and OWD database (https://ourworldindata.org/), and the missing data is interpolated. Results are shown in ten year intervals. Given imperfect data, trends are relevant rather than scales in a particular year.

Until the 1800s, the global population remained below one billion people, followed by growth to about 6 billion from the year 1800 to 2000 due to lower mortality as the livelihood improved. The growth rate of the global population was below 1.4% a year throughout the last two centuries. The rate of 0.6% from 1800 to the 1950s accelerated to 1.7% during the next fifty years due to lower mortality in the South, followed by a decline of the rates after the year 2000. Meanwhile, the global energy use grew faster than the population. The growth rate was on average 1.5% a year from 5.6 PWh in 1800 to 112 PWh in 2000. These growth rates were 0.9% during the 1800s and 2.1% over the next hundred years. They were faster in the West than in the South. Global income grew even faster. This growth rate was 2.1% annual average starting from USD_{2011} 842 billion in the year 1800 to nearly USD_{2011} 63,100 billion in 2000. They were below 1.0% from the year 1800 to 1850, then accelerated, followed by a slow-down during the first half of the 1900s when World War I and World War 2 (WW2) were fought, and accelerated to 3.7% during the second half of the 1900s. Incomes in the South grew slower than in the West until the late 1900s, followed by the acceleration above the Western growth rates during the 2000s. It is also found that the countries that import fossil fuels have generated faster economic growth during the second half of the 1900s than the countries that produce and export fossil fuels if several decades are considered. It underpins that decoupling of income and natural resources (Krozer, 2022).

Incomes grew when political oppressions and rigid norms of social behaviour are released. The income growth continued throughout the last centuries along with slower growth of energy use, and even slower population growth. This decoupling is observed across countries.

3.4 Expansion of Services

The decoupling of income and the energy use can largely be explained by changes in the composition of businesses when economies grow. Main changes are driven by faster growth of services than agriculture and industries which enlarge the share of services in the country's GDP. Given that services are labour-intensive compared to land-intensive agriculture and material-intensive industries, economies use more labour, while less energy and other natural resources per income. Rather that the substitutions of the natural resources for capital in equipment, which are often addressed from the environmentalist perspective, the substitutions for labour and knowledge evolved throughout the last century. These substitutions are addressed with regard to all services, and the knowledge work within services. The scales of change, as well as the factors that drive changes and their effects on the natural resources are assessed.

Services grew worldwide faster than agriculture and industries during the last century when the global population tripled to more than 6 billion people and the global GDP grew fifteen times to USD_{2015} about 50 trillion. Along with the growth of population and income, the composition of businesses changes across countries, measured by value. The share by value of land-intensive agriculture in the global GDP decreased from 13% to 5%, and the share of material-intensive industry from 37 to 31%, contrary to services which share by value increased from about 50% to 63% from 1900 to 2000 year (PBL, 2023). The remaining about 3% of the global GDP covers the costs of natural resources. As the labour-intensity of economies increased, meaning higher costs of labour per output value, the material-intensity of economies decreased. This implies lower uses of the natural resources, thereby, lower environmental impacts of economies. This is the driver of the decoupling of the value from material uses as observed in nearly all countries. Larger uses of capital, labour, and knowledge compared to natural resources all in constant prices evolved on all continents. Furthermore, economies grew faster on the continents with larger shares of services. Differences between countries on the continents are also significant, but they are not relevant for the argumentation about the decoupling driven by services. Graph 3.2 shows the shares of value-added in agriculture, industries, and services on continents during 1905, 1945, and 1995, based on data in the HYDE mode data shown in the PBL reference.

Globally, agriculture grew by 2.0%, industry by 2.9%, and services by 3.2% on the annual averages from 1895 to 1995. In effect, the share of service in the global value increased yearly by 0.2%, while the shares of industries and agriculture declined by −0.1% and by −0.9%, respectively. Minor annual change generated

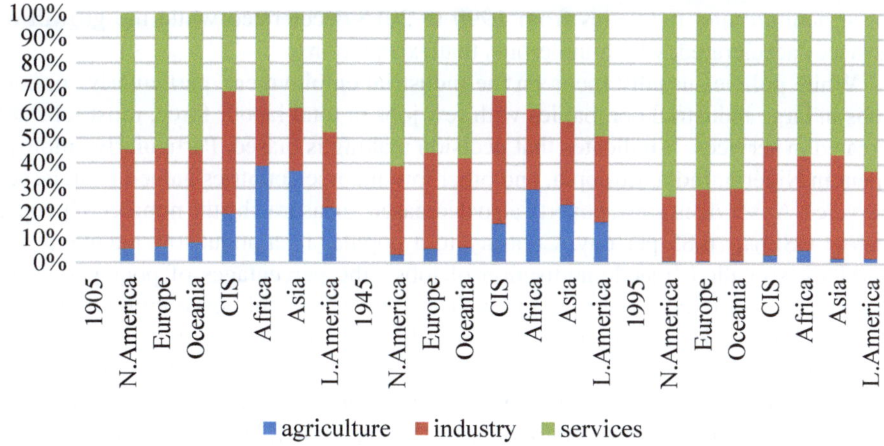

Graph 3.2 Shares of agriculture, industry and service in the Global Value Added

a 26% increase in the share of services throughout the last century. Patterns vary from continent to continent. In 1905, the share of agriculture and industries was about 40% in the West, nearly 70% in Russia, it is a CIS on the Graph, and between 50 to 60% in the South. The share of services in the West reached 60% in 1945 and exceeded 70% in 1995, while they were smaller in lower income countries throughout the last century. In particular, the communist Soviet Union (Russia) and China remained industrialised, but services covered about 50% of their GDP in 1995. Those changes in business compositions of economies evolved across countries despite policy support for metal, construction, chemicals, power and others basic industries, often considered as strategically important for the domestic economies. Former communist countries in particular supported their basic industries in order to compete with the 'West' and to enlarge their military force.

In 2015, the global average income per capita of 11,000 USD was composed of 4% agriculture, 27% industry, and 64% services. Even in China, considered the global manufacturing hub, 51% of GDP that year were values delivered by services. From 1990 to 2015, the share of agriculture in GDP decreased in nearly all countries, as well as the shares of industry in the focus countries, except in China. This indicates that the idea about emigration of the Western industries to lower income countries, so called offshoring, is only a minor factor in the changes in compositions of businesses across countries; more about this issue in Section 3.6. Growth of services is observed in all focus countries, except Brazil and Bangladesh. The correlation between GDP and the services share across the focus countries is high ($R^2 > 0.8$). Moreover, services grew faster than GDP growth in most countries. A fastest growth of services compared to GDP growth was also observed in lower income countries. Apparently, lower income countries catch up in generating services, which suggests that services remain key businesses for economic growth in the next decades. Furthermore, the growth rates of agriculture and industries from 1990 to 2015 decelerated while the growth of services accelerated, which underpins that expectation.

While policies usually focus on the industrial employment, particularly support jobs in large industrial companies with few jobs in total labour force, most jobs are created in services. It indicates that decision making is biased. Particularly employment in Nigeria, India, Ethiopia, and other low-income countries gained from larger services. As services grew, poverty also decreased, measured by the number of people below USD_{2015} 6.85 per day. Contrary to a popular idea about low payments for services, so called 'macdonaldisation of jobs', the percentages of poor people in populations declined as services grew. The USA is the only exception among the focus countries. Hence, high negative correlation between poverty and the service values is found across the focus countries throughout the period 1990–2015 ($R^2 < -0.80$). Moreover, addition of costly labour resources in economic activities did not impede but accelerated economic growth. Apparently, labour-intensive services delivered greater value than more material-intensive products; more about this subject in the next chapter.

Within the services, knowledge work grew rapidly throughout the 1900s. Knowledge work is about resolving issues. It serves economic growth through management of complex relations, generating ideas for new qualities, converting the ideas into novelties, and communication about the novelties, as well as preventing negative social and environmental impacts. Therefore, higher skills are obtained through education, financing and other services. Regarding diverse activities, definitions of knowledge work vary from a narrow focus on the processing of information up to inclusion of all kinds of art, craft, technical and intellectual capabilities (Pyöria, 2005). Knowledge work is also defined by several statistical categories. Based on the statistical categories, it covers: management, business and financing, computer and mathematical operations, architecture and engineering, life, physical, and social scientists, legal, healthcare practitioners, community and social services, education, training, as well as library, arts, design, entertainment, sports, media (Davenport, 2005). The narrow and broad definitions are used in this study. In the broad sense of knowledge work, the number of artists, craftsmen, scientists, engineers, educators, policymakers and other experts enlarged during the 1900s from a few percent of specialists in population of the West to one-fifth of all labour globally, even a quarter of the labour force in high-income countries. It did, while the global population grew fourfold. Knowledge work is also relevant for the material-intensity of economies as information and communication, education, and culture are the least material-intensive businesses, and the results of knowledge work can improve performances of the material uses. The share of knowledge workers in global labour force also increases in the narrow definition. This is measured by the number of workers in Research and Development (R&D), while R&D workers cover only a small fraction of all knowledge work in the broad definition. R&D work is higher in high-income countries than lower income ones while they catch up quickly. Another indicator of growing knowledge work is larger expenditure on education. Globally, these governmental expenditures increase in total and in percentage of GDP. Though these expenditures are higher in high-income countries, they increase faster in lower income ones.

Explanation of the growing service work and knowledge work within that puzzles many economists. Below only a brief explanatory note is drawn in order to underpin the growth of services and knowledge work in the future. From the mainstream, neoclassic economic perspective, growth of services is a peculiar process because the number of services workers increases despite the decreasing costs of natural resources and the increasing labour costs. Furthermore, policy interventions aim to maintain material-intensive economies through low taxes on materials and high taxes on labour. However, such taxes do not help, neither the subsidies for food, fuel and other basic goods in many countries with the aim to reduce market prices of material-intensive products. It is puzzling why the uses of natural resources decline along with the decreasing costs per unit as a trend contrary to larger uses of labour whose costs increase. Apparently, labour-intensive services increase value of the resource uses. Hence, services, in particular knowledge work, are instrumental for economic activities in the future and for sustainable development regarding the material-extensive activities in services.

What are the explanations? The mainstream, neo-classical economic theory considers those changes as anomalies in the market trend toward an optimal allocation of resources, meaning towards the lowest unit costs of all resources. From this perspective, the costly labour should be saved while cheapest materials used. Services would be productive insofar they reduce the transaction costs of firms due to finances, insurances, transport and suchlike distributive allocations of capital and labour (Coase, 1937). From this mainstream perspective, the growing shares of health care, education and other services for the moral goods which are largely paid by the states, are perceived as deficiencies on markets. This idea reflects the mercantilist focus on transactions. It persists although such services for the moral goods are costlier when privatised, but in the mainstream axioma higher costs of the privatised services for moral goods underpin this market deficiency, The growing share of services for moral goods in GDP is also explained by contributions of services to productivity in agriculture and industry. Larger public expenditures are assumed to enhance welfare growth as long as they increase productivity in the traditional businesses of economies (Baumol, 1967). From this viewpoint, the growth of services is explained by the spillovers of services to agriculture and industry. Services, being less productive services would be a bandwagon of more productive agriculture and industry, labelled 'Baumol paradox' (Lee, 2017).

In addition, services for health, education and other activities for moral goods add value in itself, which increases productivity. From this perspective of behavioural economics, value additions of these activities foster well-being which contributes to labour productivity (Schettekat and Yocarini, 2003). Services in research and development add to comprehension and engineering, which generate innovations (Muyed, 2008). They also serve consumer preferences for higher order of needs on the Maslow pyramid when food, shelter, and other basic consumption are satisfied, and when higher social status is emulated (Patsiaouras and Fitchett, 2012). In conventional estimates, the productivity of services is low and decreases when wages in services increase.. However, this way of measuring is biased because the resources are accounted in terms of costs, but many deliveries of moral goods and environmental qualities are imponderable in the money terms. These deliveries of services can be measured as the longest lifetime, larger enrolment in education, and other indicators of well-being and innovations. Services dedicated to maintaining availability of environmental qualities can be measured with indicators in physical terms.

Higher income improved living conditions, which generated faster growth of services than agriculture and industry. The share of services increased and within that the increase of knowledge worker was particularly fast. This was driven by the demands for health, education, knowledge and other moral goods.

3.5 Uses of Natural Resources

It is plausible that services use less energy and materials regarding high labour-intensity. This is underpinned in this section. Larger use of labour compared to materials reduce the use of natural resources, thereby reduce environmental impacts. Compared to agriculture and industry, services used only a fraction of energy and materials per service value in the USA in 1990s (Rosenblum et al., 2000). Furthermore, knowledge work is found particularly material-extensive as estimated for individual institutions, even when travels and meetings of knowledge workers are included (El Geneidi et al., 2021). Numerous studies show that linking products to services in product-service systems reduces energy and material consumption along with value addition. Even more possibilities for such reduction are envisaging through designs of novel product-services systems. Many cases of product-service systems can be found, but the reviews are not clear whether the studies assessed the realised results, or they compiled the envisaged ones though substantial differences between intensions and performances can be found.

Despite numerous studies, the statistical data on the uses of energy and materials in services compared to other businesses are scarce. For comparison across business and countries, only the OECD data on energy in several European countries is found (https://www.oecd.org/en/data.html). This data are used for assessing the energy-intensity in MJ energy use per Euro, while Euro is usually somewhat costlier than the US dollar. In order to avoid temporary variations, average energy uses during minimum 10 years are estimated. Table 3.2 presents annual average energy uses in MJ per Euro and annual average changes during from 2008 to 2018. This period covers seven years of high fuel prices until 2015 followed by three years of low fuel prices, which implies market-driven price incentives for energy saving during seven of ten years in that period. Ten businesses in the descending order of energy-intensity in production are shown in rows. These rows cover: all businesses, agriculture, mining, manufacturing, power production, water production, construction, information & communication, education services, health services, and arts & entertainment. In columns, annual average energy-efficiency in 8 European countries with sufficient data for minimum ten year are shown. These columns cover the averages in Belgium, Italy, Portugal, Slovenia, Sweden, Spain, and Switzerland, as well as the averages across these countries and comparisons with the manufacturing. Herewith should be noted that some data is missing, but better data across various countries is not found.

These results show large differences in energy-intensities across businesses. Most energy-intensive businesses are mining and quarrying, as well as the production of electricity, gas and air conditioning. These are 11, respectively 7 times more energy-intensive than manufacturing, whose energy-intensity is comparable to agriculture, forestry and fishery. These are 10 times more energy-intensive than construction and up to 25 times more energy-intensive compared to various services, which also somewhat vary. Hence, energy-intensities in services are more than hundred times lower than in the industry as a whole. Least energy-intensive are services in information & communication and in arts & entertainment. A decline of energy-intensity in time is observed in all those businesses, except minor increase in constructions, but the rates of decline are low. The rates of declines are not higher in those energy-intensive businesses compared to the energy-extensive services. The fastest decrease in energy-intensity of −3% a year is observed in services for Education and Health & care. These trends indicate negligible incentive for reductions of energy uses and pollution prevention in the material-intensive activities as mining, agriculture, and industries. Growth of services is encouraging while slow declines in the energy-intensity is worrying.

Also worrying is that high energy prices during the largest part of the assessed period 2008–2018 had little influence on the energetic performances in the energy-intensive sectors. This finding implies that taxes on energy might have little impact on energy-intensity unless high taxes are enforced and protectionist subsidies through grants and the regressive taxations on energy use are erased. Protectionism of the domestic energy-intensive businesses is observed. Given the international trade with energy resources and technology, similar trends in the energy-intensive sectors across countries are expected. However, large differences in the rates change across countries are observed, while similar trends should be observed. For example, mining in Slovenia is manifold more energy-intensive than in Belgium and Portugal, but its energy-intensity declines half slower than in Portugal while it increases in Belgium. Also, energy-intensity in the Belgian power production decreases while it increases in Portugal. In addition, the energy-intensity of the Belgian agriculture declines while the Portuguese increases. Apparently, the energy uses in the energy-intensive businesses are much supported in several EU28 countries instead of taxed despite commitment of the EU28 to the Paris agreements and calls to avoid the protectionist activities. Meanwhile, the energy-intensity of all services is low and their annual averages decline in most countries. This implies that the energy uses of these countries decline as services grow though many services evolve toward capital-intensive activities which use more natural resources. For example, tourism uses material-intensive constructions, and communication uses energy-intensive information technologies.

Decreasing uses of the materials should also be expected when the shares of services in GDP are high, or when services grow faster than agriculture and industry.

Table 3.2 Energy use per output value; annual average uses and their changes in 8 businesses in 10 countries in Europe during 2008–2018

MJ/€	Belgium	Italy	Portugal	Slovenia	Sweden	Spain	Slovak Republic	Switzer land	Annual average	Compared to manufacturing
All businesses										
Average	10	7	1			0.3	2	0.1	3	
Change	−3%	−2%	−3%			3%	−2%	0.1%	−1%	
Agriculture, Forestry, Fishery										
Average	9	9	11		2		18		10	1.2
Change	3%	−0.1%	−3%		0.2%		−4%		−1%	
Mining and quarrying										
Average	9	52	6	333	41				88	11.2
Change	0.1%	−2%	−4%	−2%	−0.5%				−2%	
Manufacturing										
Average	11	6	11	3					8	1.0
Change	−2%	−2%	−1%	−3%					−2%	
Electricity, gas, air conditioning										
Average	54	54	26	88					55	7.0
Change	−4%	−2%	1%	−2%					−2%	
Water supply and sanitation										
Average	4	5	3	2	0.3				3	0.3
Change	1%	−3%	3%	−5%	−0.3%				−1%	
Construction										
Average	1	1	1	2	0.2				1	0.1
Change	−2%	3%	−0.4%	4%	−4%				0.1%	

(continued)

Table 3.2 (continued)

MJ/€	Belgium	Italy	Portugal	Slovenia	Sweden	Spain	Slovak Republic	Switzer land	Annual average	Compared to manufacturing
Information and Communication										
Average	0.2	0.2	0.2	0.4	0.1				0.2	0.03
Change	−2%	2%	−3%	0.01%	0.5%				−1%	
Education										
Average	0.4	1	0.3	1	0.1				0.4	0.05
Change	−8%	3%	0.5%	−0.5%	−10%				−3%	
Health and care										
Average	0.4	1	1	1	0.1				1	0.1
Change	−3%	0.4%	−3%	−0.3%	−11%				−3%	
Arts and entertainment										
Average	0.5	0.3	0.3	0.4	0.1				0.3	0.04
Change	−0.04%	−1%	1%	2%	−8%				−1%	

Estimates based on the OECD database show growing global material consumption, but at a decelerating rate. Apparently, growing services contribute to lower material-uses, but insufficiently for compensation of the growth in agriculture and industries. The global material consumption per capita across the OECD and non-OECD countries saturated at about 13 tons per person in 2015, but differences across countries were observed. The average material consumption per capita was 21 ton in high-income OECD countries, which hardly increased after 2010. Meanwhile, the average material consumption was about 11 tons per capita in lower income, non-OECD countries, which increased slower than their GDP. That slow-down supports that expectation about better environmental performances due to growing services. However, these estimates have several limitations. Material consumption is an unspecific indicator of environmental performance, OECD data do not cover all countries, and the countries' data differ from the data in UNEP database on mining of natural resources and processing into products (West & Lutter, 2024).

Whether the growth of services reduced consumption of natural resources is estimated with the World Bank data for the period 1990–2015. Three indicators for natural resources are considered: water, fuels and forests. Per capita consumption during the period 1990–2015 is estimated. Table 3.3 shows the focus countries with their GDP in USD_{2015} and the share of services, as well as uses of water in m^3, fuels in GJ, and forests in m^2. The scale in the year 2015 and annual average changes from 1990 to 2015 are shown. Recall that GDP per capita multiplied by population equals GDP and that Table 3.3 shows the population data.

The real incomes per capita across countries match the shares of services in 2015 though the shares varied from 40% in Ethiopia to 77% in the USA. Their correlation across countries is high ($R^2 > 0.8$). While income per capita grew globally by 1.7% annual average, the share of services also increased. The uses of fresh water are not directly linked to services, which is reflected in a moderate correlation of freshwater withdrawals and services across countries ($R^2 < 0.5$). For example, freshwater withdrawal per capita is high in the USA with high share of services as well as in Pakistan with low share of services, While the shares of services increased, freshwater withdrawal decreased in all countries, except Indonesia and Ethiopia, but the share of services decreased while water use increased in Brazil. The uses of fossil fuels are closely linked to services. The energy uses were high in all high-income countries and Russia, and they decreased, but they were lower and increased in lower income countries. In effect, the cross-country correlations of services with the uses of fossil fuels are high for the scale in 2015 ($R^2 \approx 0.8$) and for their changes from 1990 to 2015 ($R^2 \approx -0.7$). Although the growth of services reduces the use of fossil fuels, the accelerating trends of the fuel uses in Brazil, China and India are particularly pressing for the climate change as these are large fuel users. Forest areas are not linked to services. The forest areas per capita are large in Russia, Brazil and the USA and small Egypt, Bangladesh and Pakistan. They declined globally and in nearly all focus countries, except slow growth in the EU, Russia and China. Neither their scale nor changes are correlated with services. Large, growing services contributed to lower uses of fossil fuels, but hardly to lower freshwater withdrawal and even less in forest areas.

Table 3.3 Trends in income, services and uses of natural resources in the focus countries

Growth, annual average 1990–2015	GDP USD2015/capita		Share service in GDP in %		Water use m^3/capita		Fuel use GJ/capita		Forest area m^2/capita	
	2015	Growth (%)	2015	Growth (%)	2015	Growth (%)	2015	Growth (%)	2015	Growth (%)
World	10,232	1.7	64	0.3	552	−0.5	81	0.6	5443	−1.4
USA	56,763	1.5	77	0.7	1366	−1.2	285	−0.7	9668	−0.9
Japan	34,961	0.8	70	0.4	628	−0.7	144	−0.2	1962	−0.1
EU28	30,485	1.4	65	0.3	456	−1.6	137	−0.6	3560	0.5
Mexico	9617	1.1	61	0.4	704	−0.2	64	0.5	5443	−1.7
Russia	9313	0.9	56	0.5	446	−1.7	201	−0.7	56,554	0.1
Brazil	8814	1.5	62	−0.1	329	0.4	64	2.5	24,643	−1.8
China	8016	9.1	51	0.3	431	−0.2	94	5.7	1524	0.4
Egypt	3563	2.2	53	0.5	816	−0.6	34	1.6	5	−1.8
Indonesia	3332	3.3	43	0.7	819	2.6	38	4.5	3678	−2.2
Philippines	3001	2.2	59	0.7	875	−0.7	21	1.8	687	−2.3
Nigeria	2687	2.2	58	2.1	69	−0.3	31	2.6	1239	−3.2
India	1606	4.5	48	1.3	494	−0.7	28	4.6	541	−1.2
Pakistan	1357	1.6	52	0.7	978	−1.6	19	1.6	197	−3.4
Bangladesh	1248	3.6	54	−0.2	230	−1.2	10	6.5	121	−1.7
Ethiopia	641	3.6	40	1.6	101	1.1	21	4.5	1729	−3.5

Services enabled dematerialization and lower use of fossil fuels in high-income countries, but lower income countries consumed more natural resources despite growth of services.

3.6 Resource-Intensity

Resource-intensity, meaning the uses of natural resources measured in physical terms per income in monetary value, indicates consumption patterns. It implies that changes in the resource-intensity of a country, businesses, or households indicate changes in their consumption. Whether these changes evolved, in what countries, and factors the generated changes across countries is assessed for the period 1990–2015 largely based on the data of the World Bank and OECD. Given the growing share of services in nearly all focus countries, a decreasing resource-intensity of economies can be expected. A trend of decreasing resource-intensity shows lower uses of natural resources, or higher value given the resources. Regarding slow decrease of global material consumption, a higher value rather than lower uses of natural is often plausible. Focus in this assessment is on the changes in resource-intensities during minimum ten years, which indicate trends. These trends in the resource use, measured in physical terms per monetary value, are estimated for all countries with particular attention to the focus countries. In order to assess the price effect of fossil fuels on the resource-intensities of countries that whole period is divided the sub period of low fuel prices from 1990 to 2004 and trice higher annual average fuel prices from 2005 to 2015. It can be expected that the resource-intensities declined during the sub period of high fuel prices compared to the sub period of low fuel as the prices of most natural resources follow the prices of fossil fuels. After a review of the resource-intensities across countries, changes are analysed with respect to the widespread idea about the outsourcing, meaning shifts of the material-intensive industries from high-income countries to lower income ones.

Results of assessed resource-intensities presented in Table 3.4 cover the world and fifteen focus countries. In addition; exceptionally low resource-intensity and large changes in other countries are mentioned in the text. Freshwater withdrawal in m^3, uses of fossil fuels in MJ and forest areas in m^2 are estimated per USD_{2015} of the countries' GDP in 2015, as well as their annual average changes from 1990 to 2015. Accelerations and convergences of the trends are indicated in support of forecasts. These are estimated as the increasing growth rates in time and similarity of changes across countries, respectively. For sustainable development, low and decreasing water-intensities and fuel-intensities are considered as positive, whereas the increasing forestry-intensity means more forest area per income. In order to avoid confusion, it is called forest per income instead of the forest-intensity.

Freshwater withdrawal per USD_{2015} varies across the focus countries. For example, water-intensity in Pakistan was about 70 times higher than in the EU28 in 2015, while the EU citizens had about 22 higher incomes pr person than the Pakistanis, on average. Countries' climates are also hardly relevant regarding similar water-intensities in the dry climate of Egypt as in the humid, tropical climates Indonesia and Philippines, all of them having similar income per capita. So, water use in Pakistan was wasteful compared to the EU, while water-scarce Egypt did not perform better than water-rich Indonesia and Philippines. Agriculture uses about 80% of all freshwater withdrawals across countries. However, countries' water uses per income and per capita are rarely directly linked to agricultural productivity regarding low correlation of the freshwater withdrawal and production of the cereals in ton per hectare across the focus countries ($R^2 = 0.2$). More plausible explanation of the wasteful practices is that installations and infrastructure for water use in agriculture are obsolete while the agricultural water use is cheap because subsidised. International support of water infrastructure could unintentionally increase the uses of water, given that this support reduces the costs of use (World Bank, 2023), From the environmentalist viewpoint it is an encouraging observation that water-intensities declined globally and in nearly all countries. From the economic viewpoint, it is also encouraging that these water uses are sensitive to prices. Higher prices of natural resources from 2005 to 2015 triggered a reduction of the water uses in most of lower income countries with high water-intensity. Increases of water-intensity in Serbia and Thailand with high use per capita during high prices are exceptions. A discouraging observation is that the rates of declines do not correspond with scales of uses across the focus countries. For example, high 0.25 m^3 per USD water-intensity

Table 3.4 Intensity in using natural resources, which means resource uses per USD of GDP

Countries	Freshwater withdrawal m^3/USD		Fossil fuels MJ/USD		Forest areas m^2/USD	
	2015	Growth 1990–2015 (%)	2015	Growth 1990–2015 (%)	2015	Growth 1990–2015 (%)
World	0.05	−2.1	6.57	−1.0	0.53	−3.0
USA	0.02	−2.7	4.57	−2.1	0.17	−2.3
Japan	0.02	−1.5	3.85	−1.0	0.06	−0.9
EU28	0.01	−2.9	3.71	−2.0	0.12	−0.8
Mexico	0.07	−1.2	6.08	−0.5	0.57	−2.7
Russia	0.05	−2.3	20.59	−1.5	5.98	−0.4
Brazil	0.04	−1.0	4.10	1.0	2.80	−3.2
China	0.05	−8.5	10.29	−3.1	0.19	−8.0
Egypt	0.23	−2.8	8.96	−0.6	0.001	−3.7
Indonesia	0.25	−0.6	8.33	1.2	1.10	−5.3
Philippines	0.29	−4.2	4.79	−0.4	0.23	−4.5
Nigeria	0.03	−2.3	2.08	0.4	0.46	−5.1
India	0.31	−5.0	11.59	0.1	0.34	−5.5
Pakistan	0.72	−3.0	7.62	0.02	0.15	−4.8
Bangladesh	0.18	−5.9	5.40	2.7	0.10	−5.2
Ethiopia	0.16	−6.1	2.73	0.9	2.70	−6.5

in Indonesia declines annually less than twenty times lower water-intensity in the EU28. The decelerating trends in water-intensity in several focus countries and the diverging trends across the focus countries are also discouraging because imply that the trend of declining water use presumably does not continue in the future and that the international coordination of water uses is laborious.

The fuel-intensities also vary across the focus countries, but the spread is smaller than in the water-intensity. Across countries, fuel-intensity is highly correlated to incomes per capita ($R^2 = 0.8$), which confirms studies on energy and economic growth in high-income countries. An encouraging observation with regard to climate changes is that the fuel-intensities decreased in all high-income countries with high fuel consumption. A discouraging one is that the fuel-intensity increased in several lower income ones, which implies a wasteful fuel use because more energy is used for income generation. Larger differences across countries cause laborious international coordination. The increasing fuel-intensities in lower income countries could be linked to their industrialisation. Although this link seems plausible, observations also show that the share of industry in GDP declines while the fuel-intensity increases among others in Indonesia, Nigeria, and Bangladesh. While high fuel-intensity in China decreases, similarly high fuel-intensity in India increases, which indicates inferior industrial performances in India. As the countries energy-intensities vary, moderate correlations of the industry share in GDP and fuel-intensities are observed across the focus countries ($R^2 = 0.6$). Difference in fuel-intensities increased between high-income countries and lower income ones during high fuel prices 2005–2015. For instance, the fuel-intensity in the EU28 decreased by −5% annual average, while it increased fast in Yemen, Cambodia and other low-income countries. Apparently, the fuel use is not sensitive to prices in many countries presumably due to large subsidies for fuels and low investments in cleaner technologies.

Forest areas in square meters per USD_{2015} hugely vary across the focus countries. Even if desertified Egypt is not considered, forest per income is about 100 times higher in Russia than in Japan. Several factors are relevant for the variation, but no one stands out as the decisive one. It is obviously related to the ecological conditions as desert accommodates less forests than tropics. Population densities are also relevant. For example, lower population density in Indonesia can explain its fivefold forest area per income compared to Philippines. Regulations aiming at afforestation and other policy instruments can explain lower forest area per income in Russia than in the USA, both in temperate climates, as well as in tropical Brazil compared to Nigeria. Income is also relevant. Generally, the rates of decrease in forest per income are usually lower in high-income countries than in lower income ones. For example, the annual average decrease in the EU was -0.8% and -8.0 in China with similar forest areas per income, while even stronger decreases are observed in populated Bosnia-Hercegovina in Europe and in Equatorial Guinea in Africa. Policies are apparently more important for the protection of forests than the countries ecology and economy. An encouraging trend is that the rates of decline slow-down and converge across countries, which indicates a slower deforestation in the near future. A discouraging observation is that only a few countries worldwide were able to increase forest areas per income, among them Ukraine and Georgia.

Generally, the resource-intensities are usually lower in high-income countries and the decreases are faster than in low-income countries. This difference can be driven by consumption, particularly larger consumption of services in high income countries than lower income ones. This explanation implies that global changes evolve in favour of the declining material consumption across countries. It supports the dematerialization hypothesis, which means reducing economic dependency on the natural resources as envisioned in sustainable development. From this perspective, consumption in many high-income countries evolves toward lower environmental impacts due to growing consumption of services, which needs an acceleration in lower income countries. Another explanation focuses on the trade-offs between high-income countries and lower income ones. A popular argumentation is that high-income countries increased imports of the material-intensive products from lower income ones. Better performances in resource-intensities of high-income countries are explained by the import growth from lower income countries. Import of the manufactured products from China and Bangladesh are often pinpointed. These imports would enlarge because industries migrated from high-income countries to lower income ones in search of cheaper labour, low taxes and lax regulations. This emigration would create industrial hubs in low-income countries that produce for consumption in high-income ones. In this migration hypothesis, migration equals net emigration minus immigration. Migration would even aggravate environmental qualities globally because of larger and longer transports. Return of industries toward locations where products are consumed is recommended, called 'reshoring'. Curiously, this migration thesis is popular among radical environmentalists and neo-liberal populists that oppose environmental demands with support of interests concerned about loss of industry, illustrated by the import tariffs imposed by the Trump administration in the USA.

It is assessed if the improvements in resource-intensities in high-income countries should be attributed to the increasing imports from lower income countries. Validity of this migration thesis is assessed with the monetary data on the agricultural and industrial production in high-income countries, and data on global trade with ores and minerals, which indicate monetary flows linked to natural resources. In addition, materials uses in million tons across countries are assessed. All monetary data in USD_{2015} are based on the World Bank database, and all material data on the OECD database. Those indicators are largely complementary given that the material consumption shows mainly bulky natural resources, which are usually low value, whereas the values of production and trade include fine, precious natural resources. It is assessed if high-income countries maintained their share in the global economy. Then, it is estimated if they imported more materials.

The production value of agriculture and industry grew in all focus countries throughout the period 1990–2015. Changes in the production value of high-income countries are assessed from 1975 to 2015. These changes are indicated by the shares of high-income countries in the global GDP, as well as in their share in trade with ores and minerals, and in the intellectual property rights (IPR) that indicate inventive activities. The World Bank data on the focus countries is used. Herewith, the trade with ores and minerals equals export of ores and minerals in the merchandise exports multiplied by the merchandise exports. Graph 3.3 shows the results of the estimates.

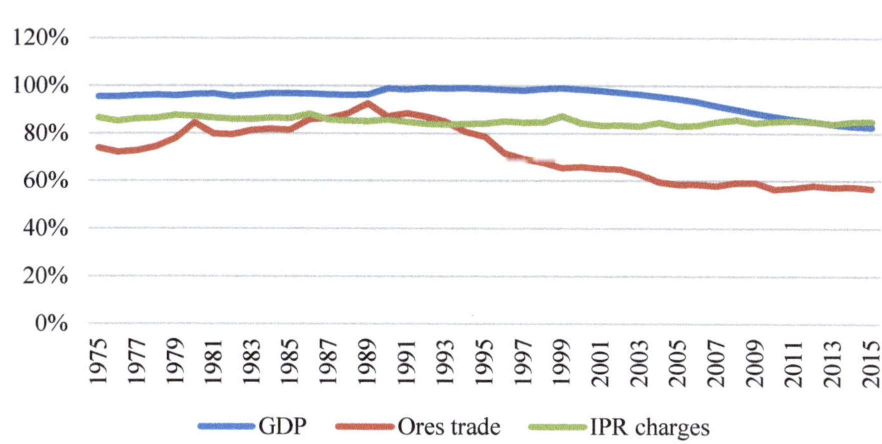

Graph 3.3 Global share of high income countries in GDP, ores trade and IPR

The share of imported ores and minerals by high-income countries increased during the 1970s and 1980s when industries migrated to the South, followed by the decline of their imports. This does not underpin the migration thesis. Meanwhile. their share in global GDP remained high until the late 1990s, followed by decline due to fast economic growth of China and financial crisis in the West. Their share declined despite continuous high share in the inventive activities. These data do not support the migration thesis, but losses of the economic performances by high-income countries despite inventive activities. Apparently, lower income countries generated higher value and became more inventive per income.

The material uses in tons per year are estimated with the OECD data. Estimates cover the period 1990–2015 as earlier data is found insufficiently reliable. These data cover high-income member countries and several mid-income non-member countries. The domestic material consumption and the material footprint in million tons are assessed. The latter adds the imported materials that are consumed in the countries of origin to the domestic material consumption. A smaller domestic consumption than the material footprint of a country shows net import of materials, whereas a larger domestic consumption than material footprint means extraction of natural resources for imports. Global material uses per income nearly doubled in twenty years toward 1.22 tons per USD in 2010, followed by a decline to 1.21 tons per USD by 2015. So, the global material consumption saturates which confirms the observation with the UNEP database as mentioned above. Insofar data is available, that saturation is observed in high-income and in lower income ones, which are OECD and non-OECD countries, respectively. Throughout that period, the material-intensity of the domestic material consumption declined from 0.5 tons per USD to 0.4 tons per USD in high-income countries, while the decline was from 7 tons per USD to 5 tons per USD in lower income countries. Lower material consumption in total and per income is a global trend that can largely be attributed to larger services.

Comparison of the material footprint and domestic material consumption in high-income countries and lower income ones largely confirms that trend in the international trade. Minor changes in the international material flows are observed. Graph 3.4 shows the material footprints and domestic consumption of the OECD countries and non-OECD countries from 1990 to 2015 in five-year intervals.

The OECD member countries have smaller domestic material consumption than material footprint. High-income countries are net material importers. These imports hardly changed during those twenty five years, and somewhat decreased during high fuel prices 2005–2015. Non-OECD countries have lower domestic material consumption than material footprint. They exported materials with minor changes throughout those twenty five years. These results show that emigration of industries to lower income countries is hardly relevant for the decreasing resource-intensity in high-income countries. Growth of labour-intensive services is decisive in high-income countries, while the domestic consumption drives higher resource-intensity in lower income countries as more incomes are spent on food, housing, and other basic goods which are usually material-intensive. Those results underpin the dematerialization of economic activities as income increase, which evolve largely spontaneously along with economic growth.

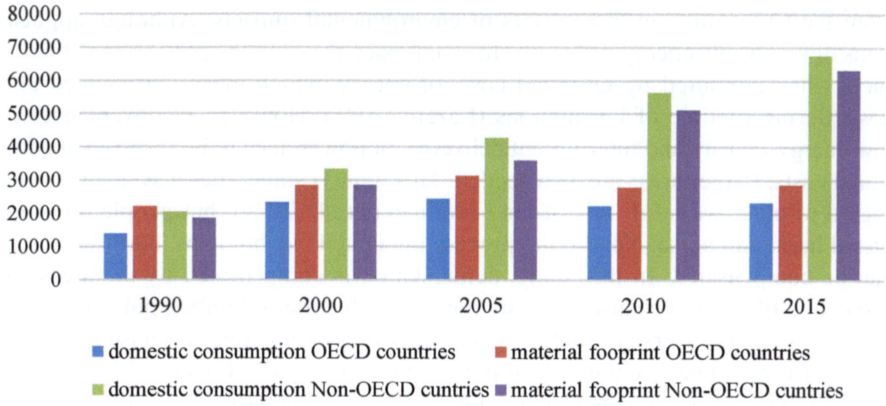

Graph 3.4 Material footprint and domestic consumption in million tons

The resource-intensities of freshwater withdrawal, fossil fuels and the forest areas per income vary a lot across countries. While water-intensity and fuel-intensity decrease in many countries mainly due to larger services, the forest areas per income decrease in nearly all countries.

3.7 Environmental-Efficiency

Environmental-efficiencies indicate effects of applied environmental technologies on environmental impacts. Wastewater treatment is linked to freshwater withdrawal, CO_2 and NOx emission reduction to combustion of fossil fuels, and nature protection areas are linked to deforestation. It is assessed if applications of environmental technologies improved environmental-efficiencies. This assessment also indicates if policies were effective, given that environmental technologies rarely emerge spontaneously because they are often costly without much private incomes. They are usually induced by the demands for pollution prevention (Nentjes & Wiersma, 1988).

Environmental technologies can be added to the use of natural resources, called add-on. They need additional costly resources, and deliver a license to operate, but rarely an income. This study covers add-on technologies for wastewater treatment, and NOx reduction with use of catalysts. Harmful emissions can also be replaced in production and products. Such process-integrated technologies are also induced by the demands for pollution prevention but they can generate income.. Herewith, CO_2 emissions that cause climate change can be prevented through substitutions of the carbon-rich coal for oil, and gas, as well as shifts from those fossil fuels to renewable energy based on biofuels, hydropower, geothermal, solar, and wind energy, and to fossil fuels-based nuclear power. Note that combustion of biofuels releases CO_2, but bioresources absorb CO_2 when plants grow, which is subtracted from the CO_2 emission in accounts of environmental impacts. Although applications of renewable energy are costly, they approach parity with applications of fossil fuels when measured by levelized costs of energy, which means discounted unit costs during lifetime of installations (Lazard, 2025). However, inconveniences of low energy-density and intermittent deliveries of power need to be resolved at additional costs. Larger areas are also needed. This issue is sometimes waved away with regard to other wasteful uses of land (Weinand et al., 2025), but people do sense visual harm and noise. Next to the process-integrated technologies, harmful effects can be compensated. In this study, deforestation is compensated by the areas for protection of nature because afforestation for production of lumber, pulp and paper does not help biodiversity. Such compensation is also imperfect because the maturation of forests takes centuries, but it helps biodiversity (Wohlleben, 2015). Those applications of environmental technologies can be demanded by regulators, firms and social organisation.

Data of the World Bank and OECD are used, but they are far from perfect. Wastewater treatments should reduce organic microbes and viruses, as well as an organic nitrogen, phosphate, and other pollutants that cause waterborne diseases and degrade ambient water while emission reduction due to environmental technologies varies. However, these data about pollutants are absent in the World Bank database and other databases that cover many countries of various incomes are not found. Therefore, the data on percentage of population with access to wastewater treatment plants is used on the assumption that sewage with the wastewater treatment prevent waterborne diseases, and some environmental impacts. This environmental-efficiency is estimated as wastewater treatment per freshwater withdrawal, both, in cubic meters of water use. Combustion of fossil fuels releases CO_2 emission, which was prevented through substitutions for renewable energy, given that technical capture and storage of CO_2 is small scale. The environmental-efficiency of these substitutions is assessed as kg CO_2 emission reduction per MJ fuel use. Fuel combustion also releases NOx emissions, which are toxic compounds that also cause respiratory problems, and acidifying moisture in the atmosphere. Major sources are power generation and car mobility. They can prevent emissions through process-integrated uses of renewable energy and better fuel-based engines, as well as through add-on catalytic reduction of NOx in exhausts of engines. The environmental-efficiency of NOx is estimated in kg NOx per MJ fuel use. Loss of biodiversity-rich forest areas can be can be compensated through nature protection areas. This environmental-efficiency is estimated by the nature protection area per forest area, both measured in square kilo metre of land. Note that higher environmental-efficiency means larger nature area per forest area.

Those environmental-efficiencies in 2015 and annual average changes from 1990 to 2015 are presented in Table 3.5. Unfortunately, the data on wastewater treatment cover only the period 2000 to 2015, and data on wastewater treatment in Indonesia and Pakistan are unavailable in the World Bank database. Insofar data are available, the environmental-efficiencies during high fuel prices from 2005 to 2015 are compared to the whole period 1990–2015. This is done with regard to the popular assumption that high fuel prices reduce emissions.

Table 3.5 Environmental-efficiencies of environmental technologies for water, air and land resources

Countries	Population without wastewater treatment		CO_2 kg/MJ		NOx kg/MJ		Nature areas km^2/km^2 forest	
	2015	Growth 1990–2015	2015	Growth 1990–2015	2015	Growth 1990–2015	2015	Growth 1990–2015
World	53%	−2.0%	0.06	−0.1%	0.005	−1.0%	0.48	3.2%
USA	2%	−2.6%	0.05	−0.4%	0.003	−0.2%	0.38	0.6%
Japan	21%	−1.8%	0.06	0.4%	0.001	−1.3%	0.29	0.5%
EU28	11%	−1.8%	0.05	−0.9%	0.004	−1.7%	0.69	4.0%
Mexico	55%	−2.7%	0.06	0.6%	0.005	−1.4%	0.40	7.9%
Russia	40%	−0.7%	0.05	−0.3%	0.002	−1.4%	0.20	3.0%
Brazil	56%	−0.9%	0.04	0.4%	0.013	−1.2%	0.49	6.8%
China	47%	−3.9%	0.08	1.0%	0.004	−2.5%	0.04	7.0%
Egypt	37%	−1.4%	0.07	0.5%	0.007	−0.9%	N.A	N.A
Indonesia	N.A	N.A	0.05	1.5%	0.009	−1.8%	0.23	1.3%
Philippines	45%	−1.5%	0.05	1.8%	0.006	−0.7%	N.A	N.A
Nigeria	72%	−0.6%	0.02	−1.0%	0.006	−0.5%	N.A	N.A
India	64%	−2.5%	0.06	1.2%	0.007	−1.9%	0.26	0.1%
Pakistan	N.A	N.A	0.04	1.1%	0.015	0.005%	N.A	N.A
Bangladesh	66%	−1.4%	0.05	3.2%	0.018	−2.0%	N.A	N.A
Ethiopia	94%	−0.2%	0.01	4.6%	0.021	−0.4%	N.A	N.A

Wastewater treatment covered most people in high-income countries but not many in low-income ones. For example, 98% of all people in the USA were connected to a wastewater treatment compared 6% in Ethiopia in 2015. As incomes per capita grew, more people are connected. Their correlation across the focus countries is high ($R^2 = 0.8$), contrary to low correlation for the water uses. Higher income consequently enlarged wastewater treatment across countries as shown with the correlations of their growth rates ($R^2 = 0.5$). This indicates that wastewater treatment for prevention of waterborne diseases is prioritised in policies. Importance attached to wastewater treatment is also indicated by an increase of applications during high fuel prices in all focus countries though these installations use energy for operations. Regarding the converging trend across countries along with accelerations of connections in mid-income countries, better ambient water quality can be expected in the near future. However, progress in low-income countries is slow. Emission reduction of medicines, heavy metals and other harmful chemicals in water also stagnates.

CO_2 emissions per MJ energy use also vary across countries. They are about 7 times higher in China, where much coal is used, compared to Ethiopia with high use of biofuels. The CO_2-efficiencies, improved in the USA, EU28, Russia and Nigeria mainly due to substitutions of CO_2-rich coal for gas and oil, and oil for gas, as well as larger use of renewable energy for power in the USA and EU. However, CO_2 emissions per fuel use increased in lower income countries mainly because more coal instead of biofuels is used. High fuel prices during 2005–2015 did improve CO_2-efficiency in many countries, but worsened in Japan and Egypt, presumably because cheaper coal instead of oil and gas is used. These environmental-efficiencies do not converge across countries but fluctuate in time, hardly. Related to higher fuel prices.

NOx is also released when fossil fuels are combusted. NOx emissions per fuel are low in high income countries where much catalytic reduction is used. Decreases of NOx emission per unit fuel use, it means higher NOx-efficiency, are observed in all focus countries, except Pakistan. As incomes per capita grow, NOx-efficiency improves in most focus countries ($R^2 = -0.5$). However, high fuel prices impeded NOx reduction in many countries. Per MJ energy, these emissions even increased in the USA, Russia, Pakistan, and Ethiopia because more coal is used, and the uses of effective but costly add-on catalysts declined. In effect, trends across countries do not converge but fluctuate in time, and higher NOx-efficiency did not accelerate across all countries. While economic growth usually enhances expenditures on low NOx technologies, higher fuel prices hinder them.

Areas for protection of nature enlarged in all focus countries, insofar data is available, but these enlargements are insufficient for the compensations of forest losses in these countries. Even worse, no one focus country increased its nature areas compared to the losses of forest areas. In effect, nature areas deteriorate at faster rates across countries. The increase of the nature areas compared to forest losses are observed only in Armenia, Kyrgyzstan, and New Caledonia. Across countries, the nature protection areas as compensations for deforestation are not linked statistically to incomes per capita, neither to density of population. For example, the nature-efficiency in mid-income China is only one-sixth of low-income India with higher population density. Policies are decisive. Important is also availability of land that is considered to be unproductive. Such land is often used for nature, whereas the expropriation of farmland is costly. It is encouraging that the nature protection areas increase fast in Mexico and Brazil. They also grew fast in China, but started at a low level. It is discouraging that the nature-efficiency declined during high fuel prices though protection of nature hardly needs energy. Budget cuts are presumably the main reason. For the international policies on biodiversity, it is encouraging that the growth rates of nature-efficiencies converge across countries, but discouraging that these growth rates decelerate across countries, which puts doubts about attainment of the objectives in the Kunming-Montreal agreement on protection of biodiversity.

The environmental-efficiency increased in wastewater treatment, which converged across countries. While CO_2-efficiency and NOx-efficiency increased in high income, they decreased in many lower income countries. The trends across countries diverged, which aggravated during high fuel prices. More nature areas are found in all countries, but the trends decelerate and they do not compensate for forest losses.

3.8 Environmental Impacts

Environmental impacts are estimated by multiplying countries GDP, which equal population times income per capita, with the resource intensities and the environmental-efficiency per country. This way, it is assessed if the environmental impacts declined during the last decades when environmental policies disseminated globally, but their enforcement is tempered by the voluntary agreements. Changing environmental impacts are considered equivalents of environmental performances defined as an annual average change during minimum ten years. These impacts could be driven by the quasi-autonomous changes in economies driven by larger services and other changes in businesses and by the societal demands that induce environmental technologies and compensations.

All basic data are presented in previous sections: 3.2 for population, 3.5 for income per capita, 3.6 for resource-intensity and 3.7 for environmental-efficiency. The impact on water, meaning water pollution, is estimated with cubic meters freshwater withdrawal per income (intensity) multiplied by cubic meters of water discharge without wastewater treatment per withdrawal (efficiency). Climate change is a result of the uses of fossil fuels per income (intensity) multiplied by CO_2 emissions per fuel use (efficiency). Impact on air, it is air pollution, is accounted by multiplying the uses of fossil fuels per income (intensity) and NOx emissions per fuel use (efficiency). Finally, restoration of nature refers to the losses of forest areas per income (intensity) multiplied by the nature areas per forest area (efficiency). Each total impact is multiplied by the country's GDP, estimated by multiplying of population and income per capita. Focus is on the changes in impacts, particularly trends in environmental performances during the period 1990–2015, but data on the water impact cover only 2005–2015. It is also assessed if the trend accelerated and converged in time. In addition, it is assessed if high fuel prices influenced environmental performances by comparison the periods of high to low fuel prices, and if these performances are driven mainly by the changes in consumption indicated by the resource-intensities, or by environmental technologies shown with environmental-efficiencies. Herewith, the average resource-intensities divided by the average environmental efficiencies above unity imply main drivers of change in consumption and below unity indicate a key role of technologies. Table 3.6 presents total environmental impacts per capita in the focus countries, and their performances as annual average changes during those periods.

Water pollution was caused by more than 2 billion m^3 global discharges without treatment in 2015, which covered about 53% of all wastewater. Large differences in water pollution per capita are found across countries. For example, it is about forty times larger in Pakistan than in the USA where wastewater treatment is widespread. Larger water pollution is observed in many low-income countries where wastewater treatment is scarce. Low water pollution in Nigeria where freshwater withdrawals are low, is exceptional. Water performances improved globally and in most countries as water pollution declined, except in low-income Pakistan and Ethiopia. These improvements are mainly driven by more water treatment, though water use is also

Table 3.6 Environmental performances of the focus countries

Growth: annual average 1990–2015	Water pollution		Climate change		Air pollution		Nature restoration	
	2015 m^3/capita	Growth total m^3	2015 ton/capita	Growth total ton (%)	2015 ton/capita	Growth total ton (%)	2015 km^2/capita	Growth total km^2
World	292	−1.3%	3.7	1.9	0.32	0.9	−2,824	3.1%
USA	23	−2.4%	14.2	−0.04	0.74	0.1	−6,000	0.7%
Japan	129	−2.3%	8.7	0.3	0.14	−1.4	−1,396	0.5%
EU28	51	−3.5%	5.4	−1.3	0.41	−2.1	−1,094	4.8%
Mexico	385	−1.7%	3.5	2.6	0.29	0.5	−3,279	7.6%
Russia	180	−1.0%	10.7	−1.1	0.38	−2.2	−45,286	3.0%
Brazil	185	−0.2%	1.3	4.3	0.47	2.5	−12,499	6.1%
China	205	−4.3%	6.3	7.7	0.35	3.8	−1,459	8.3%
Egypt	303	−0.2%	2.3	4.1	0.23	2.6	−5	N.A
Indonesia	–		1.4	7.5	0.25	4.0	−2,815	0.4%
Philippines	396	−0.8%	0.8	5.8	0.09	3.0	−687	N.A
Nigeria	50	0.5%	0.1	5.0	0.04	4.6	−1,239	N.A
India	318	−2.3%	1.1	7.6	0.13	4.2	−401	0.5%
Pakistan	978	0.6%	0.4	5.4	0.16	4.1	−197	N.A
Bangladesh	152	−1.5%	0.3	11.8	0.12	6.0	−121	N.A
Ethiopia	95	3.4%	0.0	13.8	0.04	7.0	−1,729	N.A

reduced in Russia, Nigeria, and Pakistan. As better performances increased with higher income, these trends accelerated in most focus countries, and converged across countries. Therefore, perspectives for lower water pollution are encouraging, but a comprehensive treatment of discharges is still far away. Technologies drive those improvements.

Climate change is largely caused by 27 billion tons global CO_2 emissions from 493 EJ combusted fossil fuels in 2015 (EJ $= 10^{12}$ MJ). This estimate and changes differ from the World Bank estimates, which is presumably caused by differences in subtraction of biofuels from CO_2 emissions. More than 57% of this global impact is caused by China, the USA and the EU28 with 29% of global population. CO_2 emissions per capita are only partly linked to income. For example, they are lower in EU28 than in lower income Russia and China. Moreover, CO_2 emissions in the EU28 decreased due to the shift from fossil fuels to renewable energy. Most lower income countries emit only a fraction of the EU28 emissions per capita, but their CO_2 emissions increase because of larger energy consumption along with the growing share of fossil fuels instead of biofuels in their energy mix. CO_2 emission decreased only in the USA, EU28 and Russia. Regarding the decelerating growth of CO_2 impacts, perspectives for mitigation of climate change are positive, but diverging trend across countries impedes the international coordination. Removal of subsidies could foster that convergence. While high-income countries subsidise with the aim to protect domestic industries, many lower income ones claim to support poor people but the lion's share of the subsidies delivers benefits to high incomes that use much fuel (Arze del Granado et al., 2012). Changes in consumption drive improvements.

Air pollution is largely caused by 2.4 billion ton NOx emission in 2015. This impact was spread across many countries though 38% of it was caused by China, USA and EU28 with 29% of the population. Use of fossil fuel is the cause of air pollution in the focus countries while applications of environmental technologies for emission reduction were important in Japan, EU28 and Russia. Air pollution in lower income countries was similar to high-income in 2015, and it increased fast from 1990 to 2015 because of growing use of fossil fuels without applications of environmental technology. Air pollution improved a lot in high-income countries and somewhat in lower income ones, particularly during high fuel prices. In effect, trend in NOx emission reduction diverged across countries in the last decades. As NOx emissions continue to grow globally, expansion of the respiratory diseases and losses of forests and materials caused by acidification of moisture can be expected in the future. Improvements are mainly driven by technologies.

Nature restoration through nature protection areas covered globally about 19 million km^2 in 2015, which compensated about 48% of the forest depletion. No one focus country restored its nature through compensations of forest depletion with nature areas. While these compensations were reasonable in Brazil and the EU28 they were low in most countries, insofar data is available. As more areas for the protection of nature are established, restoration of nature has increased though insufficiently fast compensation of deforestation. Given that the restorations of nature increased fast in several countries but hardly in others, these performances diverged across countries. For example, the nature restoration per capita was tenfold in Japan compared to China in 2015, but the growth rates in China were twenty times higher. Though the aggravation of nature restoration slows down a balance with deforestation is far away, as yet. Compensations, considered as environmental technologies, drive changes.

Global environmental impacts show mixed results: improvements in water pollution and nature restoration and aggravation in climate change and air pollution. Most impacts per capita are larger in high-income countries than in lower income ones. Performances of high-income countries in water treatment, climate change, air pollution and nature restoration improved faster per capita than in lower income countries whose incomes per capita grew faster. Results are shown in Graph 3.5. It shows the global shares of high-income countries in GDP, as well as in water pollution, climate change, air pollution, and nature restoration from 1990 to 2015. High-income countries cover all economies above USD_{2015} 12,000 per person in 2015.

While 20% of the global population in high-income countries generated more than 96% of global GDP in 1990 a slightly smaller share by population covered 82% of the global GDP in the 2015. High-income countries reversed the past trend of increasing environmental impacts due to the quasi-autonomous increase of services in economies and more applications of environmental technologies mainly induced by policy demands. Water pollution was lower in high-income countries in 1990

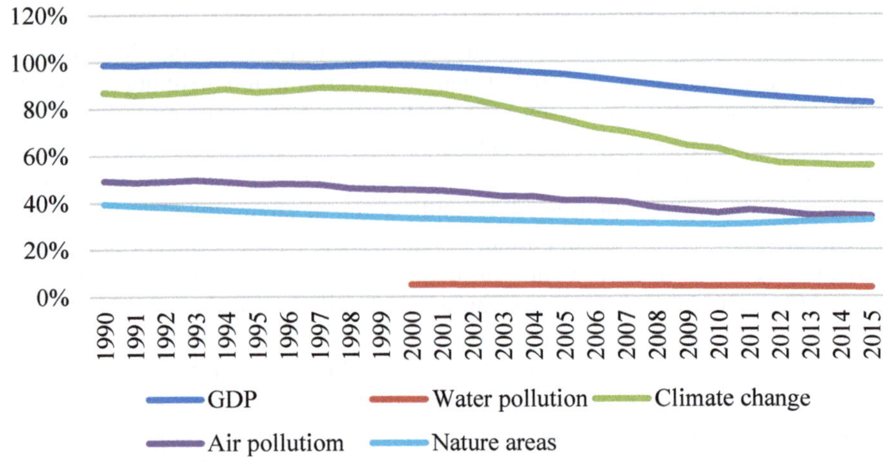

Graph 3.5 Global shares of high income countries

due to wastewater treatment and this performance somewhat improved in time. In result, high-income countries cover only a few percent of global water pollution, while better performances in wastewater treatment are observed in most countries. The share of high-income countries in the impact on climate change in the 1990s was similar to their share in the global GDP. While the global impact on climate change increased by nearly 2% a year, the share of high-income countries declined from 87% in 1990 to 56% in 2015 mainly due to lower uses of fossil fuels and lower uses carbon-intensive fossil fuels. Meanwhile, the uses of fossil fuels replaced biofuels in many lower income countries. Similar change is observed in air pollution. While global air pollution grew nearly 1% a year, the share of high-income countries declined from 49% in 1990 to 34% in 2015 mainly due to applications of environmental technologies. However, air pollution grew annually 3 to 5% in lower income countries. Nature restoration stagnated in high-income countries because additional areas for protection of nature did not match the pace of deforestation. The performances are even worse in lower income countries. In result, the share of high-income countries in the global nature restoration was nearly 39% in 1990 and 33% in 2015, which is a minor improvement compared to other performances.

Environmental technologies in wastewater treatment were essential for lower impacts on water. Consumptive changes towards services were key to reducing climate change. Technologies reduced air pollution and slowed-down degradation of biodiversity. Across countries, the performances in water pollution converged, but the countries' performances diverged with respect to climate change, air pollution and nature restoration. High-income countries cause larger environmental impacts per person, but their shares in the global impacts decrease. A declining share of high-income countries in the global income and even stronger decline in environmental impacts along with the diverging trends in most performances impede sharing burdens of environmental impacts. It is difficult to justify support of the countries whose economies compete while policies are insufficient environmental perforers. More important than justification of the aid for lower income countries would be encouraging investments in energy and material efficient production along with transfers of environmental technologies. Instead of the burden share, high-income countries can provide financial guarantees for investments in cleaner production in lower income countries. An example is the European Bank for Reconstruction and Development (EBRD) that funds investments in cleaner production and public infrastructure in the countries bordering to the EU28 in Europe and Middle Asia. Due to the guarantees, lower interest rates are acceptable.

Environmental impacts decrease in high-income countries due to more services in consumption and applications of environmental technologies, whereas the impacts increase in lower income countries. Instead of burden sharing, investments with the state guarantees for cleaner technologies are cost-effective.

3.9 High Performers

Economic growth can improve well-being and environmental qualities, or aggravate them. A large GDP is by no means equivalent of more well-being, and worse environmental qualities. As shown in Appendix C, the countries' performances with respect to sustainability indicators hugely vary across countries, and this variation is observed across high-, mid-, and low-income countries. Below is assessed, what countries improved their performance with respect to sustainability indicators during the period 2005–2015. Table 3.7 shows 26 high performing countries with their annual average rates of economic growth in the ascending order of these changes. High performers generated economic growth along with lower water pollution, impact on climate change, air pollution, and an increase of nature areas though deforestation is not compensated. Most of them also improved well-being indicated by the decreased poverty and increased governmental expenditures on education and health. The declining poverty and increasing expenditures on education and health are shown green, whereas the increasing poverty and decreasing expenditures are in red.

All high performers are high-income countries by the World Bank standards, except mid-income Romania. Most high performers are members of the EU28. While all high performers show improvements on those environmental indicators, but not all improved well-being on all social indicators. Israel, Slovakia, Poland, Czechia, Romania, Belgium, Switzerland and Germany improved their economic, social, and environmental performances during that decade. However, poverty increased in most of high performers despite economic growth in seventeen countries though the percentages poverty in their populations were several times lower than the world average in 2015. Six high performers decreased governmental expenditures on education and two decreased governmental expenditures on health.

Differences in performances are also observed with respect to environmental indicators. Water pollution was substantially reduced by high performers. Ten of them reduced water pollution by half within those ten years, which is achieved

Table 3.7 Growing countries with higher environmental performances during 2005–2015 in ascending order of economic growth

High environ. Performers	USD/cap	GDP growth	Poverty change	Education USD	Health USD	Water poll	CO_2 poll.	Air poll.	Nature restor.
Israel	35808	5%	-3%	4%	4%	-9%	-1%	-1%	3%
Ireland	62012	5%	15%	2%	4%	-4%	-3%	-3%	22%
Slovakia	16342	4%	-3%	5%	5%	-3%	-2%	-2%	8%
Iceland	52952	4%	3%	3%	1%	-4%	-5%	-4%	7%
Poland	12578	4%	-12%	3%	5%	-5%	-0.4%	-1%	4%
Cyprus	23408	3%	14%	1%	3%	-0.4%	-2%	-2%	31%
Slovenia	20890	3%	13%	0.2%	2%	-5%	-1%	-1%	10%
USA	56763	3%	2%	-1%	3%	-3%	-2%	-1%	1%
Sweden	51545	2%	5%	3%	5%	-3%	-4%	-3%	10%
Netherlands	45193	2%	10%	2%	2%	-1%	-1%	-3%	13%
United Kingdom	45405	2%	5%	3%	3%	-4%	-3%	-3%	1%
Spain	25742	2%	6%	1%	2%	-3%	-2%	-2%	6%
Czechia	17830	2%	-5%	7%	4%	-6%	-2%	-1%	2%
Austria	44196	2%	13%	2%	2%	-0.03%	-1%	-2%	2%
Romania	8969	2%	-6%	3%	2%	-6%	-1%	-1%	11%
Belgium	41008	2%	-1%	3%	3%	-7%	-2%	-4%	5%
Hungary	12721	2%	0.1%	-0.1%	0.2%	-7%	-2%	-2%	6%
Finland	42802	2%	14%	2%	2%	-2%	-2%	-3%	5%
Denmark	53255	2%	24%	-0.2%	2%	-1%	-5%	-4%	3%
Switzerland	84776	2%	-2%	2%	3%	-3%	-2%	-2%	1%
France	36653	2%	21%	0.3%	2%	-1%	-2%	-2%	4%
Germany	41103	1%	-0.1%	3%	2%	-5%	-1%	-2%	4%
Portugal	19250	1%	4%	-0.2%	-0.2%	-9%	-2%	-2%	5%
Japan	34961	1%	6%	0.3%	4%	-2%	-0.1%	-2%	1%
Greece	18084	1%	18%	-2%	-2%	-4%	-3%	-3%	6%
Italy	30242	1%	9%	-1%	0.4%	-2%	-3%	-4%	6%

mainly through wastewater treatment while water savings were limited. Iceland and Denmark reduced their total CO_2 emission by −5% annual average, which implies the reduction by half during ten years. Additional five high performers reduced these emissions by an average −4% a year, meaning by one-third in ten years. It is achieved mainly through shifts from fossil fuels to renewable energy, while reducing coal use was relevant in a few countries. Lower reduction rates are attained in air pollution. Four countries reduced NOx emissions by −4%, which is by one-third in ten years. While nature areas are enlarged in all high performing countries, even more than doubled in Ireland, Slovakia, Cyprus, Slovenia, Sweden, Netherlands, and Romania; however, no one could compensate for the losses of forest.

A few commonalities of high performing countries can be mentioned, but no specific one stands out. One commonality is that all high performers are high-income countries, except mid-income Romania, which suggests that reasonable incomes per capita are instrumental for changes in consumption and applications of environmental technologies. Another common feature is that their economic growth was moderate. It was a maximum 5% annual average, while most high performers had half lower growth rates. Their growth rates were well-below the rates in several lower income countries. Apparently, fast economic growth does not necessarily improve well-being, but impedes environmental performances. Third commonality is that all high performers show high entries in higher education with high female participation in higher education. Population of high performers is well educated, which facilitates demands for environmental qualities, and fosters acceptance of environmental policies. Fourth, most high performers are EU28 member countries, and aligned economies as Switzerland and Iceland. Economies with the coordinated social and environmental policies are apparently suitable for well-being and environmental qualities. Fifth, all high performers are democracies with involved citizens and independent environmental organisations. This kind of governance enables well-being and respectful uses of environmental qualities. Insofar data is available most high performers during 2005–2015 also performed well during the period 1990–2015, which indicates continuity in policies. This continuity fosters trust in society, thereby, reduces investment risks.

Several countries generated economic growth along with high performances on the indicators of well-being and environmental indicators. High income per capita, moderate economic growth, educated population, international coordination, and democratic governances are important conditions for high performances.

3.10 Conclusions

Economic growth goes along with reduction of environmental impacts in many countries. This is assessed with statistical data for the period 1990–2015 across all countries in the world. For this assessment, changes in countries' populations and their composition of economies are covered. Environmental impacts refer to uses of natural resources and emissions caused by these uses. The estimated impacts cover: water pollution based on freshwater withdrawal and population with wastewater treatment, uses of fossil fuels with CO_2 and NOx emissions that cause climate change, respectively air pollution, and loss of forest areas compensated with nature areas. Environmental impacts are estimated as results of the countries' GDP, their resource-intensities, meaning resources use per income, and emissions per resource. Focus is on the countries' environmental performances in the sense of annual average changes in environmental impacts. In addition, changes in well-being are assessed.

A larger, active population is often considered a blessing in the mainstream economics, on the assumption that population at work generates income growth. However, it is a threat in the environmentalist thinking as more people consume more natural resources and pollute. Smaller and skilful global populations would do for both, and this is the plausible outcome in the near future regarding the stagnating growth of populations along with increasing education of people. Aging populations in many countries cause scarcity of labour to do all necessary jobs, which impedes economic growth. This cannot be reversed in the short term, but can be mitigated by skilful labour, particularly through better educated women, and involvement of young people in low-income countries. Smaller, skilful populations emerge when policies overcome oppositions to gender emancipation and labour migration. In addition, composition of incomes changes as the shares of services grow to about two-third of GDP in most countries, though the production values of agriculture and industry increase, as well. Larger services generated many reasonably paid jobs, which increased incomes and improve well-being, including education. They also reduce material and energy uses per income given that services use a small fraction of the energy and the materials used in agriculture and industry per income. These changes toward a higher labour-intensity and lower material-intensity of growing economies evolve quasi-autonomously, it is without directives, and despite policy support of the energy-intensive production in agriculture and industry. Regarding these changes in the business composition of growing economies, decline of environmental impacts is expected. This expectation is validated with resource-intensities and environmental-efficiencies of countries.

The resource-intensities, measured in resource units per constant USD, indicate consumption of materials and energy. Water-intensities declined in nearly all focus countries, but many water-scarce countries use a lot of water. Meanwhile, fuel intensities declined in high-income countries while increased in many lower income ones. Forest areas declined in nearly all countries in the world. The declining resource-intensities in high-income countries during the last decades cannot be explained by the migration of industries to lower income countries, as they did migrate in the 1970s, but this trend reverse thereafter. International trade with minerals and ores in the USD and material consumption in tons show growth of the domestic material consumption in lower income countries next to saturating import of materials in high-income countries throughout the last decades.

Environmental-efficiency, measured in pollution per resource units, indicates applications of environmental technologies. These are induced by the demands in markets and policies. More wastewater treatment facilities were installed across countries, which reduced pollution, while populations without treatment declined in most countries. Meanwhile, global environmental-efficiency in climate change worsened as CO_2 emissions increased globally. While CO_2 emissions declined in high-income countries, they increased in lower income ones. Moreover, high fuel prices invoked renewable energy in high income countries, but enlarged emissions in many lower income countries as they applied cheaper, carbon-intensive coal. This diverging trend across countries hinders the international policy on climate change. Air pollution caused by NOx declined in nearly all focus countries and globally mainly due to more environmental technologies. This trend converged across countries, except low-income ones. Insofar data is available, the nature areas increased in many countries, but these improvements did not compensate for losses of forests.

Environmental impacts, measured by annual average changes, varied across indicators and countries. Water pollution is low and decreases in high-income countries due to low water-intensity and much wastewater treatment, but water pollution is high though decreasing in lower income countries. Per capita, the impact on climate change is high in high-income countries and decreases, while it is high and increases in mid-income ones, and it is low and increases in low-income countries. Air pollution decreases in most high-income countries, but increases in most lower income ones because environmental technologies are rarely applied. Nature areas increase in most countries, but they do not compensate for the losses of forest areas. Across countries, environmental impacts decreased in wastewater treatment and nature areas, hardly declined in air pollution, while the growth of CO_2 emissions decelerated toward saturation and decline. Sharing the burden of environmental impacts across countries is ineffective regarding the declining global share of high-income countries. Throughout the period 1990–2015, the share of high-income countries in the global GDP declined from 96% in 1990 to 82% in 2015 while their environmental impacts declined faster. Their share in global water pollution was only a few percent thanks to wastewater treatment, impact on climate change decreased from nearly 90% to 54%, air pollution to 34%, and nature losses to 33% of the global impacts. Meanwhile, these shares of fast growing mid-income economies increased. Economies of lower income countries grow faster, services in consumption are smaller, production is less energy-efficient and investments in environmental technologies are low. Larger investments in advanced production technologies and environmental technologies with support of the state guarantees provided by high-income countries are instrumental.

Economies grew and environmental impacts decreased in 26 countries from 2005 to 2015. Meanwhile, well-being is also improved. These experiences show that economies can grow and reduce environmental impacts, and that trade-offs between environmental qualities and well-being can be avoided. High performers have several features in common. Their income per capita is high, the rates of economic growth are moderate, expenditures on education are high, most of them align with the EU policies and they are all democracies with independent environmental organisations. Most of them have been high performers for a few decades, which means continuity in the performances. Compared to high performers, many lower income countries grew faster, but performed worsenedin on the indicators of well-being and environmental performances. These experiences show that incomes can grow and improve performances in well-being and environmental qualities. Moderate income growth reduces environmental impacts thanks quasi-autonomous changes in favour of services and application of environmental technology induced by the societal demands.

References

Alcott, B. (2010). Impact caps: Why population, affluence and technology strategies should be abandoned. *Journal of Cleaner Production, 18*, 552–560.

Arze del Granado, F. J., Coady, D., & Gillingham, R. (2012). The unequal benefits of fuel subsidies: A review of evidence for developing countries. *World Development, 40*(11), 2234–2248.

Ayres, R., & Voudouris, V. (2014). The economic growth enigma: Capital, labour and useful energy? *Energy Policy, 64*, 16–28.

Baumol, W. (1967). Macroeconomics of unbalanced growth: The anatomy of urban crisis. *The American Economic Review, 57*(3), 415–426.
Beaudreau, B. C., & Lightfoot, H. D. (2015). The physical limits to economic growth by R&D funded innovation. *Energy, 84*, 45–52.
Chenoweth, J., & Feitelson, E. (2005). Neo-malthusians and cornucopians put to the test: Global 2000 and the resourceful earth rvisited. *Futures, 37*, 51–72.
Chertow, M. R. (2001). The IPAT equation and its variants. *Journal of Industrial Ecology, 4*(4), 13–29.
Coase, R. (1937). The nature of the firm. *Economica, 4*(16), 386–405.
Davenport, T. H. (2005). *Thinking for a living.* Harvard Business School Press, Boston, Massachusetts.
Desa, U. N. (2022). *World population prospects 2022.* United Nations.
Ehrlich, P. R., & Holdren, J. P. (1971). Impact of population growth. *Science, 171*(3977), 1212–1217.
El Geneidy, S., Baumeister, S., Marini Govigli, V., Orfanidou, T., & Wallius, V. (2021). The carbon footprint of a knowledge organization and emission scenarios for a post-COVID-19 world. *Environmental Impact Assessment Review, 91*, Article 106645.
Fang, Z., Kang, S. H., & May, S. M. H. (2024). Does automation really reduce jobs?, *Asian and the Global Economy*, *4*(2). Retrieved April 25, 2025, https://www.sciencedirect.com/science/article/pii/S2667111524000239.
Fitchett, P. G. J. (2012). The evolution of conspicuous consumption. *Journal of Historical Research in Marketing, 4*(1), 1–32.
Gilleard, C., & Higgs, P. (2011). Consumption and aging. In R. A. Settersen, & J. L. Angel (Eds.), *Handbook of sociology of aging*. New York: Springer.
Hoffmann, R. C. (2015). *An environmental history of medieval europe.* Cambridge University Press.
IMF- blog. (2024). Retrieved September 6, 2024, from https://www.imf.org/en/Blogs/Articles/2024/09/04/sustained-economic-growth-hinges-on-productivity-gains-as-populations-age?utm_medium=email&utm_source=govdelivery.
Kalimeris, P., Richardson, C., & Bithas, K. (2014). A meta-analysis investigation of the direction of the energy-GDP causal relationship: Implications for the growth-degrowth dialogue. *Journal of Cleaner Production, 67*, 1–13.
Koyama, M. (2010). Evading the taint of usury. *Exploration in Economic History*, *47*(4). Retrieved April 25, 2025, from https://papers.ssrn.com/sol3/papers.cfm?abstract_id=1829062.
Kremer, M. (1993). Population growth and technological change: One million B.C. to 1990. *The Quarterly Journal of Economics, 108*(3), 681–716.
Krozer, Y. (2022). Economics of renewable energy. *Springer-Nature, Dordrecht, Section, 3*, 2.
Lander, D. S. (1998). *The wealth and poverty of nations.* New York-London: W.W. Norton & Co.
Lazard. (2025). Levelized Costs of Energy+. Retrieved March 17, 2025, from https://www.lazard.com/research-insights/levelized-cost-of-energyplus/.
Lee, T. B. (2017). William Baumol, whose famous economic theory explains the modern world, has died, *Vox*, May 4, 2017. Retrieved November 5, 2023, from https://www.vox.com/new-money/2017/5/4/15547364/baumol-cost-disease-explained.
Muyed, S. (2008). *The tertiary sector is going to dominate the world economy; should we worry*? MPRA Paper No. 14681. Retrieved November 6, 2023, from https://mpra.ub.uni-muenchen.de/14681/
Nentjes, A., & Wiersma, D. (1988). Innovation and pollution control 22. *International Journal of Social Economics, 15*(3/4), 51–70.
PBL. (2023). Netherlands environmental assessment agency. *Historic Database on Global Environment* (HYDE). Retrieved June 17, 2023, from https://themasites.pbl.nl/tridion/en/themasites/hyde/index.html.
Pommeranz, K. (2000). *The great divergence.* Princetown University Press.
Pyöria, P. (2005). The concept of knowledge work revisited. *Journal of Knowledge Management, 9*(3), 1–16.

Ridner, J. (2020). The dirty history of soap. *The Conversation*, 12–5–2020. Retrieved February 6, 2023, from https://theconversation.com/the-dirty-history-of-soap-136434.

Rosenberg, N., & Birdzell, L. E. (1986). *How the west grew rich.* I.B. Tauris & Co.

Rosenblum, J., Horvath, A., & Hendrickson, C. (2000). Environmental implications of services. *Environmental Science & Technology, 34*(22), 4669–4676.

Schettekat, R., & Yocarini, L. (2003). *The shift to services: A review of the literature.* IZA Discussion paper 964, Bonn.

Smil, V. (2019). *Energy and civilization.* The MIT Press, Cambridge Massachusetts.

TASS. (2024). Putin sets task to achieve steady rise in births in Russia within next six years. February 2024. Retrieved September 6, 2024, from https://tass.com/society/1753719.

Maddison Project Database, version 2018. Jutta, B., Inklaar, R., Jong de, H., & Luiten van Zanden, J. (2018). *Rebasing 'Maddison': new income comparisons and the shape of long-run economic development.* Maddison Project Working Paper, nr. 10. Retrieved February 9, 2023, available for download at www.ggdc.net/maddison.

Waggoner, P. E., & Ausubel, J. H. (2002). A framework for sustainability science: A renovated IPAT identity. *PNAS, 99*(12), 7860–7865.

Wallerstein, I. (1974). *The modern world system I: Capitalist agriculture and the origins of the European world-economy in the sixteenth century.* Academic Press.

Ward, J. D., Sutton, P. C., Werner, A. D., Costanza, R., Mohr, S. H., & Simmons, C. T. (2016). s Decoupling GDP growth from environmental impact possible?. *PLOS One, 11*(10). Retrieved April 7, 2023, from https://www.ncbi.nlm.nih.gov/pmc/articles/PMC5065220/.

Weinand, J. M., Pelser, T., Kleinebrahm, M., & Stolten, D. (2025). Countries across the world use more land for golf courses than wind or solar energy. *Environ. Res. Commun., 7*(021012), 1–8.

West, J., & Lutter, S. *Global material flow database*, UNEP. Retrieved November 17, 2024, from https://www.resourcepanel.org/global-material-flows-database.

Wiedmann, T. M., Lenzen, L. T., Keyßer, J. K., & Steinberger. (2020). Scientists' warning on affluence. *Nature Communications, 11*, 3107.

Wohlleben, P. (2015). *Das Geheime Leben des Bäume: Was sie fühlen, wie sie kommunizieren – die Entdeckung einder Verborgene Welt*. Ludwig Verlag.

World Bank. (2023). *Water in agriculture.* Retrieved June 29, 2023, from https://www.worldbank.org/en/topic/water-in-agriculture.

Chapter 4
Capabilities for Sustainable Development

Capabilities for sustainable development are assessed. The quasi-autonomous innovation-mechanism improves performances when cost-savings on natural resources are used for higher-value products. Performances are reasonable in global agriculture and transport, but low, decreasing in global industries caused by low-value products. Consumers reveal preferences for valuable, labour-intensive services. While the success rate of innovation is low and varies across countries, moderate competition due to demands for higher value deliveries is advantageous. The induced innovation-mechanism is driven by larger leisure time, and knowledge work, along with larger public investments and stricter pollution controls. Pivotal for sustainable development is the generation of higher value product-services combinations.

4.1 Introduction

How can societies pursue sustainable development in the future? Regarding the improving economic and environmental performances shown in the previous chapter, capabilities for sustainable development are assessed. This assessment is based on the estimates of societal changes in the past, on the assumption that these changes determine policies rather than other way around. Societal changes address innovations in the broad sense of using novel, value adding qualities across value chains entailing numerous adaptations within the chains. Regarding spontaneous growth of services and demanded environmental technologies, it is assumed that innovations are generated quasi-autonomously in competition and they bare driven by the societal demands for better performance. Both are addressed in this chapter.

The term 'capability' needs a brief introduction as it is interpreted in various ways. Originally, capability is defined as an individual access to resources for the value generating activities. This is defined with regard to poverty that is assumed to be caused by the deficient individual access of to education, care, and other services that enable to generate resources (Sen, 1983). This idea is converted into the Human

© The Author(s), under exclusive license to Springer Nature Switzerland AG 2025
Y. Krozer, *Economic Growth and the Environment*,
https://doi.org/10.1007/978-3-031-99181-3_4

Development Index (HDI) that indicates countries' performanes in education and health, called human capability. This interpretation of capabilities is used by the United Nations Development Program for assessments of well-being. As economic growth is prioritised in policies, a similar index is developed and used by the World Bank aiming to enhance economic growth (Mehrotra, 2005). This interpretation of the capabilities, labelled the Human Capital Index, can be found in the World Bank database.

In addition to those concepts of human capabilities and human capital, the idea of social capabilities is used with regard to interactions between interest groups in societies, called stakeholders. Social capabilities are assumed to determine successful interactions within societies, which enable welfare growth in a broad sense. Social capabilities are supposed to be influenced by many factors. Particularly important would be education and citizen participation in decision making (Temple & Johnson, 1996). Other scholars mentioned responsibilities for environmental qualities (Ekins, 2002); stakeholders' participation in decision making (Freeman & McVea, 2006), and political leaderships (Gasper, 2011). Social capabilities would benefit from the cooperation between stakeholders in regions (Gończ et al., 2006), and in value chains (Li, 2017). Those ideas are also criticised for poor definitions and lack of empirical tests (Ali et al., 2018). A common feature of various ideas about social capabilities is the advocacy of decision making about the common good in communities comprehended as a network of individual in a group with affection to each other and a common culture. This idea is usually labelled as the Communitarism. The communitarian governance is assumed to exert moral suasion on individuals, which enables to maintain ethical values, environmental qualities and other goods for the benefit of societies (Etzioni et al., 2003). With respect to the natural resources, the polycentric governances of communities are observed (Ostrom, 2009).

To avoid confusion, capability in this study is defined in the sense of the individual access to resources. Larger capabilities are assumed to generate innovations quasi-autonomously due to competition and being induced by the societal demands for environmental performance and other valuables. The former addresses changes without policy intervention, the latter refer to the demands posed by the authorities and stakeholders. While innovations are considered as qualitative changes in business activities across value chains, adaptation address to minor changes within a value chain. This definition of innovation covers economic activities in a broader sense than technologies as production tools. For instance, it includes changes in services and communication.

Brief introduction to the idea of innovations aims to avoid blur. It is observed that innovations in the narrow sense of novel technologies applied in machines, constructions, and other capital goods are usually driven by the interests of innovators rather than executed on demand by a customer. Innovations emerge when firms compete for a market share, thereby more profit, even when the specific demands are intangible (Mowery & Rosenberg, 1979). New qualities are realized with the knowledge resources that are used for understanding events and converting them into practical knowledge, called know-how, or skill. Know-how enables conversions of the natural resources and man-made resources into valuables. It was focused on land in agricultural economies, on energy and materials in industrial economies, but shifted to labour during the last century as services grew (Mokyr, 2002). A forecast is that innovations in knowledge become decisive in the twenty-first century as artificial intelligence expands (Harari, 2017). When innovations disseminate across businesses and countries due to the sales of novelties, numerous adaptations reduce costs and improve the qualities in production and uses. Such adaptations continue for decades, even centuries as observed in machines (Grübler, 1991), transport (Nakićenović, 1991), lighting (Nordhaus, 1994), and other businesses. Innovations and adaptation are driven by competition and induced by the demands of authorities and stakeholders.

After introducing innovation-mechanisms in Sect. 4.2, performances driven by competition are estimated in agriculture, industry, and transport are assessed in Sect. 4.3. Household consumption is addressed in Sect. 4.4. The innovating processes are covered in Sect. 4.5, and their financing in Sect. 4.6. The inducement of environmental technology is covered in Sect. 4.7, followed by introduction of the distributed in sanitation, renewable energy and nature in Sect. 4.8. Conclusions are drawn in Sect. 4.9.

4.2 Capabilities in Innovation-Mechanisms

A question is if the countries' capabilities for generation of economic growth and reduction of environmental impacts decrease, or increase. An answer is important for assessing these performances in the future. A pessimistic opinion and an optimistic one can be drawn based on the mainstream economic train of thoughts. They are assessed with regards to quasi-autonomous innovation-mechanism and induced innovation-mechanism for sustainable innovations, which are defined as innovations that improve economic, social and environmental performance combined. A mechanism refers to several linked activities as shown in models below.

Measured by the Human Capital Index of the World Bank, a pessimistic idea about the capabilities for global economic growth can be concluded. This index shows data for 2010 and for all years from 2017 to 2020. If the data between 2010 and 2017 are interpolated, and absent data for the EU28 are replaced by the data for Germany, which is the largest economy in the EU28, this index shows the increasing capabilities until 2017. This increase is followed by a decline of capabilities globally and in the focus countries, except the increases in India, Nigeria, and Pakistan. However, this index is biased as the literacy rates and life expectancy approximate their maxima in many countries. More than 100% literacy rate cannot be achieved, while the literacy rates already exceeded 92% of the global population between 15 and 24 years in 2015. It is above 50% in nearly all countries. More ambitious education is needed for wider capabilities in innovating. The average lifespan also approaches the maximum asymptote of about 95 years in most countries if data of the last decade is extrapolated. Aging societies are assumed to impede capabilities but global labour force still grows faster than population.

More optimism about capabilities for economic growth can be derived from trends in capital and labour. In the mainstream thinking, economies grow due to larger scale and higher productivity of capital and labour. These trends are assessed with the World Bank data. Savings, which is the main resource of capital, determine the scale of capital. Globally, savings grow faster than all capital, which implies sufficient resource of capital in the future, though savings stagnate in Egypt. Productivity of capital can continue to increase, if the total savings grow faster than all capital, as it is observed, and if all capital grows faster than the fixed capital in machines, constructions, and other goods for value addition, as it does. As those two trends are observed, capital can be allocated into profitable novelties, while risky mistakes can be avoided. Those trends have evolved globally since the 1990s, but fixed capital declined in the Japanese and Russian economies. The global scale of capital and capital productivity can continue to grow in most focus countries. So, there are sufficient resources for new equipment, which enables new technologies. Labour trends are also encouraging. The scale of global labour is sufficient regarding faster growth of labour force than all populations. In addition, the global labour force is more skilled due to wider and higher education. If the growth of labour force is slower than population in particular countries, it can be mitigated through immigration of labour from low-income countries, flexibility in retirement and education, as well as robotics with artificial intelligence, and other technologies. Labour productivity, which is estimated by the increasing GDP per worker, also increases. Difference between the labour productivity and income growth attributed to technological change, so called Solow residue, also increases. Trends of these factors indicate that global economic growth can continue unless policies undermine these factors, or the incentives for innovations vanish because businesses pursue other objectives. Appendix 4 underpins the scales and productivity.

Environmental impacts can continue to decrease due to sustainable innovations as a result of competition mechanism. This mechanism is explained. When businesses save costs through lower use of natural resources, profits are generated which can be used for development of higher value products that will enable profits in the future. Higher environmental performances are generated spontaneously, if a part of profits due to the cost-savings on natural resources are used for funding innovations that add to the value in economies. As this process evolves when firms compete for lower costs and higher values it is labelled as a quasi-autonomous innovation-mechanism. However, there are impediments. A major impediment is that low prices of the natural resources reduce the cost-savings. High prices of the natural resources and resistance to the cost-saving on the man-made resources facilitate the cost-savings on the natural resources. While the prices of natural resources fluctuate, resistance to the cost-savings on the man-made resources are widely observed. The cost-savings on labour are effectively opposed by the labour organisations, the cost-savings on capital are objected by investors, and the cost-saving on knowledge is countered by entrepreneurs. Obstructions of cost-savings on man-made resources foster cost-savings on natural resources. Another major impediment is shareholder demands for high dividends. Greed for high profits causes that profits are not allocated for the development of higher-value activities, but misuses capital which impedes productivity. Greed is unethical and impedes economic growth. In addition, efforts in research and development (R&D) of novelties can fail because of technical deficiencies in the realisation of inventions and insufficiently competitive new qualities and prices of innovations during sales.

Capabilities for the quasi-autonomous innovation-mechanism that generates economic growth and reduces environmental impacts are presented in a model shown in Table 4.1. This model presents a cash flow of a firm that generates value based on the costs-savings that are allocated into R&D for development of a novelty, and for profit that delivers shareholders value. Columns show the timeline: situation before the start in columns 2 to 4, initial period 1 in column 5, and growth periods 2 to 4 in columns 6 to 8. Rows show allocation. Assumptions about the allocation per period are: 80% of the value are costs, 20% of the costs are cost-savings, 20% of the cost-savings are spent on R&D and 80% of dividend, and the R&D delivers 20% additional value in the next period. Based on these arbitrary numbers, it is shown that continuous growth is generated due to larger cost-savings and higher value after the initial period. Hence, economies in competition generate sustainable innovations as long as cost-savings obtained from lower uses of natural resources are partially allocated in the value adding R&D. This model is used in the next section for assessing progress toward sustainable development in businesses.

Many studies show the decreasing uses and costs of energy and material throughout the last century. They are shown on the levels of countries, firms and individual products (e.g., Larson et al., 1986; Herman, et al. 1989; Tilton et al., 1991; Wright, 1997). Estimates for lower income countries, which use much natural resources per income, underpin the decreasing energy-intensities in agriculture and industry due to the improving technologies (Goldenberg & Reddy, 1990). Improving performances of innovations through the cost-reducing and effect-increasing adaptations that evolve for many decades, even centuries, are observed in the cases of equipment (Rosenberg, 1982), and utensils for daily uses (Petrovsky, 1994). These adaptations are often as cost-reducing technological change. Those improvements in environmental performances are the side-effects of economic growth driven by competition. They are considered side-effects because they are not intended to reduce

Table 4.1 A model of the quasi-autonomous innovation-mechanism; assumed per period, 20% cost-savings, of it 20% for R&D that brings 20% additional value in the next period

Action	*Assumption for the start*			1	2	3	4
	Initial	*Cost-saving*	*R&D addition*	Starting innovation	Continuous growth		
Value	*100*			100.8	105.6	110.7	116.0
Costs		*80*	*80*	80	84.5	88.6	92.8
Saving	*0*	*20*	*0*	20.2	21.1	22.1	23.2
R&D	*0*	*0*	*4*	4.0	4.2	4.4	4.6
Profit	*0*	*0*	*16*	16.1	16.9	17.7	18.6
Growth				1%	5%	5%	5%

environmental impacts even though the reduction through services is substantial. Growing human capabilities can provide similarly positive side-effects on environmental qualities. For example, higher female enrolment in higher education is considered an effective policy for mitigation of climate change with regard to lower birth rates of skilled female labour (Hawken, 2017). Statistical data on those capabilities in businesses and in consumer expenditures is presented in the next section.

In addition, sustainable innovations are also induced through social demands for environmental qualities. These social demands also evolve partly spontaneously as higher incomes allow more demands than 'bread and butter' for basic needs. Those demands intentionally trigger investments that induce innovations, which improve economic, social and environmental performances. When firms face stringent demands for environmental quality, an innovation-mechanism is induced. Figure 4.1 shows conventional deliberations of firms that face demands for environmental qualities. Vertical axis represents unit costs, and horizontal one the stringency of demand.

Firms can comply with the demands through additional available technologies at the increasing unit costs, or innovate at an initially additional cost but lower, possibly decreasing, costs than the available technologies when the stringency increases. Moderate demands induce available technologies and stringent demands induce innovation (Krozer, 1996). Cost-savings due to innovations are illustrated by the areas B minus A in the figure. Experiences show that changes of purchased qualities, resource-efficient production, reformulation of products, linking services to products, and other cost-effective actions are pursued when stringent demands are faced (Krozer, 2008). When the demands strengthen, firms' strategies dissociate into innovators that pursue competitive advantages of compliance with the demands and

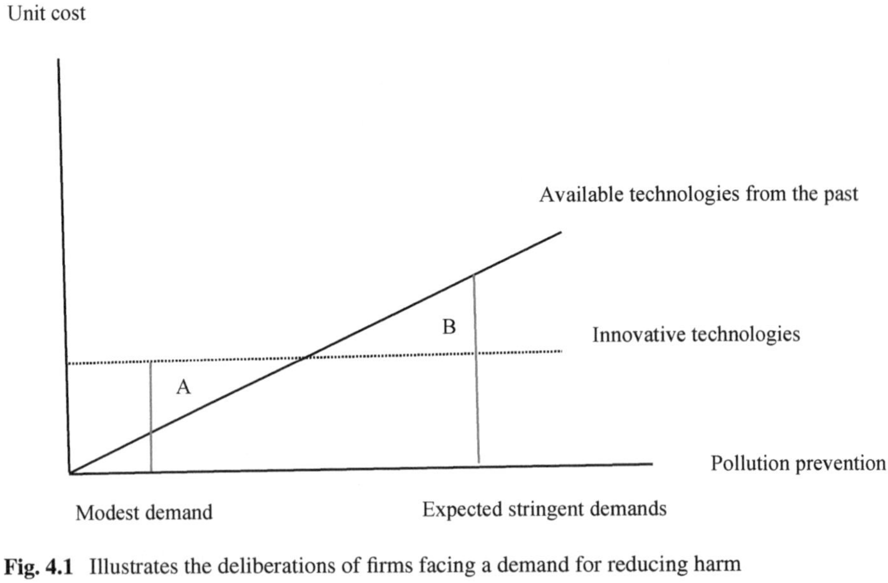

Fig. 4.1 Illustrates the deliberations of firms facing a demand for reducing harm

laggards that oppose demands. Eventually, innovators introduce numerous adaptations which reduce costs and improve qualities while laggards seek rents of public support.

Far reaching demands can induce innovations when threats to public health are sensed; for example, caused by water pollution, or fine particles and NOx emissions to the air. However, policies are sluggish. An example is the policy on climate change. Nearly hundred years after signalling about the greenhouse effect of CO_2 on climate change in science in the late 1800s, and fifteen years after signals in businesses in the early 1970s, this effect is acknowledged by the international policies in 1988 when the scientific committee on climate change (UN IPCC) is established. Mitigating climate change is agreed internationally in Kyoto in 1997, and tangible demands are agreed in Paris in 2015. Three decades of the policy preparation from the acknowledgment until demands is faster than nearly forty years from the early 1950s to the late 1980s for pesticides, but slower than ten years for the policy preparation on substitutions of chlorofluorocarbons that destroy ozone in the atmosphere with the risks of cancer. Protection of the domestic firms hinders enforcement. For example, electric cars were demanded by the California state in 'zero emission regulations' by the late 1980s. While the car manufacturers in the USA opposed it, an Indian developer introduced a small electric car (REVA) in India in the mid-1990s, but it could not enter the USA, neither the EU because of the protectionist regulations. Similar barriers are observed in replacing asbestos, recycling packaging, and other environmental issues.

Capabilities seem sufficient for sustainable innovations. Sustainable innovations emerge quasi-autonomously when cost-savings due to better use of natural resources are allocated to value-adding innovations and they are induced when far reaching environmental performances are demanded.

4.3 Producers Performances

It is assessed if the quasi-autonomous innovation-mechanisms are observed in agriculture, industry and transport. Lower uses of natural resources, which generate cost-savings, along with higher value activities can be expected. These changes should be reflected statistically in the declining uses of natural resources measured in physical terms and money terms, as well as the increasing value of deliveries in money terms. Changes during two decades, or longer are considered, being sufficient periods of time for replacing most equipment. In addition to the World Bank data, specific databases on energy and materials are used. Results are presented as indexes in time. Note that the physical and monetary data are separated in order to avoid the bias of material-intensity when higher values without decrease of material can falsely suggest improved performances.

In **agriculture**, three indicators are considered in the period 1990–2020. These indicators are: efficiency of land uses in USD per hectare of land, productivity of land use in kg production of cereals per hectare of land, and effectivity in use of natural

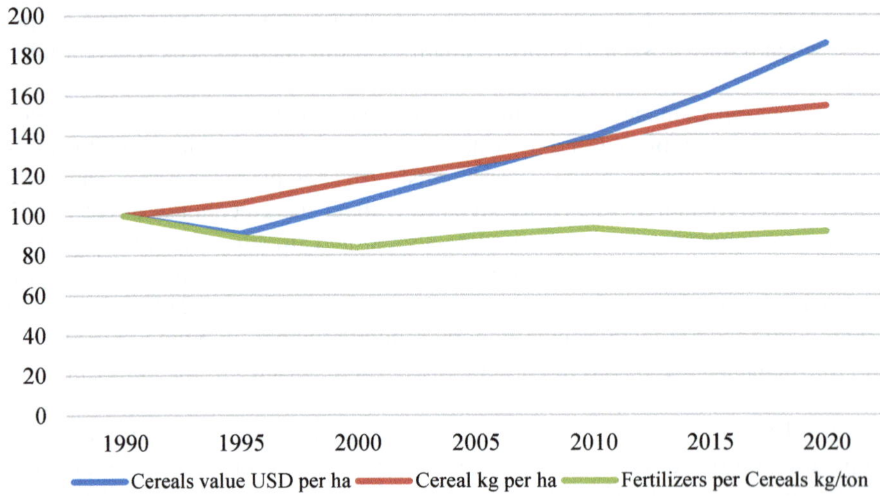

Graph 4.1 Indexes of global agricultural value per land use, products per land use and products per resource use

resources measured in kg fertilizers per kilogram of cereals. All those estimates cover global changes based on the World Bank data. Graph 4.1 shows indexes of these indicators (1990 = 100).

Uses of fertilizers per cereals in kg per ton declined by 1% annual average while this trend decelerated. This indicates cost-savings on uses of natural resources which can be used for novations in production. Meanwhile, the productivity of arable land in tons of cereals per hectare has increased by nearly 2% per year, but also decelerated. Production could increase at lower fertilizer use, but that productivity growth saturates. The global value per hectare of land increased by more than 2% annually and accelerated. Higher prices of cereals aggravate poverty. This quasi-autonomous innovation mechanism enabled more productive deliveries, while growing demands for cereals generate higher prices. Differences across countries are observed. Values increased slower than the uses of the fertilizers, being key natural resources, in most high-income countries, while they increased faster in lower income countries. In high-income countries, productivity of the material uses declines while innovations for higher value agriculture stagnate. Insufficient data hinder similar assessment in other agricultural businesses.

In **industry**, an active quasi-autonomous innovation-mechanism is expected regarding high costs of energy and materials in total costs. For example, these costs cover about 30% of the total costs in food industry, up to 20% in chemicals, and above 5% in electronics in several EU Member countries (Wilting & Hanemaaijer, 2014). Global industry performance is assessed using three indicators. One is the material use in kg product per kg mined natural resources. Second indicator is global industrial energy use in MJ per kg products. Third one is industrial production value in USD per industrial energy use in MJ. The period 1990–2015 is covered. The value data are derived from the World Bank database, the energy data from the International Energy Agency (IEA, 2024), and materials uses are based on the UNEP database on mining and processing of natural resources compiled by West and Lutter (2024). Indexes (1990 = 100) of these indicators are shown in Graph 4.2. Unfortunately, data on the industrial uses of energy and materials are imperfect. For example, the UNEP data on materials differs from the OECD data on domestic material consumption and material footprints, while both databases rely on statistics of international trade with monetary and physical values. Data on the industrial energy consumption per country are also not found.

The material uses per product increased in line with larger energy consumption per kg per MJ. It indicates that industry did not improve performances in materials and energy performances. These performances declined even during high prices of fossil fuels. The value per energy use in USD per MJ increased as fast as the material and energy uses, but economic performance declined during high fuel prices. The value per energy uses decreased during the 2000s and then increased in the 2010s during high prices of fossil fuels. Industries did not reduce energy consumption when fuel prices increased but produced cheaper products. All those indicators of environmental and economic performances increased about 2% annual average during those twenty-five years. These results show that industries generated lower value during high fuel prices presumably in response to economic crisis after the financial collapse in 2008. These trends indicate a deficient quasi-autonomous innovation-mechanism in industries. Industries become more wasteful and less value adding per unit of used energy and material. It is a worrisome trend because industry is the main cause of environmental impacts.

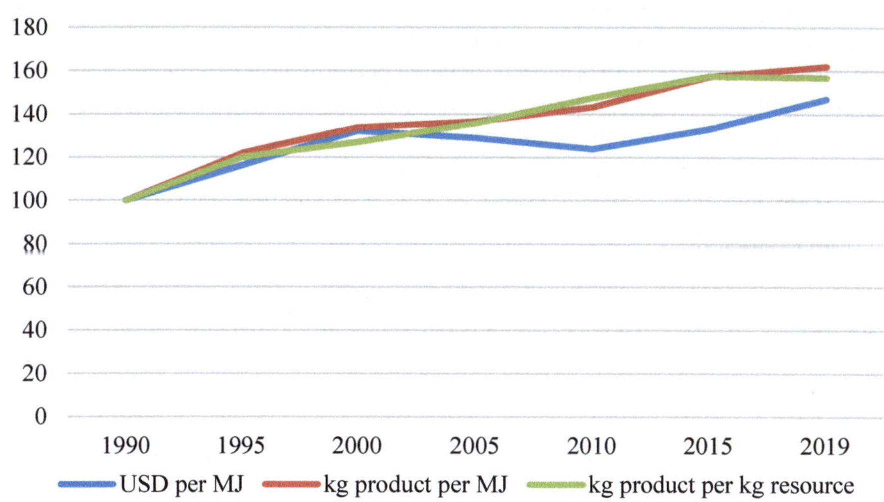

Graph 4.2 Indexes of global industrial value per energy use, products per energy use and products per mined resources

A plausible explanation for this worrisome trend in the industry is that large scale of low-value production impedes higher economic and environmental performances. As the scale enlarges, the value per products evolves toward the unit costs. This trend allows only little, or nil margin for research and development in addition to shareholder value. Indeed, low-cost, low-quality products expandedin hygiene, fashion, durables and other industrial products. Concentration of manufacturing in China, Bangladesh, and other countries striving for an accelerated industrialisation with support by public funds generates large scale of low-cost, low-quality production. This concentration enables high dividend for shareholders, which encourages short-term profits above continuity through innovations in high-value products. Changes in services also put pressures on the prices and qualities. For example, online services generate advertising while decrease sales prices and product quality (Fisman, 2013). This trend toward sales prices at equivalent of the unit costs causes a cul-de-sac in global industry because innovating for higher value is unattractive, though differences across businesses and firms could be found but not assessed because of insufficient data.

Reversing this trend requires a turnaround towards quality products, which needs forceful demands for higher value deliveries. Examples are the electrification of energy consumption, bioresources in constructions, 'slow' food and hygiene, design in fashion, and suchlike. Compliance with such demands requires life cycle management that is capable to improve performances in value changes, taking into consideration social and environmental harms. In order to invoke higher values, liabilities for harm caused by deficient qualities in life cycle of products are needed and can be imposed by policies. They would invoke actions that mitigate information asymmetry between consumers and producers about product qualities. Craftsmanship, guarantees, product circulation, and suchlike actions would foster high quality, which would justify higher product prices. In addition, public investments in networks, afforestation and other infrastructure is needed for better performances in industry. A managerial possibility is creating governance networks of front-running businesses and social organisations, along with the regulatory incentives as backstop for the laggards in alignment to the front-runners (Cramer, 2022).

In **transport**, data is found on services in air, rail, and road transport. For air and rail transport, the number of passengers per MJ energy (effectivity), and service value per energy in USD per MJ (efficiency) are used. For road transport, the passenger kilometres per MJ (effectivity) are used, but data on revenue is not available. Multiple data sources are used. All energy data is derived from the statistics of the IEA. The revenues in air transport are based on the annual reports of the International Aviation Transport Association. The passenger data for aviation and rail refer to the World Bank database, and for road transport to the OECD database. It is assumed that the energy performances in mobility are similar across countries, which is plausible given that technologies for transport are traded internationally. This assumption is relevant for the road transport as data on China, Indonesia, Philippines, Nigeria, Pakistan, Bangladesh and Ethiopia are not found in those databases. In sum, the transport data are imperfect but suffice reliable assessment; better global data is not found. Graph

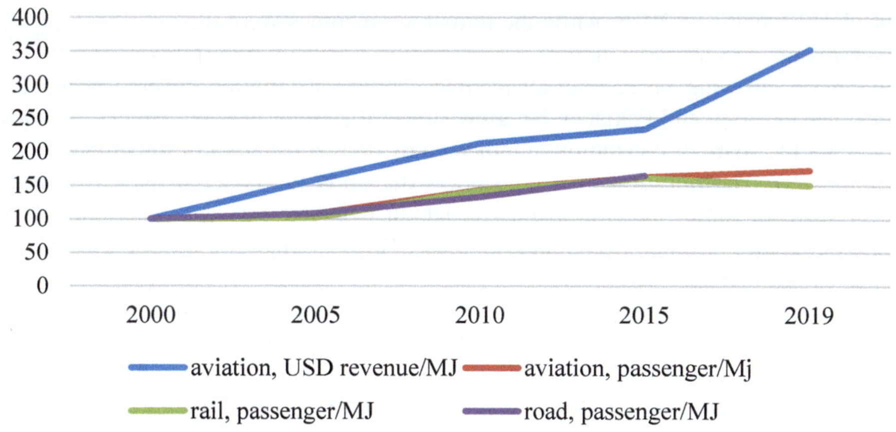

Graph 4.3 Indexes of energy performances in air, rail and road transport

4.3 shows indexes (1990 = 100) of energy performance in global aviation, rail, and cars during the period 2000–2019.

Although the revenue in aviation is only USD 1.3 per passenger, which is based on USD 1300 billion for nearly 900 billion transported passengers, the service value in USD per energy use in MJ increased three times faster than the number of passengers per energy use in MJ. This indicates high capability in cost-savings of energy use and allocations for value-adding activities. Unfortunately, similar data is not found for rail and road transports. Nevertheless, global rail transport is an energy-efficient service regarding nearly 1000 times more passenger kilometres by rail than by aviation which are delivered with about 10,000 times lower energy use per passenger kilometre rail. Moreover, energy uses per passenger in air, rail and road transport decreased by 2 to 3% throughout those twenty years. These improvements in energy performance are faster than the improvements in global economies. Higher energy performance in rail transport indicates that improving energy performance can continue despite low use of energy per passenger kilometre.

Global assessment of the quasi-autonomous innovation-mechanisms shows better economic and environmental performances in the agricultural land use, stagnation in the industry caused by focus on low-quality deliveries, and moderate improvements in transport. The industrial production is trapped by the decreasing prices and performances.

4.4 Consumer Purchases

A popular argument in industries is that consumers demand cheaper products. This argumentation is assessed. No doubt that preferences in consumption are decisive for the generation of innovations given that global consumption covered about 74%

of global income in 2015, while the remaining incomes were the savings used for investments and across countries. Consumption was only two-thirds of income in Indonesia, growing faster than all income, while consumption covered nearly all incomes in Egypt and Pakistan, but grew slower than their income. Higher incomes increase the share of consumption indicated by high correlation of the growth rates ($R^2 > 0.9$). The question is if consumers demands for material-intensive products grow, or rather material-extensive, labour-intensive services. Therefore, it is assessed if the consumer preferences are geared towards material-intensive products, or to labour-intensive services.

Assessing the consumer preferences for environmental performances is challenging because opinions and actions differ. Usually, the consumers' preferences are assessed based on their willingness to pay. Assessments reveal high willingness to pay for environmental performance, which is used by environmentalists for justification of the consumer responsibilities and motivation of interests in environmental qualities. However, the sales of products that are considered to be environmentally responsible are disappointingly low, though they grow faster than all sales. A wide gap between the consumer intentions in stated preferences and the revealed behaviour in purchases is observed (Kahneman & Knetsch, 1992). Revealed purchases of such environmentally responsible products would be reliable, but data across countries and products during several years is not available, except across main product groups for the purchases in the United Kingdom. Regarding those limitations, the consumer expenditures in several categories of material-intensity are estimated on the assumption that material-intensities indicates environmental impacts. The OECD database is used. This database covers household expenditures for purchases in several high-income and mid-income countries, but misses low-income countries. In addition, the Eurostat database on the EU countries and a few low-income countries is used. Both databases divide the expenditures into 15 categories.

With regard to material-intensities, those categories of consumer expenditures are grouped into three clusters. The first cluster, called 'Products', covers the material-intensive consumption of foods, beverages, clothes, housing, and furniture, which are based on industrial supplies to retail. The second cluster, labelled as 'Physical services', includes consumption of services in health, transport, restaurants, hotels, and miscellaneous, which are capital intensive as they involve constructions and equipment. Being capital intensive, these services can be material-intensive and polluting. With regard to a review of life cycle assessments in the EU of 25 member countries (Tukker and Jansen, 2006), it can be concluded that nearly all environmental impacts are caused by consumption in the clusters of 'Products' and "Physical services'. If the consumer expenditures grow while consumption in those two clusters declines, environmental impacts of consumption decline. The third cluster, called 'Upgradation services', covers consumer expenditures in communication, recreation, and culture, as well as in education. These consumer expenditures are dedicated to labour-intensive services for interactions between people, which are material-extensive and hardly polluting.

Based on those assumptions about the household purchases, two issues are assessed. One is if larger consumption expenditures are associated with 'Physical services', and with 'Upgradation services', and if the 'Upgradation services' grow faster than the expenditures on 'Products' and on 'Physical services'. If this is observed, consumers have tangible preference for labour-intensive services above material-intensive products. This implies that additions of services in life cycle management are attractive. In addition, second, it is assessed if the growth of 'Upgradation services' is related to the countries-specific culture and policies. If so, the costs of labour have minor importance compared to innovations tuned to the particular consumer preferences.

The consumer expenditures are estimated with the OECD data for Australia, Canada, Costa Rica, Iceland, Israel, Japan, Korea, Mexico, New Zealand, Norway, Switzerland, UK, USA, and EU27 as if a country. The period 1995–2019 is covered. Results are presented in Table 4.2. Per capita incomes, as well as the shares and growth rates of the clusters (vertically) per country (horizontally) are displayed.

Consumption expenditures on 'Products' covered about half of the total expenditures in all OECD countries. Exceptions are the USA where the expenditures on physical services were larger and Japan where 'Products' covered 80% of the total, the latter can be caused by differences in definition of products in the data. The expenditures on the 'Physical services' covered about one-third of the total in most countries. Nearly 20% of all expenditures are spent on the 'Upgradation services', but lower percentages in the USA and Japan. The growth rates of those expenditures are reciprocally to the shares. The expenditures on 'Products' grew half as fast as on' Physical

Table 4.2 Consumer expenditures on 'Products', 'Physical services' and 'Upgradation services', average shares and growth rates during the period 1995–2019

OECD Countries	Incomes per capita		Products		Physical services		Upgradations services	
	Average	Growth (%)	Share (%)	Growth (%)	Share (%)	Growth (%)	Share (%)	Growth (%)
EU27	28,519	2	50	1.0	36	1.6	13	3.5
Australia	51,206	2	48	1.0	39	1.5	14	2.9
Canada	39,138	2	47	1.4	41	2.1	12	2.7
Costa Rica	9653	3	52	1.4	35	3.0	14	3.9
Iceland	48,246	2	52	1.1	34	3.8	14	3.5
Israel	31,555	2	53	1.2	36	1.8	11	3.3
Japan	33,109	1	83	0.3	14	−0.4	3	0.3
Korea	23,012	4	45	1.0	38	3.0	17	4.1
Mexico	9017	1	55	2.4	36	3.4	8	4.4
New Zealand	34,954	2	56	1.4	30	2.4	14	4.1
Norway	71,364	1	50	1.4	36	1.9	13	3.4
Switzerland	79,137	1	46	0.0	43	1.2	10	1.2
UK	42,351	1	50	0.9	39	1.3	11	3.0
USA	52,443	2	39	0.9	57	1.7	4	0.6

services', which grew slower than on 'Upgradation services.' A methodological note is that high growth rates of smaller scale 'Upgradation services' cannot be explained by the statistical phenomenon that new activities grow faster than ones vested in the past because larger consumer expenditures on communication, education, recreation, and culture is observed for many decades. Those differences in the scale and growth of consumption expenditures enable reliable assessment. Across countries, the correlation of economic growth with the growth of consumer expenditures on 'Products'. is low ($R^2 = 0.1$), while the correlations with the 'Physical services' and 'Upgradation services' are moderate ($R^2 = 0.6$ and $R^2 = 0.5$, respectively). These estimates suggest that services are more important for consumption growth than products, which indicates that the labour-intensive services are often preferred consumer expenditures. These results confirm the observation of growing services.

The influence of the country's culture on the consumer expenditures is assessed with the Eurostat data on 28 EU member countries and 9 non-member countries between 1995 and 2020. Based on the World Bank standard for incomes, all EU member countries are high-income, except mid-income Bulgaria and Romania. Non-members of the EU28 are high-income Iceland, Norway, and Switzerland, mid-income Bosnia-Herzegovina, Montenegro, North Macedonia, Serbia, and Turkey, and low-income Albania. Graph 4.4 shows the index (1995 = 100) of consumer expenditures on 'Products',' Physical services', and 'Upgradation services.

Throughout 1995 to 2021, the average expenditure on 'Products' was about 51% of all consumer expenditures in those countries, varying from 43 to 69% across the countries, compared to 37% of' Physical services', and 12% of 'Upgradation services'. This is in line with the data on other OECD countries. The consumption of 'Products' steadily declined, except during a few years. These expenditures decreased in all those countries, except Netherlands and North-Macedonia where more 'Products' were purchased during that period. Meanwhile, the purchases of 'Physical services' stagnated, or declined in all countries, except in Lithuania and Poland where they grew. The expenditures on the 'Upgradation services' changed

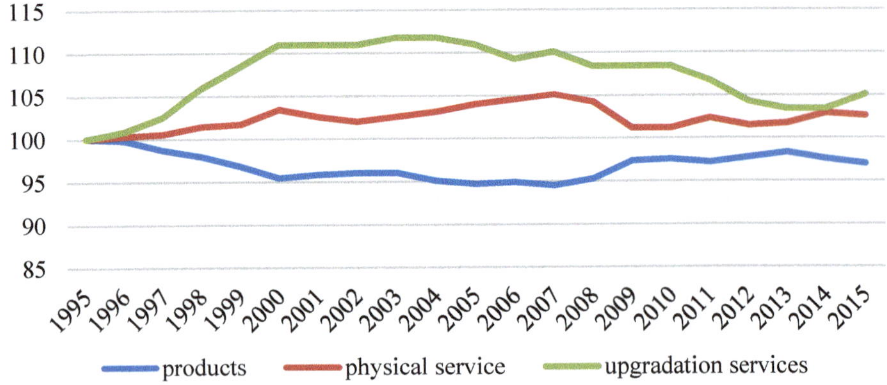

Graph 4.4 Index of consumer expenditures in Europe with Turkey

in line with economic growth. They increased faster during the 1990s when the economies grew, but their growth slowed-down during the early 2000s and decreased during the economic crisis after financial collapse in 2008, followed by the growth during economic recovery in the 2010s.

The increasing consumer purchases of 'Upgradation services' converged across countries, which means that the shift from products to services tends to continue in the near future despite cheaper industrial deliveries. Within this convergence trend, differences across countries relate to culture rather than the labour costs. For example, the Norwegian households with high labour costs dedicated 14% of total expenditures to the 'Upgradation services' in 1995, which hardly changed during those years. Low-income Albanians dedicated only 6% of total income in 1995, but surpassed that percentage in Norway by the mid-2000s to end up with 20% expenditures on the 'Upgradation services' in 2019 as their incomes per capita grew. Meanwhile, mid-income Lithuanians purchased less 'Upgradation services' than the Albanians in 1995 but more than the Albanians in 2020 while the Lithuanian incomes per capita grew faster than the Albanian ones. Income growth facilitates purchases of labour-intensive services. However, low correlation of the "Upgradation services" to income per person across countries indicate that cultural factors have stronger influence on consumption expenditures than high labour-costs. Consumers prefer labour-intensive services above material-intensive products and services when their incomes grow and the services are tuned to the cultural preferences.

Larger services within consumer expenditures is an attractive perspective for sustainable development because consumer preferences can be satisfied along with lower materials uses and associated pollution. Linking services to products is widespread in housing, care, mobility, and other durable consumer products. Business strategies also add services to products. This is done through guaranteed and warranties for repairs and recycling of high value products, as well as lease, rents, and performance services that substitute ownership for uses with take-back and deposit-return instruments. The consumer preferences for such action can be enhanced through the shift of taxation on labour to the natural resources. Such shift would increase the consumer expenditures on labour-intensive services compared to material-intensive products.

As incomes grow, consumer expenditures and consumer preferences for labour-intensive services increase faster than material-intensive products. Adding services to products matches consumer preferences, increases employment and reduces environmental impacts, which can be facilitated through shift of taxes on labour to the natural resources.

4.5 Innovators Success Rates

An issue is if there are sufficient capabilities and interests in innovating with regards to the consumer demands. This is assess on the assumption that the quasi-autonomous innovations mechanism is driven by entrepreneurs motivated by n the perspective of success in competition. Therefore, the success rate of investments in an innovation in the focus countries is estimated. This success is defined as a new firm or a new activity in a vested firm, called a startup, that survives competition during minimum of ten years in order to generate sufficient income for coverage of all costs and a profit.

The success rates are estimated based on a conventional model for innovation processes. In this model, an innovator is successful when research and development (R&D) deliver novelties for profitable sales, which is possible when the purchasers perceive advantages compared to the propositions of rivals that also innovate (Kamien & Schwartz, 1982). Realisation of a novelty needs costly efforts in research and development (R&D), which can deliver an invention that is protected from misuse and theft through Intellectual Property Rights (IPR). An IPR can be a patent, author right, trademarks and design for ownership that provides rights to use and sell the invention, and prevents rival uses (Abramovitz et al., 1995). An IPR facilitates starting new activities in a vested firm, or a new firm, both are considered as startups, and the start-up needs to sell inventions in competition for the cost-coverage and profit. This mainstream model focuses on R&D and IPR for successful innovations though informal, tacit activities are often profitable (Soleas, 2021). Given that those innovation processes involve financiers, experts, authorities and other interests, innovations is considered a system that generates economic growth when it acts successfully (Fagberg and Srholec, 2008). Many studies underline innovations as the driver of economic growth. Indeed, the cross-countries R&D and GDP during the period 2008-2017 were correlated ($R^2 > 0.8$), while R&D and IPR were moderately correlated ($R^2 > 0.5$), as well as IPR and startups ($R^2 > 0.6$).

The challenge of innovators is that the costs must be made up front, but profits generated after a period of time are uncertain because the realisation of an invention and its sales in competition can fail. In order to assess the profitability of investments in R&D, the rate of successful innovations is estimated. This rate is compounded by the rates of obtaining IPR based on R&D and starting a firm with an IPR, as well as the rate of startups that survive copetition during ten years. These rates of success are estimated per USD million spent on R&D, equivalent of 2–3 PhD's, which approximates the average cost of turning ideas into an IPR in high-income countries. The number of IPR per R&D expenditures, and the number of startups per IPR are the rates that indicate successful realisation of inventions. Multiplication of these rates shows the inventor rate, or the performance of R&D investments. This estimate is similar to the conventional R&D planning based on expected present values of costs and revenues (Sullivan et al., 2009). In order to make a profit, an inventor must generate income that covers all costs after discounting. Therefore, the sales must outcompete rivals during several years. Ten years of survival in competition are assumed sufficient for the cost-coverage and profit, or withdrawal from competition because of losses. This survival rate is estimated based on the annual average of additional firms during ten years divided by the number of startups during the same period of time. The survival rate is positive when the number of additional firms increases, but when the number of additional firms decreases because more firms die than start, the survival rate is negative. Multiplication of the inventor rate and survival rate shows the innovators rate, or the innovation performance per USD million investment in R&D. High innovator performance contributes to the economy, but larger death of firms than startups cause high social costs of starting firms but bankruptcies after several years. This estimate is based on a plausible assumption that profitable businesses usually re-invest parts of their profits in R&D for innovations rather than consume profits though such rent-seeking behaviour is observed.

All estimates cover the period from 2008 to 2017. All inventor performances are estimated with the World Bank data. Appendix 5 shows them for all focus countries, the EU28 countries and most R&D-intensive ones. The survivors', meaning the annual average of additional enterprises during ten years, are estimated with the country's statistics of enterprises because the World Bank database does show the birth rates of firms but not the death rates of firms. Among the focus countries, several low-income countries are excluded because their data on the firms' deaths are deficient, or include micro-enterprises that rarely innovate. In the result, the innovation performances of 8 out of 15 focus countries are estimated, as well as the innovation performances of the R&D-intensive Israel, Korea and Singapore. For the survival rates in China, Indonesia, and India, only industrial firms are used, excluding micro-enterprises, which can somewhat underestimate all innovators. Table 4.3 shows the rates that constitute the inventors and innovators performances. The rows display countries. Columns present the numbers of IPR per USD million of R&D in column 2, and the startups per IPR in column 3. Their multiplication delivers the inventor performance which is shown in column 4. The average of the additional firms per startup shows the survival rate in column 5. This rate is multiplied with the inventive performance to obtain the innovators performance in column 6.

The R&D-intensive USA, Japan, EU28 and China, which are countries with more than 2% R&D expenditures in GDP, generate many IPRs and startups. Together, they covered 63% of the global GDP, 74% of the global R&D, 73% of all IPR, and 71% of startups in 2015. Korea and Israel spend more than 3% of GDP on R&D, the R&D-based Singapore even more, and they generate many IPR and startups, as well. Other countries are R&D-extensive. Their R&D results vary. Russia and Brazil generate many IPRs and startups. Many IPR without much R&D but based on the skills of entrepreneurs are found in Indonesia and India. Deficient data on the additional firms do not allow reliable estimates for Mexico, Philippines, Egypt, Nigeria, Pakistan, Bangladesh and Ethiopia. Insofar data is available, the growth rates of R&D converged across the focus countries, while the numbers of IPR and startups diverged during that period, which implies that the results per USD million R&D diverge more widely, and that more effective R&D investments are possible.

The success rates vary across countries. Generally, IPR per R&D expenditures are lower in high-income countries than in lower income ones. In lower income countries, where R&D expenditures are low, IPRs are rarely patents while more often the authors rights, trademarks, and designs which require more social effort but less engineering. Startups in Russia and EU28 are inventive compared to ones in Japan, China, India, and Korea as they obtain more IPRs per R&D. Indonesia, Russia, and Brazil have the highest inventor performances, which indicates efficient R&D investments. Japan, known as the industrial powerhouse until the 1990s, has low inventor performance.

Table 4.3 Success rates of large economies in innovating per R&D million USD_{2015}, all average 2008–2017

Countries in ascending income per capita in 2015	IPR's per R&D million USD_{2015}	Number start-ups per IPR	Inventor performance	Survivor per startup	Innovator performance
	A	B	C = A × B	D	E = C × D
Focus countries, ascending order of income per capita					
World	5.0	0.5	2.2	2.2	5
USA	2.0	0.8	1.5	0.02	0.03
Japan	3.1	0.03	0.1	−7.8	−0.7
EU28	2.1	2.3	4.8	0.2	0.9
Russia	6.2	3.3	20.5	−0.2	−4.0
Brazil	7.5	1.7	12.5	0.1	1.1
China (*)	18.5	0.1	1.4	0.02	0.03
Indonesia (*)	81.6	1.0	81.8	−0.1	−5
India (*)	19.0	0.3	6.5	0.4	3.0
Highest R&D per GDP innovative countries					
Israel	1.6	0.9	1.4	0.5	0.7
Korea Rep	8.2	0.2	1.5	0.8	1.2
Singapore	6.1	0.9	5.6	0.5	0.3

World Bank data for the inventor success, the survivors are based on the countries statistical compendia, but for India https://fred.stlouisfed.org; (*) only industries

Cost coverage of R&D expenditures depends on the survival in competition, but the cross-countries' correlation of the survival rates and inventor performance is low. It shows that efficient R&D investments do not guarantee successes in competition.

Success in innovation, indicated by the innovator performance, depends mainly on survival in competition. The innovator performances in Japan, Russia, and Indonesia are low given that the survival rates of the startups are negative because the number of additional firms decreases. Contrary to low inventor performance in Japan, the inventive performances in Indonesia and Russia are high, but their R&D expenditures do not pay off, measured by the survival of startups. Not many startups survive in the USA and China, presumably because of tough competition. Per million USD, their rates of the innovator success are low, below the chance of success in a casino roulette. This implies that the R&D expenditures hardly pay off and success of a startup is unpredictable. The highest innovation performance was observed in India, where 3% of R&D-based novel ideas generated with one million US Dollars turn into profitable companies, while only 1% were successful in Israel, EU28, Brazil, and Korea. Apparently, moderate competition facilitates innovators and reduced the social costs of firms' failures.

Innovation processes involve R&D, IPR, and startups as well as competition in sales. At best, only a few percent of well-elaborated R&D ideas are successful. Survival in competition is crucial for the payoff of innovation processes.

4.6 Financing Innovations

Regarding growing expenditures on innovations but low rates of success, an issue is if larger funding can generate more innovations, or more failures in competition. For an answer, financing innovations is assessed. The mainstream idea about the financing is displayed in Fig. 4.2. It represents a profit function of an innovator in time with main steps in an innovation process on the horizontal axis and real profits on the vertical axis. A "real" means adjusted for inflation. The private financing options with typical real rents are shown italics, the public financing ones are shown with interrupted lines. The innovation process is costly. The costs are shown in the figure as negative profits during a period of time, called the 'Valley of Death'; it is when many inventors fail because cannot bear all costs before generating incomes from sales. Profits are made when innovations generate sufficient sales several years after the start of an innovation process. Private financing of innovations is often covered by venture capital, meaning participation in the startups. Loans are also given despite high risks. Public financing covers subsidies and guarantees, meaning the financed up front and assurances of the sales, respectively.

Private financiers are initially employers, promoters, family and other personal relations, as well as small investors generated with crowdfunding. Rewards of these 'informal investors' do not exceed the chance in roulette, but they have reasons to show goodwill through this kind of funding. The early-stage venture investors, known as the 'Angels', participate based perceptions that an invention will provide profitable sales in the future. If the invention is successfully demonstrated to customers, larger financing by the venture investors can be obtained for scaling up activities. Given that many inventors fail in the sales, this financing is high-risk. For mitigation of the risks, venture capital is usually invested in shares and these investors demand high real return on investment, which can exceed 25% a year to cover all costs within 3 years. These investments are often divided into seed money, early stage, and later stage in line with the steps shown on the horizontal axis. These processes usually take several years before incomes from sales cover all costs and generate profits. While the risks of failure usually decrease in the course of innovations processes because more customers are found, the investments increase.

The scale of all informal investments is unknown because they are unregistered and vary per innovator, but it is presumably small compared to all venture capital. All venture capital is small compared to all financial transactions. For illustration, the USA financing is used as a benchmark due to its largest venture capital. During 2010s in the USA, these high-risk investments covered 0.7–1.6% of annual assets, compared to 8–32% of low-risk investments derivates, which are investments with guaranteed returns at low real interest. Meanwhile, venture capital above 1% of all

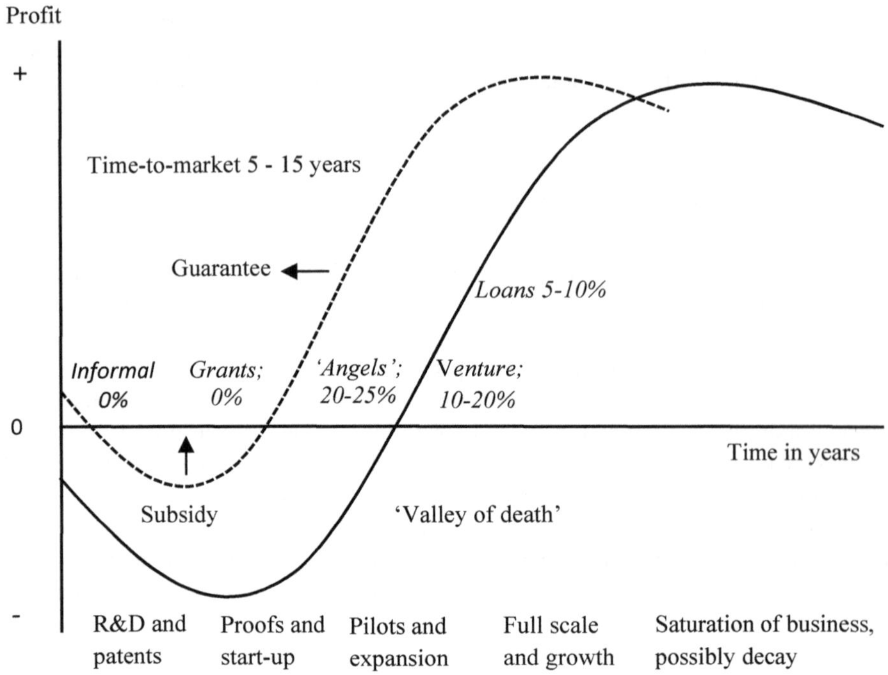

Fig. 4.2 Options for financing of an innovation process

assets was found only in a few EU countries and was below 10% of all financing of startups, while the lion's share of the start-up financing was covered by loans and subsidies. Only Denmark had a higher percentage of private funding for the startups defined as 'young high-growth firms' (Invest Europe, 2019). Much policy attention to the venture capital cannot be justified by the scale of funding, neither by large incomes as only a few percent of investments generate profits, whereas costly failures need huge back-up funds. These back-up funds are usually delivered from the public funds as subsidies for the innovators and tax exemption for the investors in innovations.

A question is about how to enhance innovations; in particular, if public funding should mainly support innovators or investors. For an answer, it is assessed whether venture capital attracts innovators, or other way around. This is assessed for the situations in the USA and the EU during the period 2007–2018 with the World Bank data for startups and Statista data for venture capital (https://www.statista.com/). Venture capital in the USA exceeded USD 63 billion annual average during the period, growing to USD 345 billion in 2021 followed by saturation. That average financing in the USA was three times higher than in the EU28 that hardly grew, though the USA venture capital was on average lower than the average in China where venture capital fluctuated annually. Venture capital in other countries was lower. Global annual average venture capital was about USD 270 billion throughout that period, steadily growing from 2007 on mainly due to the growth in the USA. A few hundred thousand startups a year in China and a similar number in the USA obtained on average above USD_{2015} 100,000 per startup. The funding could have been more per startup on Philippines and in Indonesia with less startups. However, more than one million startups in the EU28 received only USD_{2015} 20,000 per startup, while similar average funds are provided to the startups in Russia, Nigeria, Ethiopia among the focus countries. Hence, larger investors in innovations do not necessarily generate more innovators. Did larger funding in time invoke more inventors? Regarding limited data, an answer is given for the USA in comparison to the EU28 based on trends in the scale venture capital compared to the number of startups from 2007 to 2018 when both economies were recovering from the financial crisis in 2008. The annual venture capital and number of startups in the USA and EU28 are indexed in the period 2007–2018 (2007 = 100). Graph 4.5 shows these indexes.

Despite fivefold larger funding per startup in the USA, and faster growth of venture capital than in the EU, the number of startups in the USA did not grow faster than in the EU. Apparently, larger venture capital did not generate more startups, which implies that public support if innovators is effective Venture capital in the USA increased during economic recession after the financial crisis in 2008 when they gained public support through tax exemptions for the investments in startups. These tax exemptions for venture capital was a key instrument in the USA policy aiming to generate economic growth after that crisis. It successfully generated private funds for the financial participations in startups. In the course of 2010s, these tax exemptions included compensations for the eventual losses on the participations in startups, which turned venture capital into nearly risk-free investments (Kruze, 2024). However, this policy failed measured by the number of startups as these numbers did not increase though several startup became extremely profitable. The financial policy in the EU28 was different. This one aimed at the revitalization of bank transactions

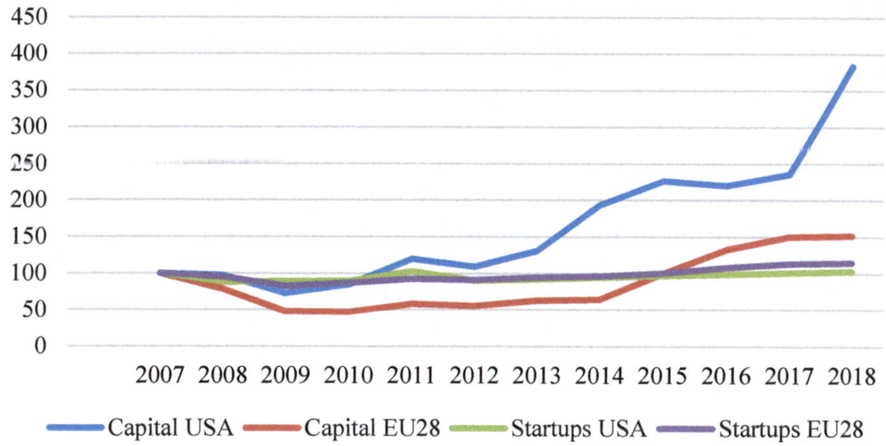

Graph 4.5 Indexes of venture capital and startups in the USA and EU28

because many banks in the EU28 were reluctant with provision of loans as they had large liabilities in firms with worthless collaterals. The European Bank, the public institution for controlling inflation and banking, purchased these collaterals at any price. It became known as 'whatever it takes', a phrase of Mario Draghi who was director of the European bank in 2012. Participations in startups had low priority.

As a result of different financial policies, developments of venture capital and startup differ in the USA from the EU28. Until the financial crisis, the venture capital in the USA declined faster than the number of startups, but turned around in 2009 due to the tax exemption into a faster increase of the venture capital than startups. While the venture capital increased fourfold from 2007 to 2018, even more compared to the lowest point in 2009, the number of startups somewhat decreased after those tax facilities in 2009 and continued at the same level until 2018. The USA tax policy was a success for the financiers, but a failure for the startups, except for a number of extremely profitable ones. Moreover, these tax exemptions fostered an oligarchy of investors in the information and communication technology (ICT), known as 'high-tech' on the USA stock market. Several investors in the ICT-based firms that emerged in the late 1900s became extremely wealthy after the financial crisis in 2008 thanks to nearly risk-free investments in new ventures. The worth of 174 multi-billionaires that invested venture capital in 'high-tech' increased from 272 to billion USD in 2008 to 1750 billion USD in 2021 (Forbes, 2025). They are influential though that venture capital covers only 2.8% of USD 62,204 billion on the USA stock market in 2021 (Siblis, 2025), which covers 44.6% of the worth of whole USA economy (Barrons, 2026). As financiers of fast growing 'high-tech' and media, their influence on politics surpasses the economic value of larger food, energy, construction, tourism and other businesses. By contrast, the EU28 venture capital decreased after the financial crisis by 2014, which is followed by slow increased. Meanwhile, the number of startups increased despite lower investment by venture capitalists than in the USA. Manifold larger venture capital in the USA than in the EU28 did not generate more startups. Better results in other countries should not be expected regarding higher innovation performance in the EU compared to other countries. This experience shows that provision of larger venture capital does not generate more innovators.

Public support covers subsidies and guarantees. Subsidies, paid upfront, reduce the costs of innovation, whereas guarantees assure sales if innovations match predefined criteria. Subsidies include grants, tax exemptions and other upfront support without repayments, as well as soft loans and credits with repayments, which encompass a few hundred different instruments across countries (Ermen, 2007). Subsidies for R&D are supposed to support mitigation of climate change, maintaining of biodiversity and other the objectives in policies (Horizon 2020, 2021), While they reduce the costs of the private beneficiaries and increase assets for collaterals in borrowing, subsidies cause losses in public finances as most innovations fail. Subsidies that do generate successes foster monopolies due to the cost-advantages of the beneficiaries. This is often criticised (Petrin, 2018; Ziesemer, 2021; Zuniga, 2024) although an innovators needs a temporary monopoly in sales of novelties in order to recover all costs and make profits. Advocates of subsidies underline the benefits for particular policy targets in the 'mission oriented' policies as experienced in development of

Table 4.4 Comparison of subsidies in the USA with guarantees in the EU28 for renewable energy; data are annual averages in the period 2009–2015

USA with use of mainly subsidies	
All establishments × 1000	7484
Energy establishments × 1000	13
Support in USD per kWh	0.12
Additional establishments × 1000	1
Public support in USD per additional establishment	30,320
EU 28 with use of mainly price guarantees	
All establishments × 1000	24,878
Energy establishments × 1000	118
Support in USD per kWh	0.4
Additional establishments × 1000	15
Public support in USD per additional establishment	5,880

internet and exploration of space, among others (Mazzucato, 2018), but there are also costly failures in nuclear energy, energy fusion, and other areas. Various pros and cons can be found without final verdict as everybody likes to benefit from subsidies.

Guarantees are payments for innovations with demanded qualities. Such guarantees can assure sales prices, purchases of particular qualities, volume of sales, liabilities for harms, and other performances. Guarantees are generic as they do not specify a particular innovator while reduces the innovators risks in competition. Less risky sales encourage investments, but also invoke disputes about the demanded performances. Experiences in the EU are obtained with the price guarantees for agricultural products, quality guarantees for durable products, take-back guarantees for disposal, and other activities. There are also various certificates and labels aiming to guarantee products qualities. These experiences indicate that they enlarge the guaranteed activities, but involve large funding because involve many interests, even if the guaranteed payment per service is low. Funding to rival interests is presumably the reason for lower popularity compared to subsidies.

Illustrative for the effects of subsidies and guarantees is comparison of the subsidies for renewable energy in the USA to the price guarantees for renewable energy in the EU28 during 2009–2015. The USA subsidies were a part of the package for restoring the economy after the financial crisis in 2008, while the guarantees in the EU28 were payments for delivery of electricity based on the renewable energy resources to the power grid, so called feed-in tariffs. Note that several states in the USA also used feed-in tariffs and many EU countries also subsidised renewable energy, and that the public expenditures on subsidies in the USA were larger than the guarantees in the EU28. Table 4.4 presents the effects and costs of subsidies in the USA and guarantees in the EU, which are measured by the number of establishments in energy business, the costs per unit of renewable energy and public support per new establishment. A new establishment indicates an innovator.

While GDP of the EU28 was 34% smaller than GDP of the USA along with nearly 50% lower energy consumption in 2015, the EU28 had three times more establishments of all firms and 8 times more establishments in energy business. The EU firms were smaller scale than the USA firms, particularly in the energy business. Although the average feed-in tariff in the EU guarantees per unit kWh was only 3 times higher than the average subsidies in the USA per kWh, they created nearly 150 times more new establishments throughout the period 2009–2015. Guarantees in the EU28 generated many innovators, whereas subsidies in the USA enlarged the scale of energy firms vested in the past. In effect, the USA subsidies were 6 times more costly per innovator than the EU guarantees. The guarantees in the EU were costly in total, but generated many successful firms, which enabled to take a global lead in renewable energy until the 2020s when China enhanced its businesses in renewable energy with similar guarantees as the feed-in tariffs in the EU28, along with the directives for purchases of renewable energy.

Advocates of subsidies point out the need for public funding of research and development of novelties because private risks are too high for private investors. This need is undeniable. Nevertheless, stronger effects of guarantees on innovators compared to subsidies can be explained if R&D is comprehended as an infrastructure for the knowledge capabilities. Based on this idea, R&D provides IPR and generates positive external effects of larger knowledge capabilities in societies, so called tacit knowledge. Possession of such knowledge capabilities enables fast conversion of knowledge into innovations at low costs when demands are announced and sales are assured with guarantees and other policy instruments. Many examples can be found with regard to public health and environmental qualities. Illustrations are wastewater treatment that expanded when charges are announced in the 1970s, prompt reduction of NOx and other air pollutants due to regulations in the 1980s (Krozer, 2002), growth of biofuels driven by the guaranteed payments to farmers in the 1990s, expansion of wind and solar power with the feed-in tariffs during the 2000s, fast delivery of vaccines for COVID due to guaranteed purchases in 2022, and so on. Such innovations are explained by conversions of the available technologies towards new demands (Sarasvathy, 2001) and local conditions (Bhaduri & Kumar, 2011). These conversions are driven by unregistered capabilities of staff and entrepreneurs in firms, as well as skills in communities (Venkitachalam and Busch, 2012). R&D is needed for generation of these knowledge capabilities that render faster response to the pressing demands than would be expected based on the mainstream model of innovation process. The policy instrument of guarantees proved to be effectove

Larger private venture capital for innovators hardly increased the number of innovators, but improved the earnings of financiers. Larger subsidies facilitate innovators, but pose financial risks to societies. Guarantees for delivered performances increase success rate of innovators, though need sound definition of demanded performances.

4.7 Induced Environmental Performances

Innovations for the improvements of environmental performances are mainly induced by the demands. It is assessed what are the drivers of these demands and what investments are induced during the last decades. Demands for availability of water, soil, forest and other natural resources have been expressed for centuries. They triggered melioration of water, nitrification of soil, afforestation and other innovations in agricultural economies. When industries expanded, threats of pollution on human safety, health, and on properties are issued. Environmental technologies for pollution prevention are induced in addition to the improvemenents in land uses. This is followed by larger consumption of environmental qualities for education, leisure, in media as services grew within economic activities. Demands for environmental performances broadened, and so the inducement of sustainable innovations (Stern, 2000).

Meanwhile, demands for environmental performances that induce innovations can be put in five categories. Traditional demands induce innovations that improve production. Within the traditional demands, the first category is about effective uses of natural resources, which refer to renewable energy, uses of bioresources, closing of material circulation, and so on. The second category is about cost-effective pollution prevention as wastewater treatment, de-NOxing catalysts, nature protection areas, and pthers. In addition, environmental qualities for consumption are demanded. The third category of demands addresses purchases of products defined as environmentally friendly. Natural, ecological, fair and other attributes of this ethical consumption are pinpointed. It is as if people want to buy environmental qualities. Meanwhile, these innovations cover a few percent of total consumption in foods and personal products in high-income countries, though lower percentage in other types of purchases. The fourth category of the environmental demands is about the use of nature in generating tourism, leisure, wellness, and similar services delivered by businesses. Such business grow faster that other services. These demands induce innovations for staying in nature. The fifth category is about environmental qualities in cultural expressions in film, music and other media. When all these demands are summed up, they constitute a substantial inducement of sustainable innovations. Estimates for the year 2010 show nearly 3.7 trillion (10^{12}) USD_{2010} global sales of sustainable innovations, equivalent of nearly 6% of the global GDP. However, even larger subsidies are provided for the activities vested in the past that degrade environmental qualities, which are rival to sustainable innovation. Policies are ambivalent in the inducement of innovations (Krozer, 2015).

When the traditional environmental demands emerged by the 1970s, it is often argued that higher income would spontaneously strengthen them as people pursued safety and pleasant life through more pollution controls (Thurow, 1980). This argument implies that demands for controls of industrial pollution were considered a luxury, affordable when more pressing issues are resolved. Indeed, demands for better environmental performances strengthen when basic needs are satisfied, but they are a few additional reasons. Drivers of the traditional demands also secure properties and well-being. Hence, modern demands for the consumption of environmental qualities and their inducement of innovations need an explanation. In line with the behavioural thinking in economics, it is assumed that they emerge due to changes in economic activities. Two main drivers of modern demands are underpinned below. One is the elongation of leisure time, which generates services that use environmental qualities for their income generation. Another driver is the growing influence of knowledge workers who need good environmental qualities for high performances, and the institutions pay for these qualities. Both drivers are briefly underpinned.

Leisure time increased in many countries during the last century due to shorter work hours and longer lifespan of people. Throughout the last century, the annual working hours in high-income countries shortened by third or more. For example, the annual working hours in France declined from 3115 to 1550 h, the equivalent of −0.7% annual average change, and in the USA from 2938 to 1845 h, which equals −0.5% annual change (OWD, 2024). The trends of shorter working hours in high-income countries continued during the last decades, but slowed down. From 1990 to 2015, the working hours have shortened in most OECD countries; it was by −0.3% annual average as in France, and −0.1% in the USA (https://data-explorer.oecd.org). Minor increases in yearly working hours were observed only in Russia, Sweden, and Lithuania, among about fifty countries found in the OECD database. Similar data about lower income countries are rare. Nevertheless, a trend for shorter work time is tangible in nearly all countries as the legal maximum hours of the workday decreases, though the maximum is often longer in lower income countries than 8 hours in high-income countries. For example, the working days are maximised at 9 hours in India and 10 hours in Egypt.

Meanwhile, the lifespan increased in nearly all countries from 1990 to 2015. Life span decreased only in several low-income as Lesotho, Namibia, Eswatini, and Dominica. Estimates based on the World Bank data show that the global lifespan increased by 0.4% annual average, but the increases varied across the focus countries from 0.1% in China to 1.4% in Ethiopia. The life expectancy increased yearly even by 6% a year in Rwanda and South Sudan, where it was short compared to other African countries. Those elongations of lifespan accelerated in most countries, and diverged across countries as the increases were slower in high-income countries than in lower income ones. Apparently, the livelihood in nearly low-income countries improves albeit slowly.

When the declining working hours are combined with the increasing lifespan, the leisure time grew during the last decades by more than 0.7% annual average. The spread in the growth rates of leisure time was small across high-income countries and larger across low-income ones due to rapidly increasing lifespan in several of them. The leisure time elongates along with global income growth. Globally, about 20% additional leisure time is realised, while the real income per person increased by 50% between 1990 and 2015. More leisure time can be expected in the future given the shortening working hours and acceleration in the elongation of the lifespans in lower income countries as their incomes per person grow. Longer lifespans along with higher income is a trend in nearly all lower income countries. They emulate a similar trend in nearly all high-income countries at a faster rate of changes. It is enabled by the health and educational services, among others.

As people live longer while their incomes increase, they are better able to pay for the services that foster longer and better lives, and for the services that facilitate activities during the leisure time. In effect, tourism, wellness, hospitality, sports, and other services for leisure time expanded. For example, services for international tourism services grew annually by 5% annual average from 1995 to 2019 and accelerated during the late 2010s. They offer environmental qualities for leisure. Clean seas and beaches are examples of these qualities. As nearly 25% of all tourists prioritise nature and culture during their leisure time the tourism services demand higher environmental performances, though they also put more pressures on nature through polluting travels and stay. While many leisure services become capital-intensive with higher uses of materials and energy, they also need to improve their environmental performance as an element in corporate strategy and image. Their positive and negative impacts on environmental qualities cannot be overestimated as global revenues of international tourism, which are receipts minus expenditures, grow by 18% annual average from 2005 to 2015. These revenues increased three times faster than the expenditures on education and health, which grew nearly twice faster than global GDP growth. Meanwhile, the leisure services constitute the largest global business.

In addition to leisure services, knowledge work has increased globally. The R&D expenditures that indicate knowledge work increasedfast. While the knowledge work was a driving force of income growth throughout the 1900s, the knowledge workers also demanded environmental quality. Their demands are expressed as the above mentioned traditional concerns about environmental degradation, as well as more modern appreciation of natural amenities. Those concerns and appreciations are observed across all social classes and professions. Special about the knowledge work is that they need environmental qualities for high performances and their institutions can afford improvements because the knowledge work is well-paid. Knowledge workers by its profession must be interested in environmental qualities, because it is a subject of much of their work. In addition, space, tranquillity, and other elements of environmental qualities are necessary for high performance; if you doubt that, try to think and exchange thoughts at the construction sites. As the numbers of knowledge workers in the population increased, services that facilitate environmental qualitieson university campuses, at student housing, around incubators, and suchlike expanded. Many knowledge services mimic wildlife on the locations with high concentration of knowledge work in cities because considered necessary for innovations. This mimicry is expressed as parks, lawns, and suchlike quasi-nature in urban areas (Florida, 2002).

Those demands of knowledge workers are also reflected in larger expenditures on environment protection. As the expenditures on knowledge work grew as a trend, as indicated by the R&D expenditures, the expenditures on environmental protection increased in line with them at a higher rate. These observations are based on the OECD data. These OECD data are available for 42 high-income and mid-income countries during the period 2015–2018. Although those expenditures vary across the countries, they are closely correlated to the knowledge work measured by R&D

expenditures ($R^2 > 0.9$). A longer period from 1995 to 2015 is covered by those OECD data for 22 high-income countries, which is an approximation of global expenditures as these countries are large spenders on the environment protection. This data enables to show trends. A trend is that the expenditures on environment protection grow faster than on R&D while their cross-countries correlation increases with time (from $R^2 > 0.7$ in the 1990s to $R^2 > 0.9$ in the 2010s). These growth rates accelerated in most high-income countries, which implies that this trend continues in the future across countries. Though a correlation is not a proof but an indication, linkage between the expenditures on knowledge work and environment protection is plausible regarding the capabilities of knowledge workers to pay for environmental qualities and vocal expressions of their demands for better environmental qualities through environmental organisations.

This plausibility is also illustrated. Graph 4.6 shows changes in the environmental expenditures with the IMF data (IMF, 2024), as well as in R&D expenditures, and number of R&D staff with the World Bank data from 2000 to 2018. They are shown as indexes of 2000 year (2000 = 100) on the vertical axis and timeline for horizontal one. Unfortunately, earlier R&D data is insufficiently reliable for extrapolations, and data on environmental expenditures are deficient as they miss the USA and India among the focus countries. Another data deficiency is that the OECD data differs from the Eurostat data for the EU countries, but better global data is not found. Similar data on environment protection in lower income countries is not found, which is a major omission as their changes evolve, presumably, faster than in high-income countries. While the knowledge work in the societies of lower income countries is smaller, it increases faster than in high-income ones, if measured by R&D.

R&D expenditures grew somewhat faster than the number of R&D staff, which indicates that knowledge work becomes more capital-intensive due to increased use of laboratories, equipment, and other capital-intensive facilities. Meanwhile, the

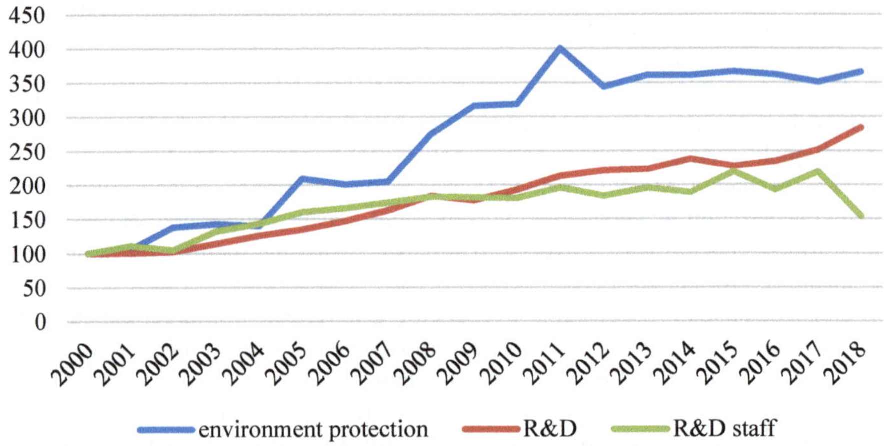

Graph 4.6 Indexes of environmental expenditures, R&D expenditures and R&D staff

expenditures on environmental protection, increased in line with the global GDP during the 1990s, followed by an acceleration during the 2000s when their growth rates were fourfold of global GDP and nearly fivefold of agricultural and industrial production. This underpins the observation that demands for environmental qualities expand far beyond traditional concerns about squandering of natural resources and pollution in agriculture and industry. Throughout the whole period from 1995 to 2018, the expenditures on environment protection grew about twice as fast as R&D expenditures. These results underpin the hypothesis that growing knowledge work is a major driver for increasing demands for environmental qualities, which trigger expenditures on environment protection. These trends in the environmental expenditures indicate growing opportunities for the sales of novelties, thereby inducement of innovations.

In addition to broad concerns about environmental degradation in agriculture and industries, interests increase in consumption of environmental qualities. Growing leisure time and knowledge work invoke demands for environmental qualities, which generate services for improving of environmental performances.

4.8 Governance of Environmental Qualities

So far, the capabilities of businesses and individuals in sustainable innovations are addressed. What about the societal capabilities as expressed by policies? Therefore, it is assessed if the societal capabilities in sustainable innovations increase due to the governance of environmental qualities. Public governance is important for sustainable innovations because private expenditures are costly but often unprofitable. Growing demands for environmental qualities are reflected in governances, comprehended as enforcement of policies through institutions vested in administrative and social organisations purposed for the uses of scarce resources. A question is what sustainable innovations are induced by governances, and if this induction increased societal capabilities in sustainable innovations.

For answering that question is hypothesised that governances induce public and private investments in environmental technologies while they tend to avoid risks. Such governances pursue investments that enable cost-saving and income-generation, but postpone investments without such economic benefits. This hypothesis is assessed for investments in water supply & sanitation, renewable energy and in the areas for protection of nature on the assumption that renewable energy enables income generation, water supply & wastewater treatment generate incomes only from sales of water, whereas protection of nature usually rejects commercial activities.

For an answer to that question, trends in global investments in renewable energy, water supply & sanitation, and in nature protection are compared. This is followed by an assessment of the trends in investments in the EU27, meaning EU member countries without the UK. Those investments are assessed for the period 2005–2020, which includes high prices of fossil fuels from 2005 to 2015 and lower prices from 2006 to 2020. Those environmental investments are also compared to all investments based

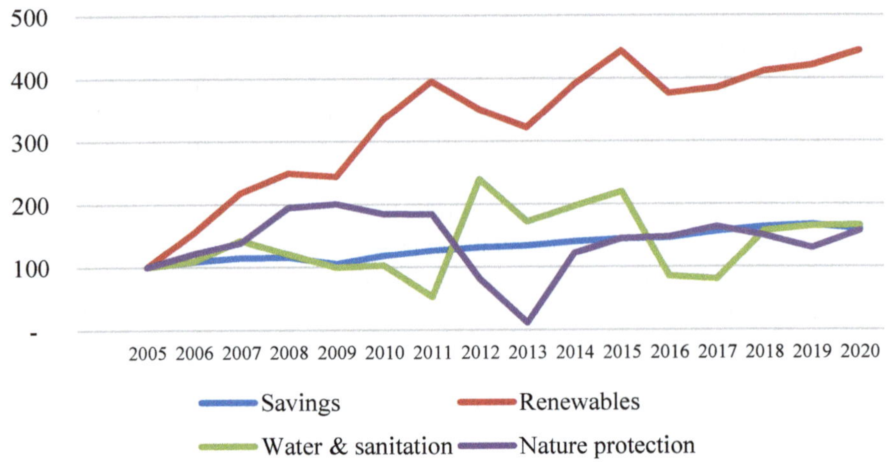

Graph 4.7 Indexes of global investments in renewable energy, water and sanitation, and nature protection

on global savings that mirror them. Global investments and investments in water supply and sanitation are based on the World Bank data, ones in renewable energy refer to the UNEP-BNEF database (UNEP-BNEF, 2025), and investments in protection of nature to the OECD database that does not cover all countries. For example, the UNEP-BNEF database shows lower investments in renewable energy than the IRENA database (IRENA, 2022), and the databases on investments in water supply and sanitation and in protection of nature miss several countries. Although those data are imperfect they suffice indication of trends. Graph 4.7 shows indexes of global environmental investments (2005 = 100). Larger investments induce innovation as they increase the possibilities for selling novelties.

Indexes do not show the scale of investments, though they differ a lot. During those fifteen years from 2005 to 2020, all annual investments fluctuated between 22 and 28% of global GDP, while those investments in environment protection did not exceed 1.5% of all investments. The shares of environmental investments in all investments varied across countries. These shares were a few times higher in the EU28 than globally and manifold higher than in low-income countries, while even the EU performances could not meet all its commitments with international agreements. Regarding that low investment in environment protection, pledges about performances often remain 'paper tigers'.

Meanwhile, investments in environment protection confirm the hypothesis about risk-avoiding governances. Investments in renewable energy of USD 221 billion annual average during that period 2005–2020 were 6 times larger than investments in water supply and sanitation, which were 37 times larger than in protection of nature. Renewable energy attracted by far most environmental investments and fastest growth. All global investments grew by 3% annual average compared to 12% growth of investments in renewable energy. Meanwhile, investments in water supply & sanitation and in nature protection fluctuated as shown in the Graph; their annual averages even declined if unreliable data about high jumps in water supply & sanitation in 2012 and in nature protection in 2014 are smoothed through interpolation. Environmental governance induced innovations in renewable energy that generated income from sales, less in water supply & sanitation, and even less in nature protection.

Trends in the EU27 confirm those global trends. Environmental investments during the period 2006–2023 are covered. Total environmental investments were 108 billion euro annual average, which grew 3% annual average. Within that total, 61% of the EU environmental investments was allocated in renewable energy, 19% in water supply & wastewater treatment, only 1% in nature protection, and 17% in air pollution, waste, safety, soil, noise, radiation and R&D put together. The share of investments in renewable energy in all environmental investments increased, while the shares of all other environmental investments decreased. The EU27 governance induced innovations in renewable energy, hardly in other environmental issues. The EU governance is as risk-avoiding as the global one.

Governances have high capabilities in inducing innovations as estimated for renewable energy in the EU28 with the OECD database for the period 2008–2017 (Krozer, 2022). This is underpinned with the rates of innovation performances in all energy compared to renewable energy. The latter is defined in that database as being the technologies for mitigating climate change with renewable energy, as well as energy efficiency and nuclear power, while nearly all patents cover renewable energy. Recall that the rates of innovation performances indicate successful innovation processes, which are calculated as IPR per USD_{2015} million of R&D expenditures multiplied by startups per IPR, and by survivors of ten year's competition per startups. Graph 4.8 shows success rates of innovating in all energy innovations (ALL) and renewable energy (RES+) for the EU28 member countries from 2008 to 2017.

The success rates in all energy innovations are substantially lower than in renewable energy in all member countries due to the policy demands for renewable energy combined with the feed-in tariffs. The innovative performances in all energy (ALL) exceeded 1% only in the UK, France, Netherlands, Belgium, Ireland, and Sweden, while it was negative in Germany and Italy due to the decline of establishments in all energy. Meanwhile, the innovation performance in renewable energy (RES+) was above 5% in nearly all EU member countries. They were above 20% in Spain, UK, Portugal, Germany, and Sweden. Denmark with the declining number of survivors was an exception. The share of environmental investments in all investments is low, except ones that generate incomes. If policies would invest more in the areas of environmental protection that did not generate incomes, more sustainable innovations could be invoked, thereby align environmental performances with value adding activities. The risk-avoiding governances in environment protection could also impede the societal capabilities in value addition.

Environmental governance triggers investments that induce sustainable innovations when income generation is expected. These are found in renewable energy, but barely in water and sanitation, and none protection of nature and other environmental issues.

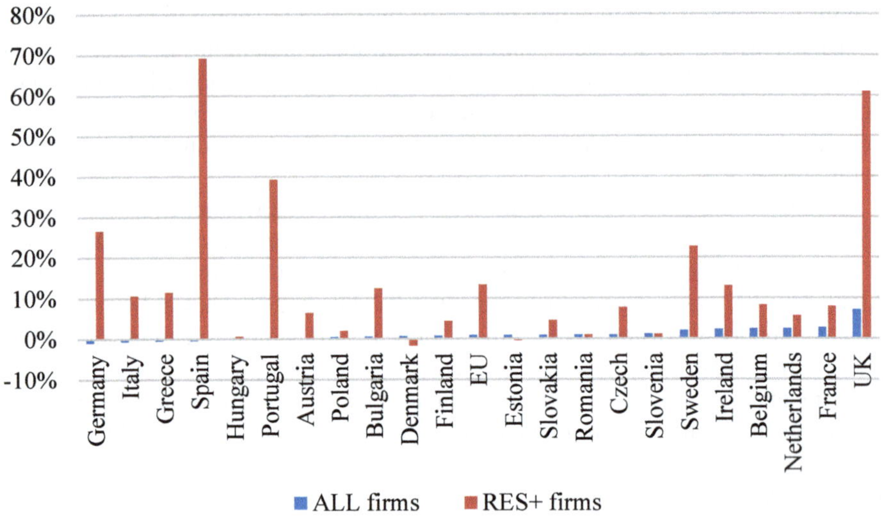

Graph 4.8 Innovation performances within EU28 by all firms (ALL) and ones in renewable ones (RES+)

4.9 Citizen Initiatives

As authorities hardly invoked sustainable innovations unless private incomes could be generated, would citizen initiatives counter this risk-avoidance. It is assessed if the citizen initiatives effectively induce risk-taking sustainable innovations. This capability is envisaged in the ideas about communitarian governances through the networking of citizen initiatives in local groups with common interests and appreciated rules. Many initiatives pursue environment protection. This 'environmental communitarism' links production to consumption, so called 'prosumption', connects individuals into networks instead of market transactions, and develops collective ownerships for the communities' common good. They are found in city gardening, renewable energy, protection of nature, biofilters for wastewater, playgrounds and other activities (Jordan & Huitema, 2023). Various kinds of governances by citizen initiatives are illustrated for renewable energy (Moroni et al., 2019).

Many scholars envision that such citizen initiatives generate 'transition' toward sustainable development based on collective learning in communities with the governmental institutions as inspirators and coordinators of the changes (Rotmans, et al., 2001). That collective learning would be driven by the citizen participation in decisions based on consent about common interests (Loorbach, 2009). This transition is assumed to be an attractive alternative for market transactions and state directives (Jordan, 2008), but it is also criticised for the mystification of trade-offs and choices, which can evolve toward autocracy in absence of checks and balances found in democracies (Meadowcroft, 2009). Imposing limits in consumption with references to the neo-Malthusian ideas could generate such autocracy (Sandberg, 2021). Rather that theorising on the environmental communitarism, results of the citizen initiatives are assessed. Globally, many citizen initiatives are found in agriculture, forestry and other land uses in lower income countries, while numerous initiatives in renewable energy in the USA and EU28 are assessed in hundreds of publications reviewed from various perspectives (Koirala et al. 2016, Mundaca et al., 2018, Lennon et al., 2019, Roberto et al., 2023). Whether such initiatives effectively induced sustainable innovations is assessed mainly using earlier studies on sanitation (Krozer, 2015), renewable energy (Krozer, 2022), nature protection (Krozer et al., 2020). This order reflects the ascending dominance of the citizen initiatives in governances. Being effective is comprehended as realisation of pursued objectives.

Sanitation covers sewage and wastewater treatment linked to it. Not many citizen initiatives are found in sanitation, presumably because sanitation is governed by municipalities and public water authorities that are perceived to take care about the citizen interests. In the course of last century, sanitation has elongated when wastewater is transported in sewage pipes far away from settlements. Wastewater treatment has also elongated as basic treatment by sedimentation of solids in septic tanks is improved with biological treatments, and sometimes with treatments of inorganic pollutants, and pathogens. They effectively reduced water pollution, but their dissemination across countries is slow because of costs and deficient policies. For example, twice richer people in Mexico than in Sri Lanka have less access to sanitation, and wealthy areas have more access than densely populated slums where the costs per person are low. Hence, access to sanitation increased by barely 2% annual average from the 1970s onward, which is half slower than the dissemination of power grid that is half slower than of the telecommunication networks. At that rate, the elongated sanitation cannot reach all people within next decades despite bold political statements. Main alternatives are the distributed sanitation and separation of sources driven by citizen initiatives. However, their coverage of wastewater is marginal, well-below one percent access despite promotion by authorities (e.g., UN-HABITAT, 2008 and EPA, 1999). The distributed sanitation treats wastewater in a closed system within communities in the septic tanks and in biodegradation fields with wetland plants (helophytes). It is cost-effective compared to the elongation, but needs an area of 1–2 m^2 person of plants on field, while half of that is needed in the elongated sanitation systems. The separation sanitation aims at the reuse of urea for fertilizers, organic matter for biogas, and water for the toilet flush at households, which can be cost-effective, but requires changes in housing and behaviour. As a result of those deficiencies in the distributed sanitation and separation at sources, interests in communities are low and citizen initiatives hardly induced sustainable innovations in sanitation.

Renewable energy covers fuels and electricity, which are produced mainly by large-scale private companies and public monopolies. Citizen initiatives are assumed to provide the alternatives for those centralised governances of energy (Walker and Devine-Wright, 2008). Many citizen initiatives for distributed energy are found in the EU28 countries. An estimate for the period 2000–2021 shows an aggregate of 10,000 initiatives that involve about 2 million people with renewable energy capacity of about 10 Gigawatts (GW) for maximum € 11 billion in value (Schwanitz, 2023). Despite mushrooming literature, all initiatives put together cover not more than a few percent of annual renewable energy production in the EU28, excluding the municipal energy companies that produce nearly half of renewable energy in Germany and Austria (Tarpani et al., 2022). Rural production of biofuels in lower income countries are presumably the largest distributed production of renewable energy, but the scale of these citizen initiatives are rarely assessed. Global distributed capacity of wind and solar power was below 1% of all global capacities, growing slower than 12% annual average growth of all capacity during 2018–2021 (IRENA, 2022). In the EU excluding the UK, the state monopoly in power transmission and distribution is a barrier. In India, where the distributed solar and wind for lights, pumps, and other applications cover abuot 12% of all renewable energy capacities, policies oblige power distributors to make such investments (IEA, 2002). In the USA, competing private distributors in several state encourages the distributed production and storage of power during peaks of electricity supplies. This is cheaper to households and to the distributors that are willing to defer investments in the power lines (Giraldez et al., 2018). Numerous citizen initiatives in the distributed renewable energy emerged.

Nature protection focuses on areas dedicated to biodiversity. These nature areas on land considered as unproductive wasteland, or wilderness, are often managed by environmental organisation created by citizen initiatives. Many areas are guided by the International Union for Conservation of Nature (IUCN) while authorities formalised and fund activities. The scales of areas vary across countries and in time. Indonesia topped all countries in 1970 with 11% of its territory dedicated to the protection of nature, which increased to 12.2% in 2019. Meanwhile, Brazil increased this share by more than 120 times to 29.8% of its territory and the EU28 by 13 times to 25.8% of its area. Globally, the areas for protection of nature increased from 2.6% of all land in 1970 to 13.2% of it in 2019, equivalent to 15.3 million km^2, though the annual growth rates declined from 7% during the 1970s to 3% in the 1980s, 1.5% a decade later, and below 1% during the 2010s. Compared to sluggish investments by authorities, these citizen initiatives effectively increased the areas. However, the areas were ineffective for the protection of biodiversity. Estimates show solely low correlations ($R^2 < 0.5$) across eight IUCN categories of protected areas in the ascending order of protection, and twelve IUCN categories of protected mammals, birds, reptiles, amphibians, fish, marine fish, freshwater fish, vascular plants, mosses, lichens, invertebrates, and all species. For this estimate, the OECD data on 37 high-income countries is used, excluding the USA and several other countries (OECD members and non-members) that do not provide data.. Another indicator of ineffective protection is the decreasing number of threatened bird species in the EU from 1995 to 2017 despite increased protection areas. Apparently, the scale of areas hardly helps biodiversity when activities outside of the areas deteriorate environmental qualities. The nature areas also became costlier. For example, investments increased 80-fold from USD 0.02 per m^2 to USD 1.64 per m^2 during that period, while private investments declined from 46% in 1995 to 16–20% based on the Eurostat database. This kind of governance evolves toward a deadlock. Improvements are possible if the areas for protection of nature incubate sustainable innovations for dissemination outside the areas. Examples are low-input agriculture, nature-based tourism, high-value bioresources, and other activities for sustainable land use. A turnaround in the citizen initiatives would be needed for an effective protection of nature.

So far, the citizen initiatives delivered mixed performances when assessed by effectivity of their objectives. Turning demands for environmental qualities into inducement of sustainable innovations requires larger organisational capabilities and supportive policies.

4.10 Conclusion

Changes that enable transition towards sustainable development are assessed. Higher performances measured in economic and environmental terms are driven by the quasi-autonomous innovation-mechanism and induced innovation-mechanism. The former evolves when firms compete with the aim to reduce costs and increase value added, while the latter emerges when far reaching improvements of environmental performances are demanded.

The quasi-autonomous innovation-mechanism acts when cost-savings due to better use of natural resources generate profits that are partly invested in value-adding novelties aiming to achieve a market share for profits in the future. This mechanism evolves spontaneously, driven by competition. However, it is obstructed by low prices of natural resources because they reduce cost-savings, and by greed of shareholders that extract profits for consumption rather than invest in innovations for higher value products and services. Pricing of the natural resources and taming of the shareholders' greed for dividends generate innovations that enable welfare growth.

Trends in the quasi-autonomous innovation-mechanisms vary across businesses. Globally, this innovation-mechanism in agriculture is indicated by the increasing value of the mass of cereal production along with larger mass at decreasing fertilizer use, all those estimated per hectare. The innovation-mechanism in industry is not observed. On the contrary, the global industry uses more energy and materials per additional value, and it focuses on lower costs of production instead of higher value deliveries. These trends show that industry is trapped into low-value mass production based on ineffective uses of natural resources, because taxes, labour costs and other production costs are easier to evade or reduce than to invest in innovation. Reversing that downward trend needs a 'hard reset' through policy demands and societal interventions in favour of higher quality products and services, liabilities for harms to well-being and environmental qualities, along with the public support of sustainable innovations. Performances in transport vary by mode. Air and rail transport generated higher value along with more transported passengers per energy use, which indicates an innovation-mechanism. Road transport show negligible improvements in passenger mileage per energy. Apparently, producers of vehicles for road transport are hardly interested in energy-efficiency.

Businesses frequently state that they are unable to improve their performances because consumers are not willing to pay for it. This argumentation is not valid. In addition to high willingness to pay for environmentally improved products, trends reveal growing purchases of labour-intensive services while stagnating purchases of material-intensive products. The consumer purchases of labour-intensive services grow despite the increasing labour costs and declining costs of material resources. Consumer expenditures on labour-intensive services in leisure, education, communication, and suchlike activities grow faster than material-intensive products and services in high-income countries and lower income ones, while these growth rates are influenced by culture and policies rather than the labour incomes. Linking products with services contributes to sustainable development; in particular when it is supported with reliable information about supplied qualities along with liabilities for the deficient qualities. This way, consumers can make fair choices.

Innovations are needed for higher value deliveries. In order to innovate, costs are made during several years of research and development (R&D), which enable acquisition of intellectual property rights (IPR) and start of firms (startups). Thereafter, firms can generate incomes for coverage of all costs and making profits, if they survive competition (survivors). While R&D, IPR, and startups are costly, the survivors generate income, thereby determine successes of innovations. Across countries, the success rates of innovators per million USD spent on R&D are rarely above 1%, and they vary across countries. Russia and Japan make costs, but failures of the startups are more frequent than continuity of the survivors. The success rates in the competitive markets of China and the USA are a small fraction of a percent. Moderate competitions in India, Brazil, EU28, Korea, Israel do better with the success rates from 1% to 3% mainly due to more survivors. More attention to the market conditions is needed for high success rates of innovators.

Innovators need funding to cover costs before generating incomes from the sales of novelties. Initial costs can be covered through informal relations. Larger funds are provided by the private investors aiming at profits through participations in ventures, as well as by the public funds through subsidies paid upfront, and guarantees for the sales that match the demanded specifications. Participations with private venture capital can support innovators. Tax exemptions for the participations provide a boost to venture capital but a few additional innovators, and a few fortunate investors. So, these tax exemptions spill public money and hinder efficient allocation of private funds. Subsidies and guarantees can work for innovator, but their impacts differ. Subsidies deliver assets to innovators at the societal costs because most innovators fail and they can distort competition when the beneficiaries can reduce costs of ineffective technologies. Guarantees do not specify a particular innovator, but support sales of all innovators that supply the demanded qualities. It is low risk for societies because paid for the qualified deliveries, if performances must be well-defined. Compared to the USA subsidies for renewable energy, the EU28 guarantees were effective and efficient measured by the number of successful innovators and unit costs of supporting renewable energy.

Innovations are also induced by the policy and citizens demands for high environmental performance. These demands grow and cover more environmental issue. Nearly all people wish amenities of environmental qualities. In addition, there are specific interests in improvements. As income grew and leisure time increased due to shorter labour times and longer lifespan in nearly all countries, the expanding businesses in tourism, wellness, culture, and other activities in the leisure services demand better environmental qualities for generation of incomes. Furthermore, knowledge work grows while knowledge workers demand silence, spaciousness, and other environmental qualities for their professional performance.

These demands invoke investments in environmental protection, which induce sustainable innovations. Most environmental investments are found in high-income countries. The largest induced investments address issues that can generate private incomes, while the environmental investments without private incomes hardly grow, or even decrease. So, investments in renewable energy grew fast contrary to stagnation of investments in water supply and sanitation, in nature protection, and in prevention of chemical hazards. These trends pose the risk that environmental issues tend to be resolved when profits are expected, while other issues remain unresolved. Citizen initiatives aiming at sustainable innovations in communities could counter that risk, but they are insufficiently effective and largely follow that pattern. Citizen initiatives in water supply and sanitation are scarce, while they mushroom in renewable energy. Although citizens initiatives enlarged the protection areas, they did not improve biodiversity while they can incubate innovations in the nature protection areas purposed for the sustainable land uses.

Capabilities for better environmental performances grow due to the quasi-autonomous and induced innovative mechanisms. Regarding trends in businesses, there is reason for optimism about capabilities for sustainable innovations in the future, if stronger demands for high quality products and services are enforced through combinations of liabilities for harms and guarantees for highly performing sustainable innovations.

References

Abramovitz, M. (1995). Elements of social capability. In B. H. Koo & D. Perkins (Eds.), *Social capability and long-term economic growth* (pp. 19–47). MacMillan.

Ali, M., Egbetokun, A., & Menon, M. H. (2018). Human capital, social capabilities and economic growth. *Energies, 6*(2), 1–18.

Barrons. (2026). Retrieved February 28, 2025, from https://www.barrons.com/articles/net-wealth-is-over-135-trillion-where-that-money-resides-d722c9c6.

Bhaduri, S., & Kumar, H. (2011). (2010), Extrinsic and intrinsic motivations to innovate: Tracing the motivation of 'grassroot' innovators in India. *Mind & Society, 10*, 27–55.

Cramer, J. (2022). Effective governance of circular economies: An international comparison. *Journal of Cleaner Production, 343*, Article 130874.

Ekins P. (2002). Introduction. In Ekins, P. (Ed.), *Social capital and environmental sustainability.* Routledge, New York.

EPA. (1999). *Constructed wetlands treatment of municipal wastewaters.* Cincinnati, mimeo: United States Environment Protection.

Ermen van, R. (2007). Comparison and assessment of funding schemes for development of new activities and investments in environmental technologies. Brussels: Fundetec, rapportnummer 044370.

Etzioni, A. (2003). Communitarism. In K. Christensen & D. Levinson (Eds.), *Encyclopedia of community: From village to virtual world, Vol 1 A-D* (pp. 224–228). Sage Publications.

Fageberg, J. M., M. Shrolec (2008). National innovation system, capabilities and economic development. *Research Policy, 37*(9), 1417–1435.

Fisman, R. (2013). Did eBay just prove that paid search ads don't work? *Harvard Business Review*. Retrieved April 19, 2025, from https://hbr.org/2013/03/did-ebay-just-prove-that-paid.

Florida, R. (2002). *The rise of the creative class* (1st ed.). Basic books.

Forbes. (2025). Retrieved February 28, 2025, from https://www.forbes.com/sites/rachelsandler/2021/11/10/inside-the-trillion-dollar-tech-factory/.

Freeman, E. R., McVea, J. (2006). A stakeholder approach to strategic management. In M. A. Hitt, R. E. Freeman, & J. S. Harrison (Eds.), *The blackwell handbook of strategic management*. Malden, MA: Blackwell Publishing.

Gasper, D. (2011). Pioneering the human development revolution. *Journal of Human Development and Capabilities, 12*(3), 433–456.

Giraldez, J., Flores-Espino, F., MacAlpine, S., & Asmus, P. (2018). *Phase I microgrid cost study: data collection and analysis of microgrid costs in the United States*. NREL report NREL/TP-5D00–67821.

Goldenberg, J., & Reddy, A. K. N. (1990). Energy for the developing world. *Scientific American, 263*, 111–118.

Goncz, E., Skirke, U., Kleizen, H., & Barber, M. (2006). Increasing the rate of sustainable change: A call for a redefinition of the concept and the model for its implementation. *Journal of Cleaner Production, 15*, 525–537.

Grübler A. (1991). Diffusion: Long term patterns and discontinuities. In N. Nakićenović, & A. Grübler (Eds.), *Diffusion of technologies and social behaviour* (pp. 451–482). Heidelberg: Springer–IIASA.

Harari, N. Y. (2017). *Homo deus*. Harper Collins Publishers.

Hawken, P. (2017). *Drawdown–the most comprehensive plan ever proposed to reverse global warming*. Penguin.

Herman, R., Ardekanin, S. A., & Ausubel, J. H. (1989). Dematerialization. In J. H. Ausubel & H. E. Sladovich (Eds.), *Technology and environment* (1st ed., pp. 50–69). National Academy Press.

Horizon 2020. (2021). It refers to evaluation of the largest EU program for R&D, called 'Horizon2020'. Of 115235 eligible R&D applications for €182 billion (USD 217) funding 12% are approved with €25 (USD 29) billion grants after competitive scrutiny by experts, but only 141 valid patents are gained, which means that € 177 (USD 186) million per patent is paid in this programme compared to average € 2.7 (USD 3) million per patent in the EU. Retrieved February 12, 2021, from, from https://ec.europa.eu/programmes/horizon2020/sites/horizon2020/files/h2020_threeyearson_a4_horizontal_2018_web.pdf.

IEA. (2002). *Electricity in India*. Providing Power for the Millions, Paris.

IEA. (2024). Retrieved September 17, 2024, from https://www.iea.org/reports/key-world-energy-statistics-2021/final-consumption.

IMF. (2024). Retrieved July 28, 2024, from, https://climatedata.imf.org/datasets/d22a6decd9b147fd9040f793082b219b_0/about.

Invest Europe. (2019). Investing in Europe, private equity activity 2019. Brussels.

IRENA. (2022). Renewable energy statistics 2022. Retrieved October 19, 2022, from, https://www.irena.org/publications/2022/Jul/Renewable-Energy-Statistics-2022.

Jordan, A. (2008). The governance of sustainable development: Taking stock and looking forwards. *Environment and Planning C: Government and Policy, 26*, 17–33.

Jordan, A., & Huitema, D. (2023). Polycentric governance. Routlegde Handbook of Environmental Policy, Taylor & Francis Group. Retrieved April 1, 2025, from, https://www.taylorfrancis.com/chapters/edit/; https://doi.org/10.4324/9781003043843-6/polycentric-governance-andrew-jordan-dave-huitema.

Kahnemann, D., & Knetsch, J. L. (1992). Valuing goods, the purchase of moral satisfaction. *Journal of Environmental Economics and Management, 22*, 57–70.

Kamien, M. I., & Schwarz, N. L. (1982). *Market structure and innovation*. Cambridge Publishers.

Koirala, B. P., Koliou, E., Friege, J., Hakvoort, R. A., & Herder, P. M. (2016). Energetic communities for community energy: A review of key issues and trends shaping integrated community energy systems. *Renewable and Sustainable Energy Reviews, 56*, 722–744.

Krozer, Y. (1996). Towards environmental life cycle costing: Decision model for environmental strategies of corporations. In Backman et al. (Eds.), UNEP cleaner production programme, *Challenges and APPROACHES to incorporate the environment into business decisions* (pp. 56–66). Opio, France: Expert Seminar.

Krozer, Y. (2002). *Innovation and the environment*. Springer.

Krozer, Y. (2008). Life cycle costing for innovations in product chains. *Journal of Cleaner Production, 1–6*, 310–321.

Krozer, Y. (2015). *Theories and practices on innovating for sustainable development*. Heidelberg: Springer. Chapters 3.3 and 3.4

Krozer, Y. (2022). *Economics of Renewable Energy*. Springer-Nature, Dordreecht.

Krozer, Y., Coenen, F., Hanganu, J., Lordkipanidze, M., & Sbarcea, M. (2020). Towards innovative governance of nature areas. *Sustainability, 12*(24), 18.

Kruze, V. (2024). *Are VC investments taxed*. Retrieved November 11, 2024, from https://kruzeconsulting.com/vc-investment-taxed/.

Larson, E. D., Ross, M. H., & Williams, R. H. (1986). Beyond the era of materials. *Scientific American, 34*(6), 24–29.

Lennon, B., Dunphy, N. P., & Sanvicente, E. (2019). Community acceptability and the energy transition: A citizens' perspective. *Energy, Sustainability and Society, 9*(35), 1–18.

Li, N. (2000, 2017). Building a network theory of social capital. In: N. Li, K. Cook, & R. S. Burt (Eds.), *Social capital, theory and research*. Routledge, New York.

Loorbach, D. (2009). Transition management for sustainable development: A prescriptive, complexity-based governance framework. *Governance, 23*(1), 161–183.

Mazzucato, M. (2018). Mission-oriented innovation policy: Challenges and opportunities. *Industrial and Corporate Change, 27*(5), 803–815.

Meadowcroft, J. (2009). What about the politics? Sustainable development, transition management, and long term energy transitions. *Political Science, 42*, 323–340.

Mehrotra, S. (2005). Human capital or human development. *Economic and political weekly*.

Mokyr, J. (2002). *The gifts of athena*. Princeton University Press.

Moroni S., Antoniucci, V., & Bisello, A. (2019). Local energy communities and distributed generation: Contrasting perspectives, and inevitable policy trade-offs, beyond the apparent global consensus. *Sustainability, 11*, 3493.

Mowery, D., & Rosenberg, N. (1979). The influence of market demand upon innovation: a critical review of some recent empirical studies. *Research Policy*, 8, 102–153.

Mundaca, l., Busch, H., & Schwer, S. (2018), 'Successful' low-carbon energy transitions at the community level? An energy justice perspective. *Applied Energy, 218*, 282–293.

Nakićenović, N. (1991), Diffusion of pervasive systems. In N. Nakićenović, & A. Grübler (Eds.), *Diffusion of technologies and social behaviour* (pp. 483–510). Heidelberg: Springer–IIASA.

Nordhaus, W. D. (1994). *Do real output and real wages measures capture realities? The history of lighting suggests not*. Yale, New Haven: Cowles Foundation.

Ostrom, E. (2009). *Beyond markets and states: Polycentric governance of economic systems*. Indiana University, Bloomington.

OWD. (2024). *Our world data*. Retrieved October 30, 2024, from, (https://ourworldindata.org/working-more-than-ever).

Petrin, T. (2018). A literature review on the impact and effectiveness of government support for R&D and innovation. *ISIGrowth*,5. Retrieved December 17, 2024, from http://www.isigrowth.eu/wp-content/uploads/2018/02/working_paper_2018_05.pdf.

Petrovsky, H. (1994). *The evolution of useful things* (1st ed.). Vintage Books.

Roberto, R., Ferruzzi, G., Negro, V., & Noussan, M. (2023). Mapping of energy community development in Europe: State of the art and research directions. *Energies, 16*(6554), 1–29.

Rosenberg, N. (1982). Learning by using. In N. Rosenberg (Ed.), *Inside the black box* (pp. 120–140). Massachusetts.

Rotmans, R. K., van Asselt, M. (2001). More evolution than revolution: Transition management in public policy. *Foresight, 3*(1), 15–31.

Sandberg, M. (2021). Sufficiency transitions: A review of consumption changes for environmental sustainability. *Journal of Cleaner Production, 293*, Article 126097.

Sarasvathy, S. (2001). Causation and effectuation: Toward a theoretical shift from economic inevitability to entrepreneurial contingency. *Academy of Management Review, 26*(2), 243–263.

Sen, A. (1983). Development: Which way now? *The Economic Journal, 93*, 745–762.

Siblis. (2025). Retrieved February 28, 2025, from https://siblisresearch.com/data/us-stock-market-value/.

Soleas, E. (2021). Environmental factors impacting the motivation to innovate: A systematic review. *Journal of Innovation and Entrepreneurship, 10*, 1–18.

Stern, P. C. (2000). Toward a coherent theory of environmentally significant behaviour. *Journal of Social Issues, 56*(3), 407–424.

Sullivan, W. G., Wicks, E. M., & Koelling, P. (2009). *Engineering economy*. Pearson.

Tarpani, E., Piselli, C., Fabiani, C., Pigliautile, I., Kingma, E. J., Pioppi, B., & Pisello, A. L. (2022). Energy communities implementation in the European Union: Case studies from pioneer and laggard countries. *Sustainability, 14*, 12528.

Temple, J., & Johnson, P. A. (1996). Socia capability and economic growth. *The Quarterly Journal of Economics, 113*(3), 965–990.

Thurow, L. (1980), *Zero sum society* (p. 197). New York: Basic Books Inc.

Tilton, J. E. (1991). Material substitution: The role of new technology. In N. Nakicenovic & A. Grubler (Eds.), *Diffusion of technologies and social behaviour* (pp. 383–406). Springer Verlag.

Tukker, A., & Jansen, B. (2006). Environmental impacts of products, a detailed review of studies. *Journal of Industrial Ecology, 10*(3), 159–182.

UNEP-BNEF. (2025). Bloomberg, frankfurt business school and UNEP (2004–2020) on investments in renewable energy. Retrieved April 19, 2025, from, https://about.bnef.com/energy-transition-investment/.

UN-HABITAT. (2008). *Constructed wetlands manual*. Nairobi.

Schwanitz, V. J., Wierling, A., Paudler, H. A., von Beck, C., Dufner, S., Knutsdotter Koren, I., Kraudzun, T., Marcroft, T., Mueller, L., Zeiss, J. P. 1. (2023). Statistical evidence for the contribution of citizen-led initiatives and projects to the energy transition in Europe. *Scientific Reports, Nature Open, 13*, 1342.

Venkitachalam, K., & Busch, P. (2012). Tacit knowledge: review and possible research directions. *Journal of Knowledge Management*, 16(2), 357–372.

Walker, G., & Devine-Wright, P. (2008). Community energy: What should it mean. *Energy Policy, 36*, 497–500.

West, J., & Lutter, S. (2024). *Global Material Flow Database*. UNEP. https://www.resourcepanel.org/global-material-flows-database.

Wilting H., & Hanemaaijer, A. (2014). *Share of raw material costs in total production costs*. PBL report 1506. Bilthoven.

Wright, G. (1997). Towards a more historical approach to technological change'. *The Economic Journal*, 107, 1560–1566.

Ziesemer, T. (2021). The effects of R&D subsidies and publicly performed R&D on business R&D: A survey. *Hacienda Publica Espanola-Review of Public Economics, 236*(1), 171–205. Mastricht University.

Zuniga, P. (2024). *The Impact and Effectiveness of Innovation Policy: Evidence from Middle-Income Countries*, World Bank, Washington D.C.

Chapter 5
Governances in Transition

What kind of governance fosters sustainable development is assessed with regard to debates about democracy and autocracy? Shifts in governances are assessed in 23 countries after the disintegration of the Soviet Union. Based on the political theories, drivers of the political transitions would be the heritage of independence, national aspirations, civil initiatives, economic liberties, and political tolerance due to free media. Successful shifts in governance are assessed. Those shifts in governances are compared to the indexes of good governance. The successful shifts closely match high scores on the indexes of democracy and institutional capability. Transitions to democracies show better performances on the indicators of economics, well-being, and environmental qualities than authoritarian governances. Lessons for sustainable development are drawn.

5.1 Introduction

Given the capabilities in generating sustainable innovations, the issue is discussed about what kinds of institutions for the policy enforcement enable economic growth, more well-being along with better environmental qualities. Instead of theorising about the ideal kind of governance for sustainable development, this assessment focuses on comparison of democracies with autocracies. Experiences with shifts in governances are used for this comparison. These experiences refer to the shifts from state directives to market-based transactions after decomposition of the Soviet Union and its satellites during the early 1990s, called political transitions. These political transitions did not aim at sustainable development, but pursued changes of governances. Many people in these countries pursued democracies. Hence, this assessment of governance reflect the aspirations of citizens and businesses rather than intensions of authorities while the results are interpreted with respect to indicators for 'good governance' and for sustainable development.

© The Author(s), under exclusive license to Springer Nature Switzerland AG 2025
Y. Krozer, *Economic Growth and the Environment*,
https://doi.org/10.1007/978-3-031-99181-3_5

Background of this assessment is discussion about what is 'good governance'. When the idea of sustainable development disseminated from the late 1980s on, 'good governance' was defined by fair elections, rule of law, participation of citizens, diversity in media, and other institutions of democracy in the tradition of the nineteenth century liberalism (World Bank, 1994). As the neo-liberal ideology strengthened during the 1990s, the 'enlightened autocracy' in Korea, Taiwan, Singapore, and other countries attracted attention due to their fast economic growth. These governances would provide prosperity because would enable continuity in politics that is assumed to facilitate decisive actions, whereas the democratically elected politicians would seek the rents of elections (Fukuyama, 2008). This argumentation evolved toward advocacy of the authoritarian ruler that represents the interests of all people in a nation, an idea referred to as the populism (Kaltwasser, 2019). In many countries, elections, parliaments, media, judiciary, and other institutions of liberal democracy remained in place, but they are subjected to the authoritarian rulers in the curse of the 2000s. Several autocracies evolved toward dictatorships where governances do not tolerate any opposition, while a few of them imposed the totalitarian ideologies of sacrificing the rights of individuals for the sake of religion, nation, and other collective ideas.

The question about what governance enables sustainable development is answered stepwise. Firstly, key factors for the generation of shifts in governance are defined based on the political theories. These factors address the processes of change, which evolve largely independent of the targeted changes. So, the drivers in political transitions are assumed relevant for various objectives, also for sustainable development. Second, these factors are used to define successful political transitions, meaning the countries that generated shifts in their institutions, not only changes in the governments. The results are used to assess whether the successful transitions evolved towards democracies, or to autocracies. Third step is about the implications of the political transitions for sustainable development. It is assessed if the democratic governances deliver better performances on the indicators for economy, well-being, and the environment than the autocratic ones, and what lessons can be learned about the process of changes toward sustainable development.

Political transitions evolved in the countries directed by the states, called socialist and communist. The governances shifted from the state directives toward market-based negotiations. These countries covered most of the global population until the 1990s, but these governances nearly vanished within one generation despite their military force and ideological appeal to many people. Necessities drove these political transitions. Various external and internal factors could explain that necessity. A popular idea in the 'West' is that the competing neo-liberal, transactional governance outperformed the directives by the states with respect to the economic performances. Ideas within the state-directed countries focus on the internal factors, particularly the demotivation to do good jobs because of oppressive elites. The expanding bureaucratic elites that governed these countries, called 'nomenclature', enjoyed privileges without delivering prosperity and freedom to population (Voslensky, 1984). Meanwhile, people that faced this oppressive elite, as well as empty purses and shops reacted by absenteeism at work and widespread alcoholism, as well as collective actions by the bravest citizens (Schlögel, 1984). Discontent about the welfare loss also ignited national rebellions within the Soviet Union and its satellites (Beissinger, 1992). As economies of those countries stagnated and tensions within the elites intensified, changes in governance emerged.

Political transitions in twenty-three countries are assessed. All assessed countries were parts of the Soviet Union, or politically bound to it until the early 1990s. Eleven countries joined the EU. Poland, Hungary, Czech Republic, Slovakia, Romania, and Bulgaria were political satellites of the Soviet Union, while Estonia, Latvia, and Lithuania were former Soviet republics, and Slovenia and Croatia were Yugoslav republics allied to the Soviet Union. Belarus, Russia, Moldova, Armenia, Azerbaijan, Kazakhstan, Uzbekistan, Tajikistan, and Kyrgyzstan, mentioned from the west to the east, were former republics of the Soviet Union that started to co-operate in the Commonwealth of Independent States (CIS) led by Russia. Meanwhile, Ukraine, Georgia, and Turkmenistan did not join the EU neither CIS; meanwhile, Moldova left CIS,. Other political transitions are not covered because only indirectly linked to that decomposition. Serbia, Bosnia-Hercegovina, Montenegro, North Macedonia, and Kosovo emerged as states after the disintegration of former Yugoslavia during the civil wars from 1991 to 1995. Albania, located in Europe, was politically allied to China. States in Asia (e.g., China and Vietnam), Africa (e.g., Angola and Tanzania), and Latin America (e.g. Cuba and Nicaragua) have different histories. Several historic studies are used for assessing political changes (Heller & Nekrich, 1982; Ash, 1989; Gessen, 2018), privatisation of the business (Svejnar, 2006), causes of economic collapse (Walder et al., 2015), and economic reforms in time (Dabrowski, 2023). Wikipedia is used for the chronology of events. Visits to nearly all of those countries and opinions of many local experts are used for interpretations of ideas and facts, but author of this study bears the responsibility for the interpretations.

Factors considered essential for the political transitions are defined in Sect. 5.2. Changes in the governance of countries that entered the EU28, the EU-entrants and those that did not enter it, non-entrants, are described in Sect. 5.3. Readers who are not interested in the descriptions are welcome to jump to the analytic Sects. 5.4 and 5.5. Successful patterns in the political transitions are defined with the transition factors and verified with indexes for good governance in Sect. 4. Performances on sustainability indicators are presented in Sect. 5.5. Conclusions with regard to changes to sustainable development are drawn in Sect. 5.6. Inter alia, labels of the governances are avoided as much as possible because they are blurred. For example, liberal-democracies by constitution can have socialist leaderships as in Austria, and socialism by constitution can be led by the liberal and religious politicians as in India.

5.2 Factors in Political Transitions

Factors that generate successful political transitions are defined. Success is understood in the sense of major changes in the vested institutions, not only political changes though politics are decisive in enabling and opposing changes in governances. These factors are defined independently of the opinions about good governance. It is focused on several key factors that are applicable across countries, and allow for nuances and exceptions in order to avoid dogmas. Several political theories are used in addition to each other on the assumption that one single theory cannot explain various political transitions, one single factor even less so.

In the mainstream idea about political transitions, governances are vested in the societal structures that continue for many generations. This idea refers to the observations by Karl Wittfogel (1896–1988) about the decentralised, transactional governances rooted in the industrial tradition of liberal societies in Europe, which is opposed to the centralised, directive governances needed for large-scale agricultural waterworks dominant in the Asian societies (Wittfogel, 1957). His idea is used by Samuel Huntington to elaborate on rival governances, called 'civilisations', when the transaction societies are in conflict with the directive governances of the Soviet Union and other communist countries (Huntington, 1993). The civilisation thesis gained popularity in the neo-liberal politics. It is used as an axiom in the assessments of shifts in governances. It misses nuances. For example, longer distances from the capitals of former Soviet republics to Düsseldorf in Germany are used for underpinning the dictatorships in former republics of the Soviet Union and liberal-democracies in former satellites of the Soviet Union (Treisman, 2010). However, it neglected harsh dictatorial regimes in Belarus and Russia on shorter distances than the moderate autocracies in Armenia, Georgia, and Kyrgyzstan. From that mainstream viewpoint, global changes in governances toward sustainable development are fictitious, whilst progress measured by sustainability indicators is insufficient from the environmentalist viewpoint. That mainstream idea is not used as an axiom, but is converted into a factor in the political transitions next to others. Several factors are assumed to drive shifts in governances. They are divided into the factors inherited from the past and the ones that evolve during the transition. The former determines the contexts, and the latter the process of change.

Two contextual factors are considered particularly important. These are experiences of statehood and cultural identity (King, 2000). In line with that mainstream idea, the images and experiences of statehoods in the past were assumed to provide a justification for the shifts in power, if necessary with violence. Such experiences also deliver formats for new institutions and other reference for new governances. The length of the countries' independence periods during the Soviet Union's existence from 1917 to 1991 is used as the contextual factor in the assessment of political transitions. It is assumed that lengthy dependence on the Soviet governance generated an elite of politicians and bureaucrats that learned to survive governmental changes, thereby generated the capability to maintain power despite inefficiencies and corruption. The factor linked to the experiences of statehood is labelled as the 'independence heritage'.

In addition, the size of cultural minorities in the population is addressed. Large minorities in populations are sources of tensions that can impede political transitions. As the minorities demand cultural autonomy, or national independence, they invoke conflicts and uprising that cause turbulent political relations (Hutchingson, 2019). In the former Soviet Union, being a colonial empire with many nationalities, the national aspirations are expressed by the cultural majorities in the republics, while the Russian minorities were privileged and had power. The decomposition of Soviet Unio ignited the national aspiration, which triggered emigration of the Russian-speaking and other non-local minorities (Glaeson, 1992). In result, the Russian and other cultural minorities in Kazakhstan, Latvia, Kyrgyzstan, and Tajikistan declined from 50–60% of the populations during the early 1990s to 30–40% in the early 2010s (Burke, 2014). The share of national minorities in populations during the Soviet Union is considered another contextual factor, called 'national aspiration'. For the transitions to sustainable development, the heritage of independence and national aspiration are also relevant for the ownership of land, minerals and other natural resources.

In addition to those contextual factors, the process of shifting governances is addressed based on political theories. Three subsequent steps are distinguished in this process: changes of governments, their consolidation through reforms, and creating new properties of institutions (Munck, 2015). For assessing political transitions in former Soviet Union and its sattelites, these are interpreted as the civil initiatives for changes of rulers, imposing new economic systems, and vesting institutional relations that tolerate opposition.

With respect to the civil initiatives, it is argued that involvement of citizen organisations in the shift of power largely determines subsequent changes in institutions, thereby creation of a new governance. Changing autocratic governments would require well-organised citizen initiatives rooted in the trade unions, church, army, and other mass organisations, which pose threats to the autocratic elite (Tarow, 1996). It is also observed that civil initiatives absorb and promote ideas and experiences in other countries (Beissinger, 2007). Such 'bandwagon effect' is widely observed. Examples are negotiations of citizen initiatives with elite, which started in Poland, followed by similar negotiations in Czechoslovakia, Georgia and other countries, or declaration of independence by the Slovenian nationalists followed by the Croatian ones, and other former Yugoslav republics entailing civil war and the disintegration of former Yugoslavia (Bruszt et al., 2010).

Second factor for successful political transitions in former Soviet Union and its satellites was the realisation of economic reform in the sense of changing economic activities from the directives by the state bureaucracies towards the transactions in markets. These economic reforms after overtaking power are often divided into two categories. Type I is the strengthening of freedom in entrepreneurial activities instead of state directives. Type II is the privatization of firms that are managed by the state. As a result of the reforms I and II, private activities expanded from close to nil in

1990 to about half of the GDP within a few years (Svejnar, 2002). While the market transactions remained in most transition countries, type II reforms are sometimes slowed-down and even partially reversed driven by social opposition against loss of income and unemployment (Estrin et al., 2009). Major changes in economies enabled to undermine corrupt elites, whereas minor changes enabled to reinforce the vested interests and directives (Turk, 2014). Success of the political transition is assessed with regard to freedom in the entrepreneurial activities (type I reforms).

Third success factor in the transition processes addresses the political relations in establishing new governances. Establishing new governances is assumed to depend on political tolerance, defined in the sense of accepting different political opinions in a country (Gibson et al., 1992). Some scholars argued that the political tolerance is a cultural capability, which can be measured with inquiries. For illustration, civil activists in the transition countries are found tolerant in the sense of being receptive for opposite opinions (Guerin et al., 2004). Other scholars dispute that cultural capability. They argue that successful political transitions generate governances that create political tolerance in the sense of high trusts in institutions (Doorn van, 2014). In this idea, trustful institutions are essential for the political tolerance. This idea is used. Trust is assessed with ranks in the freedom of media based on the assumption that free media enable trustful institutions. Therefore, countries rankings on the indexes of media freedom are used. The factors are the averages of 2004, 2008, 2012, 2016, 2020, and 2024 in the "Reporters sans frontiers" (https://rsf.org/en/index?year=2004 (started in 2002).

Independence heritage, national minorities, civil initiatives, economic reforms, and political tolerances are five factors that are assumed to determine successes of political transitions in the sense of changes in governances. They are considered as independent of each other with similar impacts on the successes. Using these factors enables to prevent several flaws. One flaw is the disciplinary bias when scholars focus on their specialisations (Welsh, 1994). For instance, economists focus on income growth and inequalities even though they acknowledge the primacy of political relations in economies (Acemoğlu & Robinson, 1999). Herewith, successes of political transitions are assessed from several perspectives on the governance. Another flaw is mixing a few factors into a single one. An example is linking the domestic political interests vested in the past aiming at privatisation of the countries' assets with the economic interests of foreign investors taking opportunity of the privatisations (Brown et al., 2006). In this assessment, each factor is assessed separately instead of combinations. Third issues is the interpretation of impacts as drivers. An example is that high economic performances indicate 'good governance' while 'good governance' is needed for economic performances (Rothstein and Theorell, 2012). Defining factors in this section before the assessment of impacts in the next sections helps to avoid this trap. Finally, scholarly fixation on a theory can neglect facts. So, radical privatisations (type I and II) are emphatically promoted (Sachs, 1994), even in hindsight (Walden et al., 2015), although they invoked dictatorship in Russia, and violence in Georgia and Ukraine contrary to the scholarly expectations. Assessing successes per factor aims to avoid this bias.

Independence heritage, national minorities, citizen initiatives, economic reforms, and political trust are defined as factors that indicate conditions for political transitions. They are hypothesised as proxies for changes to sustainable development. Those factors indicate conditions for the shifts in governances while political decisions determine changes.

5.3 Countries Political Transitions

Political transitions address changes in the regions and countries dominated by the Russian Empire that turned into the Union of Socialist Soviet Republics (Soviet Union) in 1922, five years after turning down kingdom (tsar) followed by bloody civil war. The Soviet Union was constituted as the state governed by the citizen councils, called soviets, considered as representatives of the citizen initiatives. However, the state evolved into cruel regime that appropriated all means of production and imposed the totalitarian ideology ruled by the party oligarchy. The decay of the Soviet Union in the end of 1980s enabled the satellite states and the republics within the Soviet Union to gain independence and vest national governances. Appendix F briefly describes the formation and fall of the Soviet Union. Below changes in each new country are briefly described, looking from the west to the east in geographic clusters. Firstly, the EU entrants are covered followed by non-entrants. Those five transition factors are used to describe the contexts and processes of these shifts in governances. The independence heritage and national minorities are used to describe the contexts, which cover the size of territories and populations in the early 2020s, as well as the kinds of governance before, during, and after World War II during 1939–1945 (WW2). The citizen initiatives, economic reforms, and political tolerance are used to assess the transition processes from 1989 to 2022.

Poland, Czechoslovakia, and Hungary blazed trails for political transitions and entry into the EU and NATO as the 'Visehrad Group'. It was a lobby group aiming at those entries, but this group lost relevance after these entries.

Context of Poland. Before World War II (WW2), Poland was a democratic state that evolved towards nationalist, authoritarian governance. Its territory, larger than the present one, included the western part of present Ukraine, Belarus, and Lithuania to the east, but missed Pomerania and Silesia in the south and west. Its borders are shifted about 500 km westward based on the agreement between Soviet Union and Nazi-Germany in 1939 about division of the Eastern European countries, called 'Ribbentrop-Molotov pact'. The agreed borders largely remained after the WW2 in 1945. Poland fought against the Nazi-Germans during WW2 when about two million Polish Jews were murdered, along with a million Slavic Poles. After the war, a few million Poles and Germans were forced to migrate westward with many casualties. Its communist dictatorship was harsh, but Catholic church, small private farms and craft shops were tolerated due to several citizen uprisings. The uprising in 1980 lead to the formation of an independent, trade union "NSZZ Solidarność" (*Solidarity)* that became the main opposition force. After the martial law in 1982, it acted underground, and ultimately took power in 1989 after several years of underground activism. **Transition**. Poland on 313,000 km^2 with nearly 38 million people changed government in April 1989 when the Solidarność sealed agreement at the Roundtable with the representatives of the trade union, ruling military regime, along with independent experts appointed by the trade union and the rulers. This agreement changed the military government into temporary non-elected civil leadership. Within a year, new constitution with the parliamentary system and presidential office are defined, led by the elected president Lech Wałęsa who was former leader of the Solidarność. Within a few months, the elected government enforced radical economic reforms, including free prices, trade, and entrepreneurial activities. It introduced a convertible currency, and started with the privatization of state-owned firms, so called 'shock therapy'. The privatisation was based on vouchers that are assumed to indicate the expected values of the state-owned firms. These vouchers were initially distributed among workers and citizens, but the distribution was slowed-down in order to attract foreign investors. The 'shock therapy' impoverished people because their salaries in convertible currency were low (about hundred USD monthly average), and many jobs were lost while the value of vouchers was negligible because many state firms collapsed while new private firms emerged. As the citizens' support for the reforms declined, several free elections brought nationalists, liberals, and former communists to power, which softened the hardships of the reforms. Within several years, its economy revived and incomes grew. Polish media became independent of the state, but the nationalist governments aimed to control it in the 2010s with minor success.

Context of Hungary. Hungary was a dictatorial monarchy before WW2. It covered twice larger than present territory, which included parts of present Slovakia, Romania, Moldova, Croatia, and Serbia. It joined Nazi Germany during WW2. About half million of Hungarian Jews were murdered by the Hungarian and German armies. After WW2, a few million Hungarian-speaking people found themselves in the neighbouring countries while the totalitarian communism ruled the state of Hungary. The social uprising against that ruling in 1956 was broken after thousands of casualties, followed by mass emigration. It brought a new authoritarian governances that tolerated economic and cultural freedoms in private smallholdings and the church. **Transition**. Hungary covers 93,000 km^2 and has 9.7 million people. It initiated reforms in 1990 in Parliament led by the Communist Party. These reforms allowed travels to the western countries, setting new political parties, and organised free elections for president and government. A coalition of populist and Christian-democratic parties won the elections, and the communist party went into opposition. After five years of stagnating economic reforms, being opposed by the populists, a growing budget deficit,the coalition of socialist and liberal parties took power after new election. Economic reforms are enhanced, including gradual sale of state-owned firms. Fall of income and growing employment brought the populist coalition back to power in the late 2000s. This coalition vested an authoritarian ruling that oppresses opposition, press, legal institutions, and collides with the EU.

Context of Czech. Czech was a liberal democracy before WW2. After occupation by Nazi Germany in 1939, it fought for independence during WW2 when a few hundred thousand Jews were murdered by the Nazi-German. The communist dictatorship from 1946 on enforced merger with Slovakia into one state. Cultural reforms during the 1960s led to a period of modest liberties during several months of 1968, known as 'Prague Spring', which was oppressed by the invasion of the Soviet army. Illegal civil opposition continued, including the 'Charta 99' movement. **Transition**. Czechia, which covers nearly 79,000 km^2 with 11 million people. Its governance switched from the communist regime to liberal democracy in mid-1990 after mass demonstrations. The opposition leader in the Charta 99, Vaclav Havel, was appointed as President and elected a half year later. The economy was reformed in a similar way to Poland, but the wage compensations were agreed between trade unions and the government. Vouchers were distributed among all citizens while several state-owned firms were set aside for sales to foreign investors (Brada, 1991). A few other transition countries copied this policy with minor adaptations. In 1993, the state was peacefully divided into the Czech and Slovak republics based on the national majorities within their borders. Subsequent elections brought the social-democratic, and liberal parties to power. Free elections and media brought populists to power during the 2010s as people sensed less purchasing power (Šubrt, 2012).

Context of Slovakia. Slovakia before WW2 was governed by the Czechoslovak state and the regional authority within the Hungarian state. During WW2, its nationalist government declared independence in collaboration with Nazi-Germany in 1939 and acted with the German army. The communist rulers re-established the Czech Republic and Slovakia after the war, including a part of the former Hungarian territory. **Transition**. Slovakia covers 49,000 km^2 with 5.5 million people. Founded as a state in 1993 after referendum in favour of the separation from Czechia, its first free election brought nationalists to power. Economic reforms that emerge in conjunction with Czech Republic were slowed down, and privatization was stopped. Subsequent government switched to the coalition of social-democrat with Christian-democrat parties which accelerated economic reforms. This one is followed by the populist party with authoritative leader that slowed down the reforms. While incomes grew, Slovak governance became authoritarian. By the 2010s, massive corruption and oppression of opposition threatened stability but press remained free.

Lithuania, Latvia, and Estonia, often called the 'Baltic states' due to their geography of the Baltic sea, where a Soviet republic until 1990.

Context of Lithuania. Lithuania was a democratic state that evolved into a dictatorship before WW2. Part of its territory, including the present capital of Vilnius, was occupied by Poland. Anger about the Polish occupants brought the Lithuanian political leaders to improve relations with the Soviet Union and Germany. The Soviet Union invaded Lithuania in 1940 after Ribbentrop-Molotov pact. That invasion is followed by the Nazi-German occupation when hundreds of thousands of Jewish citizens were murdered. The totalitarian Soviet regime after the WW2 deported thousands of Lithuanians to camps where many died. **Transition**. Lithuania covers 65,000 km^2 with 2.8 million people. Driven by mass demonstrations, it announced independence by the early 1990 in its parliament. Civil uprising against the Soviet army followed, which caused many casualties. After a year, the new statehood and constitution were approved, but negotiations about withdrawal of the Soviet troops took two more years. The Lithuanian state confiscated the Soviet properties. Radical economic reforms similar to Poland are implemented. As hardships of the reforms caused social unrest, the renamed communists took power in free elections and slowed down the privatisation of state-owned firms. In subsequent free elections, the political profiles of the government changed while the press remained free.

Context of Latvia. Latvia was a democracy that evolved into a dictatorship before WW2. Although neutrality was proclaimed in the 1930s, many citizens joined the Nazi-German army during WW2 against occupation by the Soviet Union after the Ribbentrop-Molotov pact. After the war, many Latvians were executed and deported to camps, while Russians moved into Latvia for work. **Transition**. Latvia is situated on 64,000 km^2 with 1.9 million people, and a large Russian minority among them. Driven by the citizen committees, it gained independence in 1990. Its communist party attempted a coup with the assistance of the Soviet army one year later, but failed due to massive civil opposition. After the first parliamentary election, a moderate government was established. Economic reforms in this industrialized republic of the Soviet Union were similar to other countries, but the privatization of state-owned firms was slow. Economy recovered after a few years of crisis and grew fast while the share of industry in economy declined by half and services expanded (Krišjane, 2005). Subsequent elections were won by moderate parties, followed by changing political profiles and free press. Tensions with the large Russian-speaking minority persist.

Context of Estonia. Before WW2, the Estonian democracy evolved towards authoritarian governance. Though formally neutral during WW2, it was occupied by the Soviet Union in 1940 after the Ribbentrop-Molotov pact. The Nazi-German army recruited many Estonians to fight against the occupant. After incorporation into the Soviet Union, Estonia experienced totalitarian rule with mass executions and deportations. **Transition**. Estonia on 45,000 km^2 has 1.3 million people with large Russian-speaking minority. It re-gained independence in 1990, driven by the citizens committees. Free elections to the national assembly followed, which formalized the statehood one year later. Negotiations about dual nationality by Russian-speaking citizens and withdrawal of the Russian army took four more years. Meanwhile, its economy is radically reformed in a similar manner to Czech with the distribution of vouchers for purchases of state-owned companies among all citizens. Losses of income in the convertible currency and high unemployment caused social riots, followed by the introduction of social security for the poorest citizens. Fast economic growth was focused on high-tech. Political profiles of governments changed while the press remains free. Tensions with Russia about borders and the Russian-speaking minority remain.

Contexts of Romania, Bulgaria, Slovenia, and Croatia. Their contexts on the Balkan peninsula are linked by several centuries of the Ottoman (Turkish) and Austrian expansions, which has dramatically changed after World War I (1914–1918) when both empires crumbled. Before WW2 (1939–1945), Romania was half the size of the present states and culturally homogenous, while the Bulgarian territory was about one-third larger. The territories of present Slovenia, Croatia, Bosnia-Hercegovina, Montenegro, North Macedonia, and Kosovo were ruled by the Serbian monarchy, renamed Yugoslavia in 1920 after the assassinations of several Croat politicians. The Romanian, Bulgarian, and Serbian monarchies evolved towards dictatorships linked to the Nazi-Germany and fascist Italy. During WW2, Romania lost the territory similar to present Moldova in the Soviet Union, and gained the Carpathian regions with large Hungarian-speaking population after the war. Bulgaria lost territory to the former Yugoslavia, which is presently part of North Macedonia. During WW2, the Yugoslav communist partizans largely based the Serb populations led by Tito fought successfully with the help of the Soviet and British armies against the Serbian monarchy, as well as the Italian fascists and Nazi-German invaders. They re-established Yugoslavia after WW2. During WW2, Nationalists in Croatia announced independence in alliance with Nazi-Germany and Italian fascists, followed by mass murder of Serbs, Jews, Muslims, and other minorities. Meanwhile, Slovenia was independently only a few weeks because captured by the fascist Italy. After WW2, Romania became a harsh totalitarian regime with a flavour of independence from the Soviet Union, while the Bulgarian regime followed neatly the Soviet Union, and was used as an experimental plot for the Soviet policies.

Yugoslavia was re-established on a larger territory than the pre-war Serbian monarchy as it included parts of Bulgaria and Hungary, as well as included Slovenia has taken over from Austria and Italy. The governance of Yugoslavia was authoritarian along with economic and social liberties unavailable in other satellites of the Soviet Union. Yugoslavia dissolved gradually after Tito's death in 1980. Its shifting leadership by nationalities evolved towards domination by the Serb and Croat nationalist leaders. Both claimed territories in the regions of Bosnia-Hercegovina and Vojvodina. Sluggish economic reforms triggered hyperinflation, while economic losses of subsidised state-owned firms brought the state close to bankruptcy. Social unrests strengthened demands for national independence. When the republics of Slovenia and Croatia demanded withdrawal of the Yugoslav army from their territories and declared independence in 1991, they were opposed by the Yugoslav army dominated by the Serbian and Montenegro republics. When the republics of Macedonia and Bosnia-Hercegovina also launched independence that year, civil war spread throughout former Yugoslavia. This war continued until 1995 causing hundreds of thousand deaths, followed by the war for independence of Kosovo with the majority of ethnic Albanians and large Serbian minority.

Transition. Romania, which covers 238,000 km^2 with 19 million people, abolished the communist ruling after the civil war that left about thousand dead and the execution of its dictator Ceausescu in late 1989. The government and presidency were captured by the renamed communist party, but they were abolished after mass civil protests. In subsequent elections, conservative, liberal, and former-communist parties formed coalitions with the Hungarian minority party. On paper, reforms similar to Poland were introduced, but the implementation was piecemeal and sluggish (Demekas and Khan, 1991). In effect, introduction of market-based economy evolved gradually during two decades, while the Romanian governance remains centralised and bureaucratic, but media remained free.

Transition. Bulgaria covers 111,000 km^2 with 6.9 million people. It underwent political reforms in late 1989. It was driven by the ecological civil organization that was tolerated during the communist regime, and reformed communists in the Parliament. One year later, the ruling communist party adopted a new constitution based on multi-party governance, and captured the political leadership. The first elections were won by the renamed communists. Delayed economic reforms brought the state near to bankruptcy. Conservative and liberal parties won subsequent elections, and introduced economic reforms which caused a decline of incomes and employment. This hardship caused social unrest. Privatization of the state-owned firms with vouchers distributed among the citizens, similar to Czech, created a group of wealthy oligarchs. This oligarchy and centralised decision making invoked massive corruption. The press is subordinated to the oligarchs.

Transition. Slovenia has a population of 2.1 million in an area of 20,000 km^2. It was the most advanced economy in Yugoslavia. A multi-party governance is introduced in 1989 before its declaration of independence in Parliament in 1991, This is followed by a short civil war against the Yugoslav army. A moderate liberal coalition was brought to power after free elections one year later. Radical political and economic reforms are introduced aiming at alignment with the EU governance. Successive moderate governments changed political profiles while media remained free.

Transition. Croatia on 88,000 km^2 has 4.1 million people. It announced independence in 1991, which was opposed by the Yugoslav government dominated by Serbs. Four years of war followed. After the end of the war in 1995, the nationalist leadership of Tujman won a few subsequent elections, His authoritarian regime delayed economic reforms and alignment with the EU. After the death of Tujman, the political profiles of governments in the 2000s changed, but freedom of the media is under pressure.

Those were the states that entered into the EU. In addition, twelve republics became independent states after the decomposition of the Soviet Union. This decomposition process evolved without much bloodshed. This is a major achievement by former socialist politicians in the Soviet Union and its satellites compared to the nationalist bloody destruction of former Yugoslavia and civil wars for power within newly created states based on the Soviet republics. However, this decomposition generated criminality linked to police, secret services, and other state institutions. The contexts and processes political transitions of these new states are highlighted from the west to the east.

Context of Russia. Creation and decay of Soviet Union briefly described in Appendix F provides the context of the Russian Federation (Russia). **Transition.** Russia covers 17,100,000 km^2 with 144 million people. It declared independence of the Soviet Union in 1991, which also ended of the Soviet Union. First free presidential elections were won by Yeltsin. In the following years, military expenses are cut and agreements are sealed with the new states about the Russia's control of nuclear weapons. The economy has been radically reformed, and vouchers for state-owned firms are distributed among citizens in a similar manner as in Czechoslovakia and Estonia. Although businesses grew and inflation was reduced, incomes of people became worthless. Meanwhile, those vouchers were mostly purchased by the elite of former Soviet Union. They became wealthy oligarchs as the privatised firms were supported by the Russia state. Given that new governance could not cope with criminality, oligarchs looked for protection of gangs, secret services, army, and other strongmen, so called 'silovniki'. Several groups also oppose reforms. For example, security forces pursued a coup directed by Yeltsin's former ally. Local insurgences were ignited by security forces, led by Putin, into wars in Moldova (Transnistria), in Georgia (South Ossetia), and in Chechnya (1st Chechen War). Wars, criminality, and corruption, along with low fuel prices for the sales of Russian oil and gas, caused an economic breakdown in the late 1990s. As Yeltsin lost credibility after re-election, he appointed Putin as his successor. Putin popularity grew due to improving economy and war against Muslim insurgence on Caucasus (2nd Chechen War), culminating in the win of fair presidential elections in 2000. Income growth due to increasing prices of oil and gas and Putin image as a strongman reinforced his power after a fraudulent election four years later. By the mid-2000s, Russia became an authoritarian state where freedom in the media, society, and the economy were curtailed. This governance evolved into a dictatorship that persecuted and murdered civil opposition, followed by the full-scale war in Ukraine from 2022 onwards.

Context of Belarus. Belarus, as it exists now, was not an independent country before WW2, but divided between the Soviet Union and Poland. During the war, nearly a million Jews were murdered by the Nazi-German, while the Belarus nationalists fought with the Soviet army against the Poles and Ukrainians. After the war, Belarus is incorporated as a Soviet Union. **Transition**. Belarus covers 207,000 km^2 with 9.4 million people. It declared independence in 1991. This is done by the communist governing body (central committee) after social unrest about deteriorating incomes. That governing body established a presidential democracy, followed by fair elections that were won by the Belarus communist leader, Lukashenko. Subsequent elections were rigged. While the authoritarian presidency kept control of prices and currency, small firms were allowed, but larger ones remained state-owned. High inflation at double digit rates, trade barriers, and inconvertible currencies remained until the early 2000s. Crushing social protests against the income loss and terrorist attacks with many casualties in 2012 paved the way to the Lukashenko dictatorship; this attack was presumably arranged by the security service. Economy improved due to more freedom for businesses and fuel supplies from Russia at discounted prices during the 2010s. Ridged elections in 2020 invoked mass protests which were crushed, followed by mass imprisonment and emigration. The state controls the media.

Context of Ukraine. Ukraine was an independent state during about a year from 1918 to 1919 during the Civil War in Russia. This was followed by the Polish occupation of the western part, and the Soviet occupation of the central and eastern parts until WW2 (Plokhy, 2023). On the Polish territories, rich landowners possessed huge areas of land. On the Soviet territories, farmers were forced to leave land for the collective farms. During the 1930s, heavy opposition to that collectivisation, mass deportation, and the killings of individual farmers caused famine of a few million deaths. During WW2, a few million Ukrainians were killed. Among them, more than a million Jews were murdered by the Nazi-Germans and the collaborating Ukrainian nationalists. As the border moved westward after the war, almost one million people migrated from the Polish territory that became the Soviet Union. **Transition**. Ukraine covers 603,000 km^2 with 44 million people, of it large Russian speaking minority. It became independent in 1991 after mass demonstration aiming at independence. The declaration of independence by the Communist Party was supported by referendum. A democratic constitution is approved. Subsequent governments during thirty years after the 1990s switched orientations from liberal-democracy linked to the EU to the authoritarian ruling linked to Russia. Economic reforms similar to Russia were introduced after the independence, but they were obstructed by the populist presidency that enforced privileges for local oligarchs. Public services and investments were hindered by corruption in weak institutions. When the democratically elected president lost to the populist leader in fraudulent elections, social uprising abolished this new presidency in 2004, called the 'Orange revolution' (Åslund, 2005). About ten years later, Euromaidan ended the presidency of a populist leader that won fraudulently elected. In 2014, Russia started the war against Ukraine on eastern regions and Crimea, culminating in the Russian invasion of Ukraine in 2022. For decades, media resisted controls.

Context of Moldova. Moldova was an independent country during a few weeks in 1918, but was captured by Romania as its Bessarabia region before WW2, followed by incorporation in the Soviet Union as its republic during WW2. **Transition**. Moldova covers 34,000 km^2 with 2.6 million people of Romanian-speaking majority with large Russian, Ukrainian, and Turkish speaking minorities. Its independence declared in 1991 was driven by a coalition of civil organizations and the Communist Party. After a few years of independence, nationalist tensions culminated in a war with the Russian army that established a separatist state in the eastern part of Moldova, called Transnistria. During three decades of independence, Moldova's elections swinged between the Russia-oriented populist party and the EU-oriented Christian-democrat and liberal parties. Economic reforms similar to Russia were introduced right after independence. They curbed inflation as private firms expanded, but impoverished people because payments did not meet prices. After social protests, economic liberalization slowed down during the 1990s while public institutions were weakened by corruption, and media are constrained. In result, the Moldovan state was on the brink of bankruptcy throughout the 2000s (Dabrowski, 2003). The EU-oriented governance in the 2010s accelerated economic reforms, and more freedom of the media.

Context of Georgia. Georgia was an independent state during a few years after 1918, but was occupied by the Soviet Union thereafter. It was considered the wealthiest and influential republic, as Stalin and several other Soviet leaders had the Georgian roots. **Transition**. Georgia covers 69,000 km^2 with 3.7 million people, including several minorities. It gained independence in 1991 after peaceful, mass demonstrations in 1989 that were oppressed by the Soviet Union. A roundtable meeting with the communist rulers and opposition evolved in a similar way to Poland. A fair election gave presidential power to the Georgian nationalist party. This result led to conflicts between political parties, which culminated in civil wars in the regions of Ossetia and Abkhazia against the separatist forces supported by Russia. Frictions with Russia mounted when the Georgian government declared the EU orientation in the early 2000s, followed by swings between the pro-EU and pro-Russian rulers that blamed each other for fraud and corruption (Sartania, 2021). Radical economic reforms similar to Russia are introduced shortly after the independence but the ongoing violence brought the Georgian economy on the brink of collapse during the 1990s, while violations of property and civil rights by corrupted institutions frustrated reforms (Papava, 2014). During the 2010s, economy improved, but the continuing violent swings between pro-Russian populist parties and pro-EU liberal ones weakened the Georgian governance (Iashvili, 2019). Freedom of the media is constrained by rival factions.

Context of Armenia. Armenia was under the rule of Iran, Turkey, and Russia for more than six centuries, except a few years of independence between 1918 and 1920, which isfollowed by the Soviet occupation. **Transition**. Armenia covers 29,000 square kilometres with 3 million people. It became independent of the Soviet Union in 1990, which was driven by the Communist party. Within a few years, war was fought against the neighbouring Azerbaijan about the Nagorno-Karabakh region. This Azeri area is conquered by Armenia with the help of the Russian army. Another conflict arose with the neighbouring Turkey about the region of Nakhichevan, an Azeri enclave between Armenia and Turkey, but it is resolved without much bloodshed. During the 1990s, Nagorno-Karabakh had an Armenian population influx, but subsequent wars against the Azeri forces in 2020 and 2023 brought the Nagorno-Karabakh region to Azerbaijan. Shortly after independence, the Russian-oriented presidents came to power in fraudulent elections. Struggles for power between the military, presidential, and governmental interests, as well as corrupted institutions triggered civil uprisings for democracy during the 2000s. By the late 2010s, fair elections stabilised governance that pursued to balance pro-Russia and pro-EU interests. After independence, prices, trade, and firms were freed, which reduced inflation, but large state-owned firms remained. Economy largely depends on local oligarchs, and on investments and remittances of the Armenian diaspora (Odling-Smee, 2024). For long, elections were fraudulent though improved during the 2010s, while media also gained more freedom.

Context of Azerbaijan. For centuries, Azerbaijan was controlled, or occupied by Iran and Russia. Its independence during several months in 1918 ended with the Soviet occupation. **Transition**. Azerbaijan has an area of 87,000 km^2 with 10 million people. It declared independence from the Soviet Union in 1991, which was driven by the nationalist civil organizations. Bloody civil war against Armenians and other minorities, as well as against the Soviet army, followed. The nationalist party took power after fraudulent elections, but was removed by subsequent social uprisings invoked by the loss of the Nagorno-Karabakh region to Armenia in 1993. A new nationalist ruler turned Azerbaijan into a dictatorship. Delayed economic reforms and control of economic activities by the state caused inflation and a decline of incomes during the 1990s. Economy improved during the 2000s when prices, trade and business are freed and several state firms are privatised, while fuel production remained state-owned (Gunes and Hajyieva, 2020). High international prices of fuel increased sales by the state firms, which triggered an economic boom during the 2010s (Suleymano and Aliyev, 2015). The economic governance is market-based, but fuel production is monopolised by rich oligarchs linked to the presidency while private firms can participate in oil and gas business. Dictatorial dynasty is vested, while media is controlled by the government.

Context of Turkmenistan. Turkmenistan was conquered by the Russian Empire. Subsequently, the Soviet Union occupied it after crushing the nationalist revolt in the 1920s, known as the Basmachi Rebellion. Local communist became the new rulers. **Transition.** Turkmenistan covers 488,000 km^2 with 6 million people, hosting large Uzbek and Russian minorities. It declared independence from the Soviet Union in 1991, which was enforced by the local communist ruler who became president and changed the constitution to secure his ruling position for life. Although nationalist governance is formally a multi-party and holds elections, it purges rivals and persecutes opposition. Meanwhile, external conflicts were resolved peacefully, including one about boarders with the neighbouring Uzbekistan. Its economic government continues in the communist style. Economic performances declined during the 1990s because of the plummeting fuel exports to neighbouring countries that also suffered economic crises after their independence. During the subsequent decades, relations to China and the Afghan Taliban improved, which enlarged fuel exports (Pomfret, 2001). The state sets prices and owns large companies. It allows small private businesses, while the state incomes are based on fuel exports (Repkine, 2004). The Turkmen economy boomed during the 2010s mainly due to growing fuel exports to China. Its governance remains totalitarian with minor cultural and educational reforms, while media is controlled by the government.

Context of Kazakhstan. Kazakhstan was part of the Russian Empire. It was an independent state during a few months of 1918, but conquered by the Soviet Union. Forced collectivization of farming and husbandry caused famines with more than one million deaths. Colonization by Russian and other nationalities followed. Sparsely populated area was used for testing and disposal of nuclear weapons, and for other hazardous activities. **Transition.** Kazakhstan covers 2,725,000 km^2 with 19 million people, including large Russian-speaking minority. Its communist ruler declared independence of the Soviet Union in 1991 after crushed civil uprising against this ruler. Independent Kazakhstan turned into presidential republic led by that communist ruler, re-elected in fraudulent elections. Close ties with Russia were kept. The economy is gradually being reformed. After 1993, prices, trade, and business were partially liberalized, and several state-owned firms were privatized with vouchers similar to those in Russia, while several state-owned firms were sold to foreign firms. Oil and gas firms were also sold, but re-nationalised during the 2000s (Larsson, 2010). After the death of the dictator in 2020, the new government aims to strike a balance in relations to Russia and the West and to diversify economy into higher-value activities, but the changes are slow (Bohr et al., 2014). Media is under the government control.

Context of Uzbekistan. The Russian Empire conquered Uzbekistan. During the 1920s, Uzbek national rulers joined the communists in crushing the Basmachi Rebellion aiming at independence. Forced collectivisation of farming caused famine with many thousand victims, while purges within the Uzbek governance continued during the 1930s until WW2. During WW2, it provided a shelter to a few million refugees from European territories. **Transition**. Uzbekistan covers 449,000 km^2 with a population of 84 million, including large Russian, Kazakh, and Tajik minorities. Its communist ruler declared independence from the Soviet Union in 1991. His, totalitarian ruling continued, despite terrorist attacks by Muslim insurgents, attempts to assassinate the ruler, and wars against the neighbouring Tajikistan and Kyrgyzstan. Opposition was defeated, and economic reforms were rejected, which avoided losses of income, but caused economic stagnation and corruption. Prices of local goods and small firms are freed, but controlled by the state. The Soviet-style economy continued for two decades after the independence (Pomfret, 2000). After the dictator's death in 2016, political and economic reforms were announced in the presidential elections, but the changes in governance evolved slowly (Tsereteli, 2018), and violence continued (Schmitz, 2020). Media is strictly controlled.

Context of Tajikistan. Tajik was an independent emirate (a Muslim kingdom) that was overthrown by the Soviet army in the 1920s. It was followed by social insurgency with large casualties and loss of nearly half of its territory to the communist Uzbekistan. **Transition**. Tajikistan covers 14,100 km^2 with 9.5 million, including large Kyrgyz and Russian-speaking minorities. Civil uprising initiated the Tajik independence from the Soviet Union in 1991. Soon, it is followed by civil war between the factions aiming at the Islamic state and at secular governance with many thousand causalities and mass emigration to Russia. Economic reforms are started after the civil war as late as 1997. Reforms of market economy were announced, but the enforcement was piecemeal (Iwasaki, 2002). Many prices and large holdings are controlled by the state while this economy floats on remittances from large Tajik diaspora mainly in Russia and Gulf countries (Amir & Berry, 2013). This presidential republic is governed by the dictator that controls media.

Context of Kyrgyzstan. Kyrgyzstan was a khanate (a nomadic kingdom) that was conquered by the Russian Empire in the late 1800s. National insurrection was oppressed by the Soviet Union in the 1920s, followed by local communist rulers. **Transition**. Kyrgyzstan covers 199,000 km^2 with 6.6 million people including and large minorities of Uzbeks, Mongols, and Slavs. It declared independence in 1991 after ethnic struggles between Uzbeks and Kyrgyz populations, which invoked the state of emergency in this republic. An independent social leader emerged during the conflicts to become an unopposed president in a fair election. Soon, he turned into an autocratic ruler with close ties to Russia. Economic reforms with free prices, trade, and business are announced, but postponed. Parts of agriculture and large industries remained state owned, and corrupt state controls continued for longer than decade (Abazov, 1999).Mass demonstrations calling for more democracy and economic reforms in 2005 brought opposition to power. A Parliamentary republic is established, but conflicts with the previous ruler continued. The civil uprising against corruption five years later, and struggles between Kyrgyz and Uzbeks with many victims changed the ruling again. The Kyrgyz governance stabilised by the late 2010s with more political and economic freedoms, but media is controlled. A short cross-border war with neighbouring Tajikistan ten years later is resolved peacefully.

Governance in the satellite countries and Baltic republics shifted to liberal-democracies after radical economic reforms, except in Hungary and Croatia, where the authoritarian rulings and slow economic reforms took place. In the former Soviet republics, wew governances dominated by local oligarchies developed in various directions. Moldova, Ukraine, Georgia, Armenia, and Kyrgyzstan swinged between authoritarian and liberal ruling. While Russia evolved toward a totalitarian state after radical economic reforms, dictatorial Kazakhstan gradually liberalised after economic reforms. Meanwhile, dictators in Azerbaijan, Belarus, Turkmenistan, Uzbekistan, and Tajikistan announced reforms but maintained strict controls.

5.4 Successful Transitions

It is assessed, what political transitions were successful measured by the transition factors, what were performances of the transition countries measured by indicators of prosperity, what were the drivers of these successes, and if good governance matches successful transitions. Successful transitions are comprehended as major shifts in governances indicated by high scores on the transitional factors. Successes in prosperity are shown in Appendix G. Changes in the transition countries are compared to the EU without changes in governances, as well as to India with minor changes, and to China with major changes in governances. The drivers of successes refer to the transition factors. Match with good governance is assessed with several indices in databases presented in Appendix H. All those issues are assessed subsequently.

Successes of the political transition reflect ideas in hindsight, which is incomparably easier to express than the forecasting of successes. Nevertheless, such reflection helps to define necessary capabilities for changes in governances though these capabilities illustrate only the conditions for the changes, but no guarantees of changes. Ultimately, political decisions determine the course of actions. This assessment of successful political transitions is based on scoring each country on the earlier mentioned transition factors. Per country, each factor is scored with 2 points for the definitely observed event, 1 point for partially observed, and no points for negligibly observed. For example, Poland experienced independence during the existence of the Soviet Union for more than two decades, while Georgia only had independence for several months, and Turkmenistan has no experience with independence during the existence of the Soviet Union. They are scored for the independence heritage with 2, 1, and 0 points, respectively. National minorities in populations before the governmental shifts scored 2 points for the minorities below 20% of the populations as in Bulgaria, 1 point for the minorities between 20 and 30% of the populations as in Ukraine, and 0 for the minorities above 30% of the population as in Estonia. When citizen initiatives were decisive for the shifts in power as in Lithuania, it has scored 2 points, whereas modest or mixed initiatives of citizens and governments scored 1 point as in Moldova, and weak initiatives scored 0 points as in Croatia. If economic reforms took place within a few years after the shift of power as in Russia they are scored with 2 points, if they are delayed or reverse as in Kazakhstan they are scored with 1 point, and negligible reforms are scored with 0 as in Uzbekistan. Free media throughout the transition period as in Romania are scored with 2 points, but if free media are limited during a period as in Kyrgyzstan it is scored with 1 point, and when media are continuously oppressed as in Tajikistan it is scored with 0 points.

Table 5.1 shows 23 transition countries in column 1, with a chronology of shifts in the governments in column 2. This chronology is based on the initial free elections in the satellite countries and declarations of independence in the former Soviet republics. The contextual factors are in columns 3–4, and the process factors are in columns 5–7. The sum of the scores is in column 8. Given equal scores of several countries, the process factors are summed up to determine the final ranking. This sum is shown in column 9. The ranking of countries in descending order of successful transition from 1 to 23 are presented in column 10. Scores of 8 to 10 points, shown in green colour in 7 countries, indicate successful transitions. Scores of 5 to 7 points, shown in yellow in 9 countries, are partially successful. Scores below 5 points, shown in red in 7 countries, indicate similar governances during two decades after the changes of governments.

Table 5.1 Patterns in the political transitions

Countries	Shift of power	Contextual factors		Factors in the transition process			Total factors score	Corrected for the process factors	Ranking successful transitions
		Heritage independence	National minority	Citizen initiative	Economic reforms	Political trust			
Czech	Jun/90	2	2	2	2	2	10	6	1
Lithuania	Mar/90	2	2	2	2	2	10	6	2
Poland	Jun/89	2	2	2	2	2	10	6	3
Romania	May/90	2	2	2	1	2	9	5	4
Estonia	May/90	2	0	2	2	2	8	6	5
Latvia	Aug/90	2	0	2	2	2	8	6	6
Slovenia	Apr/91	1	2	1	2	2	8	5	7
Slovakia	Jun/90(*)	1	2	1	1	2	7	4	8
Hungary	Mar/90	2	1	1	1	2	7	4	9
Bulgaria	Jun/90	2	2	1	1	1	7	3	10
Georgia	Apr/91	1	1	2	1	1	6	4	11
Ukraine	Dec/91	1	1	2	1	1	6	4	12
Croatia	Apr/91	1	2	1	1	1	6	3	13
Kyrgyzstan	Aug/91	1	0	2	1	1	5	4	14
Armenia	Sep/91	1	2	0	1	1	5	2	15
Russia	Jun/91	2	1	0	2	0	5	2	16
Moldova	Aug/91	1	0	1	1	1	4	3	17
Tajikistan	Sep/91	1	1	1	1	0	4	2	18
Azerbaijan	Aug/91	1	0	1	1	0	3	2	19
Kazakhstan	Dec/91	1	0	1	1	0	3	2	20
Turkmenistan	Oct/91	1	1	0	0	0	2	0	21
Uzbekistan	Aug/91	1	1	0	0	0	2	0	22
Belarus	Aug/91	0	1	0	0	0	1	0	23

2 – definitely observed, 1 – partially observed, 0 – negligibly observed.
(*) chronology together with Czech

Most successful transitions are found in the European countries, while three of them were former Soviet republics. All successful transitions entered the EU, but Slovakia, Hungary and Bulgaria among present EU members are not considered as successful transitions. Apparently, entry into the EU governance facilitated the transition process, but it is not decisive. Nearly all countries assessed as unsuccessful transitions are found in Asia. This finding largely confirms the mainstream idea about the transactional tradition of the governances in Europe that differ from the directive governances in Asia. However, politicians determine the shifts in governances and their decisions change in time. For example, political decisions turned Hungary away from democracy toward the authoritarian governance aligned with the dictatorship in Russia, whereas political decisions in Moldova, Armenia, and Kyrgyzstan turned toward more democratic governances.

Performances in improving prosperity in the transition countries are assessed as indexes of 1992 in 2002 and in 2012 compared to the EU, China, and India. Prosperity is indicated by GDP growth per capita, lower inequality, longer average life expectancy and lower share of industry in GDP. Results covered in Appendix G are summarised below. Most transition countries became more prosperous after thirty years of political transitions, but prosperity in Russia and Ukraine hardly increased. Prosperities increased despite lower shares of industrial activities in most countries. Large differences across countries are also observed, particularly between the performances of the EU-entrants and non-entrants. The EU-entrants had a better start, and most of their performances improved more than the performances of non-entrants. The EU-entrants prospered more than the EU as a whole, which implies that they gained from the entry; if the EU gained is not assessed. Non-entrants had a lower level of prosperity at the start, and their performances improved slower. While the GDP per capita of non-entrant countries grew, the living conditions of people in the EU entrant countries improved more than in non-entrant ones. Most EU-entrants and non-entrants were highly industrialized countries. The shares of industry in GDP in a few countries exceeded even the share in China that is widely considered to be the global manufacturing hub. High share of the industry is presumably the heritage of the communist ideology preoccupied with technologies for processing of the natural resources. While the share of industry in China increased, it decreased in most of the non-entrants, except in Belarus where the communist governance continued. The living conditions in the EU entrants remained better than in the non-entrant countries even after twenty years of political transition. Performances of the successful transitions improved slower than in China that also experienced the transition from the state directives to market negotiations, but faster than in India whose mixed state-market governance is liberalised. The political transition was important for the prosperity of EU-entrants and non-entrants, but it was not the panacea.

Factors that determine successes refer to the timing of changes in governments and to those transition factors. The timing of changes was important for the successes. Struggles for power within elites of Soviet Union during the late-1980s enabled the development of oppositional citizen initiatives in several satellite countries Union and

Soviet republics. They emerged during the period when countries elites were indecisive about policies, regarding deploring economic performances. Hence, political oppression was relaxed. Such situations enabled preparation of citizen initiatives and elites for the shifts in power, which eventually took place. Early shift in government, ones before the decomposition of the Soviet Union, could take advantage of that relaxation in order to realise more successful transitions than their followers. In effect, most fast movers experienced more successful political transitions than the laggards, which is indicated by high correlation between the timing of shifts in power and ranking of successful transitions ($R^2 = 0.8$). Those shifts in power evolved fast. After the first shift in the mid-1989 in Poland, 6 power shifts emerged in other countries within a few months, followed by 8 other shifts within a year. Governments changed in 15 countries before the disintegration of the Soviet Union in 1991. Mostly, the satellite countries moved fast, but also a few Soviet republics. All 23 countries changed governments after 2.5 years. The last one was Kazakhstan by the end of 1991, if the separation of Czech and Slovakia in 1993 is neglected. Countries where power has shifted later than one year after the shift in Poland have been only partially successful, shown yellow, or changed governments without major shifts in governance, shown red. Fast actions were relevant for the successful political transitions.

No specific transition factor stands out as the decisive one. All factors are relevant and highly correlated with the rankings, except for the 'national minority'. This finding underpins that mono-causalities provide insufficient explanations of the political transitions.

All fast movers experienced a few decades of independent statehood before subordination to the Soviet Union, except Slovenia that was divided between Austria, Italy, and Serbia. Most laggards experienced short statehoods, or had no states during the Soviet ruling. Long heritage of independence of Russia is exceptional. Shorter Soviet ruling is presumably more important for the successes of political transition than the mainstream idea about the European 'civilisation'.

Although the scores on 'national minorities' have low correlation to the successes in transition, they are important. Large national minorities did trigger violence in several transition countries, including wars between Armenia and Azerbaijan, Kyrgyzstan and Uzbekistan, as well as in Moldova, Georgia, and Ukraine with Russia, and among the republics of Yugoslavia. Some conflicts cooled down, but the Russian invasion of Ukraine expanded from 2014 onward. Spread of the Hungarian-speaking minority among neighbouring Slovakia, Romania, Ukraine, and Serbia did avoid large national minorities in one country, but generated national sentiments that are exploited by the authoritarian Hungarian government.

Citizen initiatives operated illegally within the Soviet Union and its satellites, but the oppression and initiatives are not directly linked. For example, citizen initiatives for changes of governments did not emerge in rather mild authoritarian regimes in Hungary, former Yugoslavia, and Georgia, compared to more oppressing rulings in the Baltic states, Romania, Bulgaria and Kyrgyzstan where citizen initiatives did emerge and prepared changes of the governments. Oppressive rulings were certainly relevant, but not decisive. Well-organized, united opposition that could influence elite in order to reach agreements with the rulers were more important and realized in Poland, Georgia, and Czechoslovakia, among others. Citizen initiatives that gained the support of mass organisations as the church in Poland, or army in Russia could shift power when window of opportunity emerged. Contrary to that, rival factions within the citizens initiatives caused collisions that undermined political transitions as in Georgia and Ukraine. National and religious struggles undermined citizen initiatives in Azerbaijan, Armenia, Kyrgyzstan, and Tajikistan.

Economic reforms emerged in the countries where new governances were introduced, whereas changes of governments in Hungary, Bulgaria, Tajikistan, among others had minor impacts on the economic governance. Economic reforms were reversed in Belarus and Kazakhstan, while they were opposed all together in Uzbekistan and Turkmenistan. Local political interests were decisive for the economic reforms. For example, the ruling parties in Georgia and Russia implemented radical reforms, while the Armenian rulers delayed them and the Azeri ones opposed them. Local political interests are also decisive for the results of economic reforms. So, radical reforms modernised Czech and Estonian economies, which fostered the democratic governances. However,similar reforms in Russia and Ukraine reinforced corrupt oligarchies that exploited the Russians and Ukrainians citizens. Such differences indicate the importance of political changes for economic relations.

Political tolerance, measured by free press, is a fluid concept. Most fast movers established political tolerance. However, Hungary and Slovakia among the fast movers evolved toward authoritarian governance with limitations for media, contrary to laggards whose initially authoritarian governances gradually liberalised as in Armenia and Moldova. Among the 'laggards', political tolerance declined in Russia as it turned into a dictatorship, while it increased in Ukraine. Meanwhile, vested dictatorships remained until the death of the dictators in Azerbaijan, Kazakhstan, Turkmenistan, Uzbekistan, and Tajikistan. As all dictators kept power until death changes of dictatorships should not be expected, unless defeated by struggles, or collapsing economy.

Good governance is compared to the ranking with the transition factors based on several indexes. Details about the indexes can be found in Appendix H. Correlations between the rankings with the indexes and with transition factors are estimated, as well as the number of matches among successful and unsuccessful transitions. These indexes cover : democracy (BST), institutional capabilities (EIU), economic liberties (IEF), corruption (CPI), governance (WGI), happiness (HAP), and ease of doing business (EDB). The match measured by correlations is indicated by regressions: R^2 above 0.8 indicates a match, R^2 between 0.5 and 0,8 shows moderate matches, and lower regressions no matches. The ranking of successful transitions matches democracy (BST) and institutional capabilities (EIU) regarding high correlations ($R^2 = 0.9$). Successful transitions are also correlated ($R^2 = 0.8$) with low corruption (CPI). Economic liberties (IEF), but the governance performance (WGI) show moderate correlation ($R^2 = 0.7$). Low correlations are found for the ranking with the happiness index (HAP), and the index for ease of doing business (EDB).

It is also assessed if the highly ranked countries with the transition factors match the countries highly rankedon with the indexes. Reasonable scores are found. Six of seven countries assessed as successful transitions match the EIU, CPI, and HAP. Five successful countries match BST and FREE, but only four matches EDB. Romania and Bulgaria, ranked among moderately successful transitions, tend to score lower on those indexes. The successful political transitions delivered democracies and capable institutions, but not per se high scores on happiness neither the best governances for doing business.

Combined independence heritage and limited nationalist aspiration, as well as citizen initiatives, economic freedom, and political tolerance enable successful political transitions, which generated prosperity and enabled good governance in the sense of democracies and capable institutions.

5.5 Performances for Sustainable Development

It is assessed if the successful political transitions enhance sustainable development compared to less successful ones. As the successful ones, are driven by democratic governance with capable institutions this outcome implies that democracies are better equipped for changes toward sustainable development than the authoritarian governances.

The performances of transition countries are defined as annual average changes on the indicators for economy, well-being and environmental qualities during 1991–2015. They are estimated for 23 transition countries, and compared to ones in the USA, EU, and China. Table 5.2 shows the performances. Rows show countries in the descending order of successful transitions. Based on the former Table 5.1 they are grouped in successful transitions in seven countries in green colours, moderately successful nine countries in yellow, and seven unsuccessful ones in red. Columns show the countries' ranking based on the index for democracies (BST) and the countries' performances on indicators for sustainable development. Below these performance indicators, the criteria for high, moderate and low performances, and correlations of the rankings based on transition factors and based on performances are presented. The ranking based on institutional capabilities (EIU) is not shown because nearly the same as with the BST.

Next to the correlations between the ranking with transition factor and the performance indicators, it is assessed how many successful transition countries match high performance on the indicators. This match is illustrated for GDP growth. Fast growth is considered above 4% annual average, moderate one 1% to 4%, and slow growth is below 1%. While correlation is low ($R^2 = 0.3$), fast growth matches 3 of seven successful transitions, one of 9 moderately successful transitions, and none of 7 unsuccessful transitions. This finding implies the successful transitions often generate fast economic growth compared to the unsuccessful ones. In addition to the match with successful transition, the matches with the indexes for democracy (BST) and for institutional capabilities (EIU) are estimated. Several indicators not shown in the Table 5.2 are used for explanations of the (mis)match with the (un)successful political transitions.

Economic indicators cover income growth and changes of economic structure. Income growth is indicated by GDP in USD_{2015} per person. Real incomes grew faster in the countries with successful transitions than in the unsuccessful ones. Although the cross-country correlation between the income growth and the transitions ranking is low ($R^2 = 0.3$), the matching shows tangible results. As income grew 0.9% in the EU28 and 9.2% in China, fast income growth in the transition countries is set in-between at above 4% annual average. Fast income growth is achieved in 3 of 7 successful transitions compared to only one among the moderately successful ones and none among the unsuccessful transitions. Among the unsuccessful transitions, the Russian and Kyrgyz incomes hardly increased, while the Ukrainian and Tajik income per capita decreased. A popular explanation of the income growth is radical reform of economies. However, Russian, and Ukrainian incomes grew slowly after radical reforms, while the Croatian income grew fast after modest reforms. Economic reforms were important but not decisive for fast income growth. Neither large inflow of foreign investment can explain fast income growth regarding high inflows into slowly growing Georgia, as well as into moderately growing Azerbaijan and Turkmenistan with large sales of fossil fuels. Meanwhile, the inflows of foreign investments decreased in the successful transitions with fast growing economies of Estonia and Latvia. Foreign investments were minor factors for the successful transitions and income growth.

Changes in economic structure were more important for the income growth. These changes are indicated by the decline of nature rents and fuel use in GDP. The declines of nature rents are moderately correlated with the successful transitions ($R^2 = 0.5$). Matching provides tangible results. Decline of the nature rents indicates changes towards higher value activities contrary to an increase of the nature rents which indicates a reinforcment of the incumbent businesses. While 3 of 7 successful transitions generated major changes in economic structure, all unsuccessful country and most of moderately successful ones increased dependency on the nature rents from minerals. Higher value adding activities in GDP in the countries of successful transitions were not driven by larger and better R&D given that their R&D and IPR per capita did not grow faster than the unsuccessful ones. Meanwhile, the successful transitions also reduced uses of fossil fuels faster than the unsuccessful ones, which is not shown in the Table. The decreasing fuel uses are observed among 6 of 7 successful transition countries and an increase in one, compared to the increases in 3 of 7 unsuccessful transitions. Highly and moderately successful transitions countries reduced fuel uses per capita faster than the USA and EU28, whereas the fuel use increased in China, as well as in the unsuccessful transitions in the fuel exporting Azerbaijan, Kazakhstan and Turkmenistan. However, agriculture in the successful transitions did not outperform the unsuccessful ones measured by the fertilizer uses per cereal production.

The quasi-autonomous innovation mechanism driven by competition was key to the changes in economies, thereby income growth. The successful transitions changed their economies for higher value activities, while the unsuccessful ones reinforced interests in low-value mineral and fuel production. The entry into the EU was more important for the establishment of capable institutions than the inflow of foreign investments.

Well-being is indicated by the decrease of poverty, enrolment in the tertiary education, and reduction of the infant mortality. Poverty is measured by the percentage of people below USD 6.85 per day per person. This was low and decreased in all successful transitions, except strong increase in Slovenia, the wealthiest country before the transition. Unfortunately, 4 of 7 unsuccessful transitions did not provide any data on poverty. Successful transition countries decreased poverty faster than the USA, EU, and China. Another indicator of well-being is the percentage of people who have enroled in tertiary education as a percentage of the population. This indicates the enlarging capabilities. Successful transitions tangibly outperformed all other transition countries given high correlation of the rankings based on the transition factors and enrolments ($R^2 = 0.8$). The successful transitions in Europe also outperformed the USA, the EU28, and China. Infant mortality indicates the capabilities of health services. Infant mortality decreased in all transition countries. The highest improvements in performances are achieved by unsuccessful transition countries where highest infant mortalities are found before the transition period, as in Tajikistan. Across countries, successful transitions did not outperform the unsuccessful ones with respect to the reduction of infant mortality. Successful transitions had lower poverty and higher health standards, and they outperformed other transition countries with respect to capabilities in education. The increasing capabilities due to higher education facilitated the economic shift towards higher value activities.

Environmental performances are indicated by freshwater withdrawal, CO_2 emission reduction, and forest areas, all per capita. Freshwater use in m^3 per person decreased in nearly all transition countries. Increases are observed in Latvia and Croatia where water uses were low, and in Armenia with fourfold larger water use. Across the transition countries, successful ones did not outperform less successful ones. CO_2 emissions in tons per person are reduced in nearly all countries of political transitions, but increases are observed in Croatia and Turkmenistan. Most transition countries outperformed the decreases in the USA and the EU28, whereas the emissions increased in China much faster than in any of the transition countries. The successful transitions did not outperform the unsuccessful ones. For example, the unsuccessful Moldova reduced CO_2 emission by nearly 5% annual average along with a 1.6% GDP growth. NOx emissions are also reduced by all transition countries, except an increase in Armenia, but successful transitions did not perform better than less successful ones. NOx emission reduction is not shown in the Table because the patterns are similar to CO_2 emission reduction. The forest area in m^3 per person increased in all successful transitions, except in Czech. Meanwhile, the forest areas decreased in all unsuccessful transitions, except for an increase in Moldova and Belarus. Across countries, the afforestation in successful transition countries outperformed less successful ones ($R^2 = 0.5$). While forest areas increased in 3 of 7 successful transitions, the areas decreased in all unsuccessful ones. The improvements in environmental performances across the transition countries can largely be attributed to the collapse of obsolete firms along with emergences of new firms that increased value and efficiency in uses of materials and fuels.

Overall, countries with successful transitions generated democratic governances with high institutional capabilities, which improved performances on nmost indicators for sustainable development. Tangibly better performances of the successful transitions compared to the unsuccessful ones are observed in the income growth, driven by shifts from low-value processing of natural resources towards higher value activities in industry and services, facilitated by the growing entry into higher education. These shifts can be attributed to the quasi-autonomous innovation-mechanism driven by competition. Larger afforestation areas in the successful transitions than in the unsuccessful ones can be attributed to the societal demands that induced afforestation. However, the inducement of innovations for other environmental improvements lagged behind the economic and social changes during the political transitions. Better environmental performances in the successful and less successful transitions can largely be explained by the collapse of inefficient firms and entry of more efficient technologies in new firms. Variation in the performances of individual countries can be explained by the country-specific policies.

5.6 Conclusions

It is assessed; what kinds of governance generate changes for sustainable development. The assessment is based on the experiences with the political transitions, which were not purposed for sustainable development, but aimed at the changes of governance. These political transitions emerged after the decomposition of the Soviet Union in 23 countries during the period 1989 to 2022. Eleven of them became members of the European Union. Among the EU-entrants, Poland, Hungary, Czechia, Slovakia, Romania, and Bulgaria were former satellites of the Soviet Union, while Estonia, Latvia, and Lithuania were Soviet Union republics, and Slovenia and Croatia were former Yugoslav republics. Non-entrants were Russia, Belarus, Moldova, Armenia, Azerbaijan, Kazakhstan, Uzbekistan, Tajikistan, and Kyrgyzstan that participated in the Confederation of Independent States, as well as Ukraine, Georgia, and Turkmenistan outside both blocks. Using theories on political transitions, five factors that drive changes in governance are defined. These are the heritage of independent statehood and percentage minorities within population, which provide the context for the political transitions, as well as citizen initiatives, economic liberties, and free media, which determine the processes of the transitions. Per country, these factors are assessed with literature, followed by scores per factors, and summing up for the ranking of the successes in political transitions. A transition is considered successful when the country's governance has changed, meaning its institutions are shifted not only government.

Governances evolve in different directions. Czech Republic, Lithuania, Poland, Romania, Estonia, Latvia, and Slovenia are assessed as successful. These seven countries were independent states before their subordination to the Soviet Union, except Slovenia. They had small minorities, aside Estonia and Latvia. Their citizen initiated the shifts in governments, though partially in Slovenia. They introduced the economic

Table 5.2 Scores of political transitions on the sustainability indicators (G—green, Y—yellow, R.—red)

Countries	Rank success	BTS rank	Economic indicators			Social indicators			Environmental indicators		
			GDP growth G,>4 Y.1 t 4 R.<1	Nature rents G,<4 Y.1 t 4 R.>4	Fuel use per capita G,<-2 Y.-2 t 0 R.>0	Poverty G,<-5 Y.0 t -5 R>0	Tert. educ. G,>5 Y.1-5 R.<1	Infant mortal. G,<-5 Y.- 4 t -5 R.<-4	Water use G,<-2 Y.-2 t -1 R.<1	CO_2 emission G,<-2 Y.-2 t -1 R.>-1	Forest area G,>1 Y.0-1 R.<0
Correlations descending success of transition and indicators (R^2)			0.3	0.5	0.1	0.2	0.8	0.1	0.0	0.0	0.5
Czech	1	2	1.8%	0.8%	-1.3%	-3.0%	6.0%	-5.1%	-1.4%	-1.7%	-0.03%
Lithuania	2	3	5.9%	-5.3%	-2.8%	-7.8%	3.3%	-4.3%	-14%	-2.5%	1.4%
Poland	3	8	3.7%	8.9%	-0.7%	-12.3	5.1%	-4.9%	-0.9%	-0.7%	0.25%
Romania	4	9	2.5%	-0.8%	-2.8%	-5.6%	7.6%	-4.7%	-3.8%	-2.5%	0.96%
Estonia	5	1	5.4%	2.5%	-2.3%	-9.3%	4.9%	-6.7%	-0.9%	-1.8%	1.23%
Latvia	6	5	5.2%	-1.3%	-2.0%	-8.2%	4.7%	-4.6%	0.4%	-2.3%	1.44%
Slovenia	7	4	2.6%	4.7%	0.1%	12.6%	5.4%	-5.4%	-0.1%	-0.1%	0.06%
Slovakia	8	6	3.8%	30%	-1.6%	-3.1%	5.8%	-3.4%	-3.9%	-2.3%	-0.05%
Hungary	9	12	2.0%	-1.1%	-1.0%	0.4%	5.2%	-4.7%	-1.5%	-1.5%	0.70%
Bulgaria	10	10	2.1%	6.9%	-1.2%	-9.0%	4.1%	-3.2%	-0.3%	-0.9%	1.32%
Georgia	11	14	1.7%	10%	-1.6%	-1.9%	1.3%	-5.8%	-2.1%	-2.6%	1.08%
Ukraine	12	11	-1.1%	3.7%	-3.2%	-6.0%	-1.8%	-2.8%	-2.6%	-4.2%	0.71%
Croatia	13	7	4.01%	7.8%	-0.7%	1.8%	4.7%	-3.5%	1.1%	0.01%	0.68%
Kyrgyzstan	14	16	0.0%	26%	-3.1%	-0.6%	2.5%	-4.1%	-2.4%	-2.6%	-0.86%
Armenia	15	13	3.95%	117%	-0.9%	-3.8%	3.6%	-4.8%	2.7%	-1.5%	0.66%
Russia	16	17	0.9%	4.6%	-0.7%	-1.7	1.6%	-3.8%	-1.7%	-1.0%	0.13%
Moldova	17	15	1.6%	2.5%	-4.6%	-3.2	N.A.	-2.9%	-3.2%	-4.6%	0.89%
Tajikistan	18	22	-0.6%	13%	-3.6%	N.A.	0.8%	-3.9%	-4.3%	-3.3%	-1.76%
Azerbaijan	19	20	3.6%	7.0%	0.0%	N.A.	0.3%	-5.0%	-2.4%	-2.5%	-0.64%
Kazakhstan	20	18	2.6%	9.3%	0.1%	-9.8%	1.0%	-5.6%	-1.6%	-0.7%	-0.11%
Turkmenistan	21	23	2.8%	8.6%	0.8%	N.A.	N.A.	-2.5%	-1.1%	0.9%	-1.64%
Uzbekistan	22	21	2.4%	9.5%	-3.0%	N.A.	-2.7%	-5.0%	-1.0%	-2.2%	-0.38%
Belarus	23	19	3.2%	4.8%	-1.6%	-19%	2.5%	-5.0%	-1.3%	-1.9%	0.72
Comparison to a few large economies	USA		0.9%	-0.1%	-0.7%	2.0%	0.9%	-2.0%	-1.2%	-0.8%	-0.9%
	EU		0.9%	2.9%	-0.6%	10.5%	3.4%	-4.1%	-1.6%	-1.0%	0.5%
	China		9.2%	-0.6%	5.7%	-3.7%	12.0%	-6.2%	-0.2%	5.5%	0.4%

liberalisation soon after the shift, and they allowed free media throughout the transition period. All successful transitions entered the EU. Partially successful Hungary, Croatia, Bulgaria, and Slovakia together with Czech also entered the EU, but Slovakia and Croatia had little independence heritage, ruling communists in Hungary and Bulgaria changed only governments with minor economic reforms and constrained media. Including those, nine countries were considered only partially successful. They had little experience with statehoods, except Hungary and Russia and had large minorities, except Croatia, Slovakia and Armenia. Their communist rulers drove the shifts in governances, except in Georgia and Kyrgyzstan. Liberalisation of economies was delayed except in Russia and Ukraine. Their media were oppressed. Russia, among them, evolved toward dictatorship while others swinged between the authoritarian and democratic governances. Moldova, Azerbaijan, Kazakhstan, Tajikistan, Turkmenistan, Uzbekistan and Belarus are assessed as the unsuccessful transitions. They hardly experienced statehoods, hosted large minorities, shifts of their governments were driven by the local communist rulers, though only partly in Moldova, economic reforms were slow, and media were oppressed. All of them vested the non-communist dictatorships, except Moldova that evolved toward democracy.

All successful transitions were first movers in the political transition as they changed governments before the decomposition of the Soviet Union. Fast shifts of the governments were important for successful political transitions because did not give time for re-enforcement of the communist elite. In addition to the experiences of statehood and small national minorities as the context of political transitions, several conditions in addition to each other facilitated these transition process. None of those five factors stands out as the decisive one for the successful political transition. Although citizen initiatives were oppressed by the authoritarian governance in the Soviet Union and its satellite, organised citizen initiatives were essential for the successful political transitions. Contrary to the that, if only governments changed without changes in institutions, authoritarian governances were re-established by the incumbent elites, entailing dictatorial regimes in several of them. After deep economic crisis, former Soviet satellites and three Soviet republics that joined the EU28 steadily evolved toward prosperous civil societies, whereas all other former Soviet republics remained authoritarian where prosperity fluctuated, or stagnated. Successful transitions vested good governance measured by the indexes for democracy, economic freedom, low corruption, and high institutional performances, though not per se highly scoring on the indexes for happiness and ease of doing business.

Most political transitions improved performances on several sustainability indicators, but prosperity hardly increased in Russia, Ukraine, Moldova, Kyrgyzstan and Tajikistan. The successful transitions performed better than the unsuccessful ones on several indicators for economy, well-being, and environmental qualities during 1990–2015. The successful ones generated faster economic growth mainly through the shifts to higher value activities largely due to more efficient uses of materials and fossil fuels. This underpins the importance of the quasi-autonomous innovation mechanism when competition is allowed. The domestic resources were decisive, whereas foreign investments hardly contributed to higher value. Successful transitions also delivered superior results for well-being. Poverty decreased in most successful transitions, except in relatively wealthy Slovenia, where it declined. Poverty increased despite economic growth in several less successful transitions. Successful transitions enabled more people to enter higher education than less successful ones, which is important for the economic changes towards value adding activities. Meanwhile, health services improved in all transition countries. Environmental performance improved in most transitions countries. Freshwater withdrawal was reduced in all countries, aside Croatia and Armenia, but unsuccessful transition countries with high uses of water hardly reduced it. Most transition countries reduced CO_2 and NOx emissions per capita, while the successful transitions did not perform better than the unsuccessful ones. Forest areas per capita increased in all successful transitions, except Czech, whereas they decreased in all unsuccessful ones, except Moldova and Belarus. Societal and policy demands rarely induced environmental performances, except for forestry in the successful transitions.

Experiences with the political transition provide several lessons in the process of changes toward sustainable development. Firstly, people find ways to go around and resist oppressive directives, while alignment to societal interests and co-operative resolutions of issues are better accepted. Second lesson is that the democratic governances generate higher performances in economy, well-being and environmental qualities than the authoritarian governances. They enable societies to generate economic growth based on high-value activities, enlarge human capabilities due to accessible education, and foster nature. Third, while politics and policies are important, changes in governances need to overcome the resistance of the dominant political and economic interests. Institutional innovations are needed for sustainable development. Last but not least, independent citizens' organisations are necessary for initiation of changes for sustainable development, while good governance is needed for balancing these initiatives with other stakeholder interests and preventing harmful events. Experiences with the political transitions show that the democratic governances outperform the autocratic ones on most sustainability indicators.

References

Abazov, R. (1999). Policy of economic transition. *Central Asian Survey, 18*(2), 197–223.

Acemoğlu, D., & Robinson, J. A. (1999). *A theory of political transition*. Cambridge: Massachusetts Institute of Technology

Amir, O., & Berry, A. (2013). Challenges of transition economies: Economic reforms, emigration, and employment in Tajikistan. In A. Berry (ed.), *Social Protection, Growth and Employment Evidence from India, Kenya, Malawi, Mexico and Tajikistan*. New York: United Nations Development Program.

Ash, T. G. (1990). *We, the people*. Grant Books.

Åslund, A. (2005). The economic policy of Ukraine after the orange revolution. *Eurasian Geography and Economics, 46*(5), 327–353.

Beissinger, M. R. (2007). Structure and example in modular political phenomena: The diffusion of Bulldozer/Rose/Orange/Tulip revolutions. *Perspective on Politics, 5*(2), 259–276.

Beissinger, M. R. (1992). Elites and ethnic identities in Soviet Union and Post-Soviet politics. In A. J. Motyl (Ed.), *The Post Soviet Nations*. New York: Columbia University Press.

Bohr, A., Brauer, B., Gould-Davies, N., Kassenova, N., Lillis, J., Mallinson, K., Nixey, J., & Satpayev, D. (2014). *Kazakhstan tested by transition*. Chatham House Report

Brada, J. C. (1991). The economic transition of Czechoslovakia from plan to market. *Journal of Economic Perspectives, 5*(4), 171–177.

Brown, J. D. J. S., & Earle, A. T. (2006). The productivity effects of privatization: Longitudinal estimates from Hungary, Romania, Russia and Ukraine. *Journal of Political Economy, 114*, 61–99.

Bruszt, L., Campos, F., Fidrmuc, J., & Roland, G. (2010). *Civil society, institutional change and the politics of reform: The great transition*. Discussion Paper No. 7825. London: Center for Economic Policy Research.

Burke, J. (2014). Post-soviet world. *Guardian*, 9–6–2014. Retrieved March, 4, 2024, from https://www.theguardian.com/world/2014/jun/09/-sp-profiles-post-soviet-states

Dabrowski, M. (2023). *A limping transition: The former soviet union thirty years on*. Bruegel.

Dabrowski, M. (2003). Moldova: major economic problems and challenges. *Background paper for the UNDP Roundtable on Social-Economic Issues organized at the request of the President of Moldova* on April 12, 2003. Chisinau, Warsaw.

Demekas, D.G., & Khan, M. S. (1991). *The Romanian economic reform program*. Washington D.C: International Monetary Fund. WP/91/80.
Doorn van, M. (2014). The nature of tolerance and the social circumstances in which it emerges. *Current Sociology Review*, 1–23.
Estrin, S., Hanousek, J., Kočenda, E., & Svejnar, J. (2009). The effects of privatization and ownership in transition economies. *Journal of Economic Literature, 47*(3), 699–728.
Fukuyama, F. (2008). About relations between the political and economic dimension of development. In: Governance, Growth and Development (pp. 25–34). Washington D.C: World Bank.
Gessen, M. (2018). *The Future is History. How Totalitarism Reclaimed Russia*. Penguin, Random House, New York.
Gibson, J. L., Duch, R. M., & Tedin, K. L. (1992). Democratic values and the transformation of the soviet union. *The Journal of Politics*, *54*(2), 329–371/
Glaeson, G. (1992). The "National Factor" and the logic of Sovietology. In A. J. Motyl (Ed.), *The Post-Soviet Nations*. New York: Columbia University Press
Guerin, D., Petry, F., & Crete, J. (2004). Tolerance, protest and democratic transition: Survey evidence from 13 post-communist countries. *European Journal of Political Research, 43*(3), 371–395.
Gunes, M., & Hajiyeva, H. (2020). The stages of development of the transition economy: The case of Azerbaijan. *International Journal of Academic Research in Economics & Management Sciences., 9*(2), 89–101.
Heller, M., & Nekrich, A. (1982). *Geschichte der Soviet Union, I and II*. Athenäum, Köningstein/Ts.
Huntington, S. P. (1993). The clash of civilizations? *Foreign Affairs, 72*, 21–49.
Hutchinson, J. (2019). Nationalism and war, a review of the literature. *Studies on National Movements* 4. Retrieved May 4, 2024, from https://stateofnationalism.eu/article/nationalism-and-war/.
Iashvili, T. (2019). The essentials of Georgia's economic transformation. *Wroclaw Review of Law, Administration & Economics, 9*(1), 1–12.
Iwasaki, I. (2002). *Economic transformation and institutional development in Tajikistan*. PIE Project Discussion Paper Series No. 120, Institute of Economic Research, Hitotsubashi University.
Kaltwasser, C. R. (2019). *Populism and the economy: An ambivalent relationship*. Friederich Ebert Stiftung.
King, C. (2000). Post-post communism, transition, comparison, and the end of "Eastern Europe." *World Politics, 53*, 143–172.
Krišjane, Z. (2005). Latvia: A centre-oriented country in transition. In B. Müller, M. Finka, & G. Lintz (Eds.), *Rise and Decline of Industry in Central and Eastern Europe* (pp. 131–154). A Comparative Study, Springer.
Larsson, J. F. (2010). *The transition in Kazakhstan*. Lund University thesis, Lund.
Munck, G. L. (2015). *Democratic transitions*. International Encyclopedia of the Social & Behavioral Sciences (2nd ed., pp. 97–100). Los Angeles: University of Southern California.
Odling-Smee, J. (2024). *The economic transition in Armenia*. IMF. Retrieved February 27, 2024, from https://www.imf.org/en/News/Articles/2015/09/28/04/53/sp073101
Papava, V. (2014). Georgia's economy, the search for a development model. *Problems of Economic Transition, 57*(3), 83–94.
Pomfret, R. (2000). *The Uzbek model of economic development 1991–99*. University of Adelaide.
Pomfret, R. (2001). *Turmenistan: From communism to nationalism by gradual economic reforms*. University of Adelaide.
Repkine, A. (2002). *Turkmenistan economic autocracy and the recent growth performance*. Retrieved February 27, 2024, from https://www.researchgate.net/publication/228155007.
Rothstein, B., & Teorell, J. (2012). Defining and measuring quality of government. In S. Holmberg, & B. Rothstein (Eds.), *Good Government, The Relevance of Political Science* (pp. 13–39). Edward Elgar, Cheltenham, UK.

Sachs, J. (1994). *Shock therapy in Poland, perspective of 5 years*. University of Utah.
Sartania, K. (2021). Struggle and sacrifice: Narratives of Georgia's modern history. *Carnegie Europe*, April, 2021.
Schlögel, K. (1984). *Der Renitente Held*. Junius Verlag.
Schmitz, A. (2020). *Uzbekistan transformation, strategies and perspectives*. German Institute for International and Security Affairs.
Šubrt, J., Vinopal, J., Hampl, S., & Pullman, M. (2012). The velvet revolution and modern Czech history in the eyes of the Czech population. *Czech Journal of Political Science, 1*.
Suleymanov, E., & Aliyev, K. (2015). Macroeconomic analysis and graphical interpretation of Azerbaijan economy in 1991–2012. *Expert Journal of Economics, 3*(1), 40–49. Retrieved February 27, 2024, from https://economics.expertjournals.com/23597704-306/accessed.
Svejnar, J. (2002). Transition economies: Performance and challenges. *Journal of Economic Perspectives, 16*(1), 3–28.
Svejnar, J. (2006). Transition economies: Performance and challenges. *Journal of Economic Perspectives, 16*(1), 3–28.
Tarrow, S. (1996). Social movements in contentious politics: A review article. *American Political Science Review, 90*(4), 874–883.
Treisman, D. (2010). *Twenty years of political transition*. United Nations University, Working Paper 2010/31.
Tsereteli, M. (2018). *Economic modernisation of Uzbekistan*. Silk Road Paper. Washington D.C: Central Asia–Caucasus Institute.
Turk, Z. (2014). Central and Eastern Europe in transition: An unfinished process? *European View, 13*, 199–208.
Voslensky, M. S. (1984), *Nomenklatura*. Edition Molden, Munchen.
Walder, A. G, Isaacson, A., & Lu, Q. (2015). After state socialism: the political origins of transitional recessions. *American Sociological Review, 80*(2), 444–468
Walder, A. G., Isaacson, A., & Lu, Q. (2015). After state socialism: The political origins of transitional recessions. *American Sociological Review, 80*(2), 444–468.
Welsh, H. A. (1994). Political transition processes in central and Eastern Europe. *Comparative Politics, 26*(4), 379–394.
Wittfogel, K. A. (1957). *Oriental despotism*. Yale University Press.
World Bank. (1994). *Governance, The World Bank Experience*. Washington D.C.

Chapter 6
Summary and Final Conclusions

Five trends are highlighted. One. Societal demands for income, well-being and environmental qualities increase across countries. Two. The neo-liberal policies and degrowth ideas fail in realising their aims, while the idea of sustainable development has robust foundations. Three. Incomes and well-being increase while impacts on the environment decrease across countries due to growing material-extensive services and environmental technologies. Four. Environmental performances improve if industries generate higher value services and authorities invest in sustainable innovations. Five. Democratic governances with capable institutions perform better than the authoritarian ones.

6.1 Aim and Method

This study underpins possibilities of sustainable development in the sense of economic growth along with improvements of well-being and environmental qualities. It is shown empirically that incomes can grow while environmental qualities be improved. This is assessed with indicators for space, minerals, energy, and organisms, with regard to the uses of man-made resources of capital, labour, and knowledge which can cause pollution and other hazards to health and the environment. Various means for improvement of incomes and environmental qualities are addressed. They encompass substitutions of material-intensive products for labour-intensive services, replacements of the mineral stocks by the flows of renewable energy, bioresources and recycling, introduction of valuable and less harmful designs, as well as pollution prevention through prudent uses of the natural resources, low hazard compounds, and safety controls. Such qualitative changes in economic activities across value chains refer to sustainable innovations, which are usually followed by numerous adaptations within value chains. They have emerged in the past, while more can be expected in the future as societal interests for environmental qualities increase. On the assumption

© The Author(s), under exclusive license to Springer Nature Switzerland AG 2025

Y. Krozer, *Economic Growth and the Environment*,
https://doi.org/10.1007/978-3-031-99181-3_6

that interests in societies determine policies, not the other way around, it is focused on the realised performances rather than on policy intentions and regulations.

For assessing the realised performances, defined as annual average changes, statistical data in authoritative databases are used. Trends in performances are assessed, measured by the annual average change during a decade or longer across countries. All 207 countries in the database on the World Bank, and the world are covered. Particular attention is given to fifteen countries with populations above 100 million people, including the EU of 28 member countries considered as one country. Together they cover more than two-third of global GDP and environmental impacts. Most attention is given to the period 1990 to 2015 with respect to available data. During that period, most countries aimed to turn away from state directives toward market transactions in their governances while the environmental governances disseminated to nearly all countries. Possibilities for sustainable development are assessed based on the ideas of economists, countries performances in the past, producers' and consumers' capabilities for the future, and changes in the countries' governances.

6.2 Ideas

Economist ideas about environmental qualities are comprehended as moral codes about the human role in nature, and as instruments for human behaviour in nature. In the morals, more than 90% of people in the world, measured by adherence to religions and ideologies, assume the supremacy of human above nature. While this idea dominates, opposition on the fringes of nearly all religions and ideologies assumes that humans are equal or even subordinated to nature. These Anthropocentric, respectively Ecocentric morals are used by economists to assess the instrumental possibility of sustainable development. Mainstream economics perceive transactions with flexible substitution of the natural resources for man-made ones as the source of all value, referred to as weak sustainability. Economic fringes consider environmental qualities as the foundation of all transactions, labelled as strong sustainability. Moderate economists tend to combine these viewpoints, but their radical opponents are vocal in science and policies.

Within economic thinking, three strings of thoughts partly support and oppose each other. Mainstream economics addresses prices as drivers of the resource substitutions. Evolutionary theorising, preoccupied with knowledge, assumes that changes in technologies can maintain availability of environmental qualities. Behavioural economics focused on value addition, addresses investments in the value adding activities and prevention of environmental impacts. Mainstream economists assume that the price competition drives toward lowest cost resources, which generates economic growth and prevents environmental degradation if harms to the environment are priced. This idea about price-driven economic activities evolved into ideology that all societal interests can be optimised through the market transactions. This neo-liberal ideology, turned into policies in the Anglo-Saxon countries in 1980s, followed by dissemination to most countries. It is claimed to generate economic growth through privatisation of public assets and mass access to capital, while environmental impacts would be resolved through the transactions between private interests without regulation. Estimates from 1990 to 2015 show that the neo-liberal policies did not fulfil their promises as the income growth decelerated globally and in high-income countries that promoted the neo-liberalism, while it accelerated in several lower income countries, particularly in China. Moreover, public expenditures did not decline globally and in most countries, aside the USA, mainly because policies and public funds turned away from the social support to the capital support. Due to this shift, rents from capital grew and accumulated in hands of a few thousand families in the world who became multi-billionaires in dollar assets with political powers, alike the aristocracy in the 1800s.

The economics preoccupied with environmental qualities address provision of natural resources, regulation of sinks for residuals, support of land uses, and cultural activities. Although the threat of the deplored environment was emphasised time and again from the late 1700s onward, societies were able to overcome collapses through innovations. Growing population with larger consumption would overexploit energy and minerals, but profitable opportunities in renewable energy and recycling were found. Pollution would become unbearable for health, but less harmful alternatives and emission reduction decreased pollution without undermining economic growth. Land for the common good would be captured by private interests, but areas for nature protection continued to enlarge due to environmentalist actions. Fair uses of environmental qualities are lauded with respect to animals and ecosystems, responsible consumption, integration of formal and informal work, shared access to natural resources, and equity in environmental impacts. Radical expressions about fairness advocate economic contractions in high-income countries with income transfers to lower income ones. This degrowth would reduce income and environmental impacts per person in high-income countries, giving access to environmental qualities in lower income ones. However, estimates based on economic recessions in high-income countries in the EU and oil-producing countries show that the degrowth would undermine well-being, and aggravate water pollution, air pollution, and nature while impacts on climate change would decline, at best, in line with the economic contractions.

A realistic alternative to the radicalism of the neo-liberal and degrowth ideas is the idea that the entrepreneurial creativity enables to release constrains posed by environmental qualities. It is realistic if economic value in money terms grows faster than the uses of natural resources measured in physical terms, called 'decoupling'. Innovations would increase value adding activities, thereby economic growth, along with improvements in well-being and environmental performances. Such 'sustainable innovations' are observed across businesses as environmental policies are disseminated from the second half of the 1900s onward. In this study is underpinned that higher performances in economy, well-being, and the environment continued, despite relaxation of the policy demands for environmental performances. Higher performances are driven by the quasi-autonomous demands for higher value services, and induced by the citizens' demands for environmental performances.

6.3 Performances

Several environmental impacts are reduced globally and in many countries while economies grew during the last decades. This is assessed based on the conventional environmentalist model in which environmental impacts are the results of population and income per person, as well as consumption of the natural resources per income and environmental impacts per resource. While the global population grew due to longer life expectancy, these growth rates stagnated in nearly all countries because the birth rates declined faster than the death rates in nearly all countries, except in Africa. Given that the birth rates decline while the maximum lifespan saturates, the global population ages and presumably declines within a few next decades. A worry for economic growth is that the labour force may stagnate. Shortage of labour aggravates as economic activities shift from land-intensive agriculture and material-intensive industry toward labour-intensive services. Services increased from one third to about two-third of GDP during the 1900s. Within the growing services, the knowledge workers expanded from a few percent to about one-fifth of global labour force that increased fourfold during the last century. These trends are observed in nearly all countries. So far, there is no shortages of labour on the global scale but in high-income countries, while lack of jobs is observed in low-income ones. The global shortage of the labour force in the future can be mitigated through better access to education, migration policies, flexible retirement, better work conditions with robotics, and other means that enlarge people skills.

As a result of growing services, pressures on environmental qualities per income decline because services use a small fraction of the agricultural and industrial energy use per income. This is also reflected in the decreasing material use per capita as observed in high-income countries and in lower income ones. Also, water use decreased in nearly all countries. Energy use decreased in high-income ones, and deforestation slowed down despite weakening environmental policies. Economies dematerialise as incomes grow in high-income countries, but the dematerialisation is insufficiently in lower income countries with lower share of services in economies.

Given these changes in economies, environmental impacts are determined by the resource uses per income and emissions per resource use. Uses of resources per income decreased during the period 1990–2015. Per USD_{2015}, uses of water in m^3, fuels in GJ, and forest areas in m^2 uses decreased in nearly all focus countries. However, low-income countries increased their fossil fuel use per income while decreased the uses of biofuels. The dematerialisation in high-income countries is often attributed to the emigration of industries to lower income countries, but this hypothesis is not valid. That emigration of industries evolved during the 1970s, but turned around from the late 1990s onward. Larger material-intensive domestic consumption and inefficient technologies are main causes of the growing use of natural resources in lower income countries. Meanwhile, the export of materials mass did not grow. Exports did grow by value. Emissions per resource also decreased when more environmental technologies were applied. Wastewater treatment covered more people in all focus countries. CO_2 per fuel use decreased in high-income countries, but increased in lower income ones and Japan. NOx emission per fuel use decreased in all focus countries, aside Pakistan. Nature protection areas per forest area increased, insofar data are available. Total environmental impacts are estimated by the multiplications of populations and their incomes per person with the resource uses per income and environmental impacts per resource. While incomes grew, water pollution declined in all countries, CO_2 emissions and air pollution decreased in most high-income countries, but increased in lower-income ones, and nature restoration increased, but rarely compensated the deforestation. While the share of high-income countries in global GDP and environmental impacts decreases due to larger services and environmental technologies, the share of lower income countries increase. Regarding the increasing share of lower income countries in global income and environmental impacts, an international burden sharing is dubious. Instead, investments in sustainable innovations in lower income countries can be enhanced through guarantees by the states in high-income countries.

A popular idea that economic growth increased well-being, but aggravated environmental impacts should also be dismissed. Insofar data is available, economic, social and environmental performance hugely vary across all 207 countries in the world as estimated for the period 2005–2015. An additional income can enlarge or reduce poverty, increase or decrease public expenditures on education and health, use more or less natural resources, and improve or aggravate environmental impacts. Interests and policies are decisive. A few dozen countries improved performances on nearly all indicators of well-being and on all environmental indicators, though the increase of nature areas did not compensate for deforestation. A few common features of high performers are defined. All high performers experienced, moderate economic growth; it is below 5% annual average. All of them are high-income countries by 2015 though several of them were mid-income and low-income twenty five years ago by the standard of that time. Their populations are well-educated measured by high access to tertiary education. Finally, all of them are considered as democracies. Apparently, these properties facilitate changes toward sustainable development.

6.4 Capabilities

Capabilities in the sense of access to resources for conversions to valuable activities are assessed with regard to innovations that improve economic, social, and environmental performances. Such sustainable innovations are generated quasi-autonomously due to competition between entrepreneurs and through inducement of the far reaching demands by policies and citizens' organisations. Sustainable innovations emerge quasi-autonomously if the cost-savings due to better uses of natural resources are allocated in development of higher value novelties. As these cost-savings deliver higher value activities they automatically reduce environmental impacts and increase income. However, this quasi-autonomous innovation-mechanism is hindered by low prices of the natural resources, which cause that the cost-savings become unattractive, and by the stakeholder greed for high dividends instead of investments in innovations. The inducement of innovation is obstructed by policies that protect laggards rather than encourage innovators.

Global capabilities of this quasi-autonomous innovation mechanism are estimated. High capabilities are indicated by the increasing trends in incomes per material in monetary terms along with the decreasing trends in material use per product in the physical terms. In agriculture, the innovative capabilities are found based on the growing value of produced cereals and decreasing uses of fertilizers. These capabilities increase in lower income countries, but saturate in high-income ones. In industry, the innovative capabilities are low and decline measured by the production value compared to the uses of energy and the conversions of minerals into materials. This worrisome finding can be explained by the business strategies aiming at the low-cost products. This drives industries into a deadlock of declining sales prices toward unit costs of production. An industrial turnaround toward higher value deliveries is needed, which can be invoked by liabilities for harms to safety, health, and environmental qualities, when they are combined with higher labour capabilities in design, take back with guarantees for repairs, ethical production, and suchlike life cycle management. In the transport, the value of transport is compared to energy per passage mile. Low capabilities are found in the road transport, presumably related to that industrial deadlock, while higher in air and rail transport. Improvements in energy performances are observed in air transport, as well as in rail transport with manifold better energy-efficiency, which implies that the energy-efficiency can improve nearly infinitely on the global scale.

An often heard complaint that sustainable innovations are not feasible because consumers are not interested is unfounded. This is based on the consumer purchases from 1995 to 2019 year mostly in high-income and mid-income countries. The consumer purchases are divided into the material-intensive products, capital-intensive services and labour-intensive services. This assessment shows that 15 to 30% of all household purchases address labour-intensive services in education, leisure, and communication. These purchases grow faster than the purchases of material-intensive products and capital-intensive services. Moreover, they grow despite the increasing costs of labour along with the decreasing prices of materials, and the growth rates of labour-intensive services are higher than other types of services. This finding underpins a mismatch between the industrial focus on lower cost products and the revealed preferences for value adding services. As incomes grow, more products linked to services are attractive, which enable innovations in the life cycle management.

The capabilities of innovators are assessed with regard to uncertainties about the profitability of innovations per million USD expenditures in research and development (R&D). It is uncertain if such investments generate intellectual property rights for novelties, which facilitate the starts of inventing firms. After the start of the firms, it remains uncertain if the invention generates sufficient sales in competition with rivals to cover all costs and generate profits. So, it is uncertain if the inventor's R&D generates a startup, and if this innovator generates profitable sales. The rates of successful investments after ten years of competition are estimated for all focus countries, and for a few R&D-intensive countries with more than 3% R&D expenditures in GDP; low-income countries hardly do R&D. The rates of inventor success and the rates of innovator success after ten years of competition differ and vary across countries. High success rates of inventors per million USD in R&D are found in Japan, Indonesia, and Russia, but their investment are not profitable as more firms fail than start. The inventor success rates were lower in the USA and China, but more startups survived competition. However, their rates of successful innovator are well-below 0.1% per million USD in R&D because not many firms survive tough competition. Investing in innovations in these countries is a gamble. Twenty-fold higher rates of successful innovations are found in Brazil, EU28, India, Israel, and Korea despite lower inventor rates. These results show that conditions in competition determine the profitability of R&D expenditures rather than the generating of startups. Given that the failures in innovations cause high social and private costs, survival of startups in competition should be fostered through demands for novel, high-value businesses.

The capabilities of investors in innovators are also assessed. Therefore, private and public investments in startups are estimated. Average private investment per startup vary from about USD 20,000 in the EU28 to more than USD 100,000 in the USA, and even higher in a few mid-income countries. High investments in the USA are driven by the tax exemptions for investors in new venture and compensations for their losses. In effect, total venture capital in the USA increased fivefold between 2007 and 2018 while the venture capital in the EU28 hardly increased, but the number of startups hardly increased in the USA while they did in the EU28. This finding implies large social costs in the USA. Much public money allocated in tax exemption in the USA is wasted because many startups failed in the competition. Investors gained from tax exemptions, but startups were more often broke. Public funding upfront shifts the costs and risks of private investors to public ones, while bankruptcies are costly to the startups, investors and to the society. An alternative is the public funding after deliveries through guarantees for the sales of innovations. Public guarantee facilitates deliveries of innovations for the demanded qualities, while private interests take the risk of investments. Experiences in agriculture, renewable energy, packaging, and other businesses illustrate that such generic guarantees need larger funds than subsidies for particular firms, but better market conditions generate many more innovators. In renewable energy, the price guarantees for deliveries to grid, so called feed-in tariffs, were cheaper per succesful innovator than subsidies. Demands for renewable energy combined with the feed-in tariffs increased manifold the rates for successful innovations across the EU28 countries.

In addition to the abovementioned quasi-autonomous innovation mechanism driven by competition, sustainable innovations are induced due to the citizens demand for environmental qualities, being expressed in policies. Demands for public health and environmental qualities are posed for centuries. They are strengthened during the second half of the 1900s due to income growth along with more leisure time driven by longer lifespan and shorter labour time. Income with leisure time trigger services in tourism, sports and other activities that demand and use environmental qualities. In addition, the growing knowledge work demands environmental qualities for better work performances. All professions like good environment in general, while silence spaciousness, and other qualities are essential for high performance of knowledge workers. Their demands generate services for the natural amenities in cities. The demands of leisure services and knowledge work generate global investments in environmental technologies. These investments grew during the past decades despite relaxed environmental policies and 'fail-soft' agreements with firms. Usually, public authorities induce these environmental investments. Most investments are made in renewable energy. These investments generate private incomes. However, investments in sanitation, nature protection, safe chemicals, and in other issues that do not provide private incomes hardly increase, though they prevent harm.

In addition to the authorities, citizen initiatives induce innovations. Their capabilities in this inducement vary, which is illustrated for sanitation, renewable energy, and nature protection. In sanitation, local authorities invest in sewage and wastewater treatment at the end of sewage pipes. These are effective but costly in thinly populated areas and in low-income countries. Citizen initiatives also induce distributed sanitation systems and separation of wastewater streams at sources, but these innovations hardly disseminate. In renewable energy, large-scale private and public energy firms are main investors in the production capacities. Many citizen initiatives emerge in communities, but these production capacities are small and grow slower than large scale ones unless they are directed by the authorities as in India and China, or facilitated by large private power suppliers as in the USA. In nature protection, citizen initiatives are decisive about establishment of protection areas. Their initiatives are effective measured by the protection areas that cover about the quarter of all global land. However, they are ineffective when measured by the protection of nature, given that the threats to biodiversity hardly decline across countries and the protected areas. Meanwhile, the costs of establishing a protected area expand. Resolving this deadlock needs innovative land uses rather than larger protected areas. Citizen initiatives can incubate sustainable innovations in the protected areas for the land uses outside the areas.

Capabilities in sustainable innovations enlarge with the increasing demands for high-value services in general and for environmental qualities in particular. These capabilities induce innovations if protection of incumbent interests and shareholder greed are contained. Although the silver bullet in policies on sustainable innovation is still to be found, guarantees for the demanded services proved to be cost-effective instruments.

6.5 Governance

Type of governance that enhances sustainable development is assessed. Democratic governances are compared to autocratic ones based on experiences with political transition in 23 former satellites and republics of Soviet Union. Based on the assumption that the process of change in governances evolves in similar ways for different goals, lessons from the political transitions for sustainable development are drawn. Authoritative theories about political transition are used for the definition of five key factors in the political transitions. The contextual factors refer to the mainstream idea that economic and cultural patterns vested in the past largely determined changes in governance. Main contextual factors are long experiences of independent statehood (heritage of independence) and low share of national minorities in the population (national minorities). In addition, the process factors are considered, which cover the involvement of civil organisations in the shifts of governments (civil involvement), the liberalisation in doing business (economic reforms), and acceptance of various opinions in the media (political tolerance). With help of these transition factors, the contexts, and processes in political transitions of satellites and former republics of the Soviet Union are described. These descriptions are used for scoring and ranking of successful transitions in the sense of shifts in the governances. Seven countries are assessed as successful transitions, all of them are in Europe, nine countries in Europe and Asia as moderately successful, and seven countries in Asia and Europe are considered as unsuccessful.

Three former Soviet republics and four Soviet satellites assessed as successful transitions entered the EU28, but a few EU-entrants are assessed as only moderately successful. A key factor in the successful transitions was early change of the government which prevented continuation of the oligarchy. Most of the successful ones were front runners that experienced a few decades of statehoods during the existence of the Soviet Union, and had small national minorities. Their citizens had independent organisations before the changes of governments, followed by reforms of their economies within a few years, and continuation of free media. Their prosperity grew measured by income, decreasing income inequalities, and longer lifespan, while the industrial shares in economies declined. Their high ranking with transition factors match the rankings on several authoritative indexes on governance. Successful political transitions highly correlate to high ranks on the indexes for democracies, economic freedom, institutional capabilities, and low corruption. Correlations of the ranking with transition factors and the rankings with indexes of 'good governance' and 'happiness' are modest, while the correlation for the ease of doing business is low. Democratic governances with capable institutions facilitate political transitions, though not always satisfy people and businesses.

Successful political transitions are compared to less successful and unsuccessful ones with regard to their performances on the key sustainability indicators. The successful ones score higher on the indexes of democracy and institutional capabilities. Their economic performances were better. The successful transitions generated faster economic growth and more high-value activities, while fuel-efficiency improved in most transition countries. Particularly relevant were the shifts to higher value activities. These shifts were largely based on domestic investments, while foreign investments were small compared to the domestic ones despite entry in the EU, and they were not larger in the successful transitions than in the unsuccessful ones. Well-being improved more in the successful transitions than in the unsuccessful ones. Poverty declined faster though it was lower at the start of the transition period. Education improved faster, but not health care. Environmental performances were better in a few areas. The successful transitions were better in reducing water pollution and protecting of nature than the unsuccessful ones, but not better in mitigation of climate change, or reduction of air pollution. Improvements of economy and well-being had priority during the political transitions.

Based on the political transitions, a few lessons about changes for sustainable development can be drawn. One is that people find ways to go around bureaucracy and resist oppression, which implies that sustainable development should align to main trends in societies and in the citizen preferences. Second is that the successful changes are attained in democracies with institutional capabilities. Imposing sustainable development as a directive has a low chance of success. Third is that capable citizens are needed, which implies the need for accessible services in education. Fourth lesson is that successes are driven by the value-adding entrepreneurial behaviour in societies rather than political choices. Support of this behaviour requires an encouragment of sustainable innovators instead of protecting laggards. Fifth, independent citizens' organisations are necessary for the initiation of changes and capable politicians for the successful continuation.

6.6 Closing Remarks

Experiences of the past decades across all countries in the world show that high-value products linked to labour-intensive services generate sustainable innovations, which enable reasonable economic growth with improvements in well-being and high environmental performances. These innovations are driven by competition and they are induced by demands for well-being and better environment, provided that the shareholder greed and protection of incumbent interests are tamed. Five non-regret actions within reach of all countries enhance sustainable development.

1. Reliable sets of economic, social and environmental indicators supports decision making with respect to various interests and render credible implementation of those decisions with science-based truth.
2. Gradual shifts of the taxes on labour into taxes on natural resources, starting with elimination of subsidies for protecting polluting interests, generate value adding labour at lower environmental impacts.
3. Wider access of populations and business to higher education, to tinkering in experiments, and to cleaner technologies enlarge the innovators capabilities in surviving competition with value adding novelties.
4. Guaranteed prices for the supplies that are highly qualified with sustainability indicators support the consumer demands for higher value services, which induce innovations in well-being and environmental qualities.
5. Independent citizen initiatives create trustful policies for sustainable development, while capable institutions are needed for strengthening links between innovators and followers.

Appendix A
Calculation Methods

Much used formulas in the book explained below.

A frequently mentioned term is 'cost'. Unless specified, this term refers to the unit cost, also called a 'marginal cost'. The unit cost, 'c', is total cost divided by total volume in a year; for example, a million USD yearly cost for 1000 pieces is USD 1000 per piece; note that the total annual cost is estimated as the sum of depreciations and operational costs.

The value added is the sale of products minus the cost of purchasing resources. It shows deliveries of capital, labour and knowledge in an organisation, excluding purchases of materials, energy and hired labour, formally represented as:

$$V_i = (P_{s,i} - P_{r,i}) \cdot Q_i \tag{A.1}$$

'V_i' is value added in monetary terms; 'P_s' is the sales price; 'P_r' is the resource price; 'Q_i' denotes the quantity of resources in terms of mass; for each resource, purchase prices are multiplied by the quantities.

Wherein historical changes are analysed, current prices of goods are converted into the constant ones of a year i.e., real prices. Estimates of constant prices 'p_r' are corrections of current prices with the inflation coefficients 'r' in databases. If uncorrected in the databases, the World Bank inflation rates are used for the most part of price estimates, formally represented as:

$$p_r = p_t / \left(\frac{r}{100} + 1\right) \tag{A.2}$$

The prices corrected for inflation are expressed in the monetary value of a particular year; for instance, US_{2011} means prices in US Dollars as per the year 2011. Note that when the annual rate of inflation is high, these corrections are laborious and somewhat arbitrary because they refer to the prices of traded goods rather than the prices of consumer goods on the domestic market.

© The Editor(s) (if applicable) and The Author(s), under exclusive license to Springer Nature Switzerland AG 2025

Y. Krozer, *Economic Growth and the Environment*,
https://doi.org/10.1007/978-3-031-99181-3

Changes are called 'growth'. Growth 'g_t' is assumed to be an exponential function of time 't' per year, formally represented as:

$$g_t = n_{t+1}/n_t - 1 \tag{A.3}$$

The growth rate 'g' is often an annual average of several years over a period of time. High growth rates generate large changes within a few years, but a low rate spanning a long period of time also causes large changes; for example, twice the volume is generated in 70 years with 1% growth $(1 + 0.01)^{70}$; in 36 years with 2% growth; and in 24 years with 3% growth. Herewith, low rates are relevant because long-time spans are assessed. Trends in the growth rate during a period are called accelerators, 'a', formally represented as:

$$a_t = g_{t+1}/g_t - 1 \tag{A.4}$$

A trend above 1 implies acceleration of growth; and below 1 a slow-down. Acceleration over a few subsequent decades is an augmenting trend; whereas, the slow-down over a few decades indicates saturation. For instance, augmenting renewable energy is an acceleration of the growth, but a saturating population means slow-down of the growth.

The trends encompass fluctuations, such as the rises and recessions, called booms and slumps of income. Herewith, the standard deviation 's' is used to indicate the scale of fluctuations. This is formally represented as:

$$\mathrm{s} = \sqrt{[1/(N-1)] \cdot \sum_{i=1}^{N} (x_1 - \overline{x})^2} \tag{A.5}$$

It is calculated in Excel. Large standard deviations compared to averages indicate strong fluctuations. Increasing standard deviation spanning a period of time indicates a diverging trend, and a decreasing one shows a converging trend; for example, divergence in CO_2 emissions per capita across countries and convergences in total energy consumption. The standard deviation, when compared to the average, is also used as an indication of the validity of conclusions; when the standard deviation is higher than the average, the validity of the conclusion is low. For example, it can be a disputable statement with respect to large fluctuations.

Links between observations are correlated; for example, the changes in income when compared to changes in energy consumption. The Pearson correlation is used because it is a reliable and well-known method that is easy to handle in Excel by the interested public. A regression is formally represented as:

$$R^2(x, y) = \sum (x - \overline{x}) \cdot (y - \overline{y}) / \sqrt{\sum (x - \overline{x})^2 \cdot \sum (y - \overline{y})^2} \tag{A.6}$$

For example, 'x', is the annual average growth of income and, 'y', is the annual average growth of energy consumption during a period. Herewith, a stringent criterion is used because regressions equal to and above 0.8 ($R^2 \geq 0.8$) are considered correlated, and between 0.5 and 0.8 moderately correlated but lower are assumed uncorrelated.

A mainstream assumption is that higher prices reduce demands. The price elasticities of demand refer to the effects of price changes on demand changes; for instance, the effect of higher prices of energy resources on the consumed volume of energy. The mid-price elasticities are calculated and formally represented as:

$$k = \frac{p_{i+1} - p_i}{(p_{i+1} + p_i)/2} / \frac{q_{i+1} - q_i}{(q_{i+1} + q_i)/2} \tag{7}$$

For $p_i = \sum_i^n p_t/n$, also for q_i; $p_{i+1} - p_i$ Is price change, $q_{i+1} - q_i$ volume change.

In energy, low price elasticity 'e' is usually assumed ($e > -1$), meaning that an increase of the unit price causes less than a unit consumption decrease. The income elasticity is estimated in a similar way for the incomes instead of prices. In energy, income elasticity above $+1$ is usually assumed; it means that a unit of additional income causes more than a unit of additional consumption.

Changes is technologies are indicated as the effect-increasing technical change and the cost-reducing one. Both are expressed in percentage annual change. The effect-increasing technical change is formalised as:

$$k_t = k_0 a^t \tag{A.8}$$

Herewith, 'k_t' is the effect due to the change; 'k_0' the initial effect; 'a' the coefficient of the effect-increasing technical change usually assumed due to know-how and scale of activities over time 't', usually in years. The costs of technologies often decrease over time. This cost-reducing technical change is expressed in a percentage average change of unit cost per year. This is formally represented as:

$$c_t = c_0 a^t$$

A popular measurement is the unit costs per doubling of outputs, formally shown as:

$$c_t = c_0 \left(\frac{o_t}{o_0} \right)^b \tag{A.9}$$

wherein 'c_t' denotes the unit cost in year t; 'c_0' the unit cost in base year; 'o_t' the output in year t; 'o_0' output in the base year; and 'b' the inclination of the curve that reflects the cost-reducing technical change. The cost reduction is measured by half-time, which is the time needed for the reduction of unit costs by half of the initial situation; it is $c_t/c_0 = 0.5$. This is much used to estimate the increases in the required scale of the production, given the cost reducing technical change. In economics, the cost-reducing changes are used to indicate impacts of technological changes on prices. These two are often combined and called 'technological learning'; whilst the effect-increasing technical change always reduces some costs, the cost changes may not influence the effect when cheaper resources are used without further effect.

The conventional indicator of the successful business is profitability. This is estimated with the Net Present Value (NPV). Firstly, the Present value is calculated followed by the Net Present Value:

$$PV_t = \sum_{t=1}^{n} C/(1 + r/b)^{bt} \tag{A.10}$$

For example, if 1 million USD is invested (also called the outgoing cash flow) 'I' and 1 million USD of income is generated per year during two years (also called the incoming cash flow) 'C' at 10% interest 'r', the NPV is:

$$1^{\text{st}} \text{ year } 1/(100\% + 10\%)^1 = 0.91$$

$$2^{\text{nd}} \text{ year } 1/(100\% + 10\%)^2 = 0.83 \text{ million Euro}$$

$$\text{PV} = 1.74$$

$$NPV = PV - I$$

$$\text{NPV is } 1.74 - 1 = +0.74$$

Positive NPV indicates potentially profitable investment, negative NPV a loss. When several investments over time are done, they are discounted much in the same way as the income. If alternative proposals with different timelines are compared, as it is often the case in this study, the present value of average annual cash flows is estimated called the 'uniform annual stream' (UAS), 'equivalent annual cost' (EAC), 'present value annuity', or suchlike names. These terms are often used to express annual capital costs of investments. It is calculated as the present value or net present value divided by the annuity factor. The annuity factor A_t is the sum of the discount factors over time, and the uniform annual streams (UAS) are NPV (or PV for nil investment) divided by A_t:

$$A_t = \sum_{t}^{n} 1/(100\% + r)^t$$

$$UAS = NPV/A_t$$

Based on the above: $A_t = (100\% + 10\%)^1 + (100\% + 10\%)^2] = 1.1 + 2.21 = 3.31$. UAS = 0.74/3.31 = 0.22 average profit a year.

Appendix B
Progress in Environmental and Social Goals

In this Appendix is illustrated if sufficient progress in achieving Environmental and Social Goals (ESG) within framework of Sustainable Development Goals (SDG) is made. Indicators for environmental and social goals are shown in Table B.1. Rows present indicators of ESG's. Columns present the situation in 2015, annual average change during 3 subsequent periods, as well as acceleration or deceleration of the changes in performances. The periods are 1990–2004 when annual average prices of fossil fuels were low, 2005–2015 when the average prices tripled and 2016–2020. The accelerations and deceleration compare those averages during 2015–2005 to 1990–2004, and 2020–2016 to 2005–2015. Colours indicate the rates of changes: green means much progress, yellow moderate and red aggravation. Finally, several remarks about data are shown. Empty boxes show lack of data or unreliable data in a few cases. For 42 ESG indicators, data is generated by the World Bank, which covers nearly half of all indicators.

Table B.1 Indication of trends and shifts in trends after approval of Sustainable Development Goals in 2016

World Bank database: Environmental Social and Governance (ESG)	Situation	Annual average changes during three periods			What is policy effect? Changes in the periods		Remarks about the changes
Indicators; empty boxes mean no data	2015	1990-2004	2005-2015	2016-2020	2005-2015 to 1990-2004	2016-2020 to 2005-2015	Focus on the last period
Access to clean fuels and technologies for cooking (% of population)	64%	1%	2%	2%	1.41	1.01	
Access to electricity (% of population)	87%	1.5%	0.8%	0.8%	0.51	1.08	
Adjusted savings: natural resource depletion (% of GNI)	1%	5%	1%	20%	0.12	30.15	more depletion
Adjusted savings: net forest depletion (% of GNI)	0.1%	-3%	4%	-3%	-1.38	-0.73	less depletion
Agricultural land (% of land area)	37%	-0.4%	-0.1%	0.1%	0.24	-1.17	
Agriculture, forestry, and fishing, value added (% of GDP)	4%	-3%	2%	0.3%	-0.76	0.16	
Annual freshwater withdrawals, total (% of internal resources)	9%		*0.04%*	*0.2%*		*6.89*	

(continued)

© The Editor(s) (if applicable) and The Author(s), under exclusive license to Springer Nature Switzerland AG 2025

Y. Krozer, *Economic Growth and the Environment*,
https://doi.org/10.1007/978-3-031-99181-3

Table B.1 (continued)

Annualized average growth rate in per capita real survey mean consumption or income, total population (%)							
Cause of death, by communicable diseases and maternal, prenatal and nutrition conditions (% of total)	20%						
Children in employment, total (% of children ages 7-14)							
CO_2 emissions (metric tons per capita)	4.6	0.4%	1%	-1%	2.21	-1.68	
Coastal protection							
Control of Corruption: Estimate							
Cooling Degree Days							
Economic and Social Rights Performance Score							
Electricity production from coal sources (% of total)	39%	0.5%	-0.03%		-0.07		few data
Energy imports, net (% of energy use)	21%	3%	-85%				
Energy intensity level of primary energy (MJ/$2017 PPP GDP)	4.8	-1%	-2%	-1%	2.45	0.74	
Energy use (kg of oil equivalent per capita)		0.3%	1%		3.25		few data
Fertility rate, total (births per woman)	2.5	-2%	-0.5%	-1.5%	0.31	2.90	pressure on environment
Food production index (2014-2016 = 100)							
Forest area (% of land area)	31%	-0.2%	-0.1%	-0.1%	0.69	0.81	
Fossil fuel energy consumption (% of total)	80%	-0.01%	-0.1%		11.65		few data
GDP growth (annual %)	3%	11%	-62%	-89%	-5.86	1.43	
GHG net emissions/removals by LUCF (Mt of CO_2 equivalent)							
Gini index							
Government Effectiveness: Estimate							
Government expenditure on education, total (% of government expenditure)	14%	1%	0.4%	-2%	0.44	-5.21	
Heat Index 35							
Heating Degree Days							
Hospital beds (per 1,000 people)	2.7						
Income share held by lowest 20%							
Individuals using the Internet (% of the population)	40%	52%	10%	8%	0.19	0.77	saturation of growth
Labor force participation rate, total (% of total population ages 15-64) (modelled ILO estimate)	66%	-0.1%	-0.2%	-0.2%	1.43	0.80	
Land Surface Temperature							
Level of water stress: freshwater withdrawal as a proportion of available freshwater resources							
Life expectancy at birth, total (years)	72	0.4%	0.4%	0.04%	1.06	0.10	
Literacy rate, adult total (% of people ages 15 and above)	86%	1%	0.3%	0.2%	0.48	0.71	
Mammal species, threatened							
Methane emissions (metric tons of CO_2 equivalent per capita)	1.1	-1%	-0.3%	-1%	0.34	2.67	
Mortality rate, under-5 (per 1,000 live births)	43%	-2%	-4%	-2%	1.56	0.55	
Net migration							
Nitrous oxide emissions (metric tons of CO_2 equivalent per capita)	0.39	-1%	-0.2%	-0.2%	0.33	1.26	
Patent applications, residents	1972500	3%	7%	3%	2.59	0.50	
People using safely managed drinking water services (% of the population)	69%	1%	1%	1%	0.97	0.96	
People using safely managed sanitation services (% of the population)	49%	2%	3%	2%	1.39	0.78	

(continued)

Table B.1 (continued)

PM2.5 air pollution, mean annual exposure (micrograms per cubic meter)	46.5		2%	-2%		-1.24	
Political Stability and Absence of Violence/Terrorism: Estimate							
Population ages 65 and above (% of total population)	8%	1%	1%	2%	1.05	1.92	
Population density (people per sq. km of land area)	57	0.2%	1%	1%	5.84	0.89	
Poverty headcount ratio at national poverty lines (% of population)							
Prevalence of overweight (% of adults)	38%	1%	1%	1%	1.04	0.87	
Prevalence of undernourishment (% of population)	8%	-1%	-4%	3%	4.04	-0.68	
Proportion of bodies of water with good ambient water quality							
Proportion of seats held by women in national parliaments (%)	23%	5%	3%	2%	0.74	0.67	
Ratio of female to male labour force participation rate (%) (modelled ILO estimate)	68%	0.1%	-0.04%	0.2%	-0.45	-5.57	ratio increased after 2016
Regulatory Quality: Estimate							
Renewable electricity output (% of total electricity output)	23%	-1%	2%		-3.98		few data
Renewable energy consumption (% of total final energy consumption)	17%	0.1%	0.3%	3%	4.50	7.80	
Research and development expenditure (% of GDP)	2%	0.03%	1%	4%	23.29	6.14	
Rule of Law: Estimate							
School enrolment, primary (% gross)	101%	0.3%	-0.1%	-0.2%	-0.20	4.06	
School enrolment, primary and secondary (gross), gender parity index (GPI)	0.995	1%	0.5%	-0.2%	0.74	-0.41	
Scientific and technical journal articles	2275681	4%	5%	5%	1.31	1.03	
Standardised Precipitation-Evapotranspiration Index							
Strength of legal rights index (0=weak to 12=strong)	5		3%	4%		1.28	
Terrestrial and marine protected areas (% of total territorial area)				2%			
Tree Cover Loss (hectares)							
Unemployment, total (% of total labour force) (modelled ILO estimate)	6%	1%	-1%	0.3%	-0.46	-0.67	
Unmet need for contraception (% of married women ages 15-49)							
Voice and Accountability: Estimate							

Appendix C
Variations in Country Performances

This Appendix shows whether an additional income improves or aggravates well-being and environmental qualities, and if trade-offs between well-being and environmental qualities are observed. The period 2005–2015 is covered, because earlier data are deficient. Prices of fossil fuels and other natural resources were high during this period, and economies of many countries were severely hit by the financial crisis after the collapse of banks in 2008. Insofar data is available, economic, social and environmental indicators of 207 institutional entities in the World Bank database are covered. These entities are independent countries and parts of countries as the Caribbean islands within the Netherlands state. Within those entities, 75 are high-income countries with annual average incomes per capita above USD_{2005} 12,000, 51 are mid-income ones with the incomes from USD_{2005} 4000 to USD_{2005} 12,000, and 81 are low-income countries below USD_{2005} 4000 per person. These incomes are based on the GDP per person. Well-being is indicated by poverty that is measured by percent people below USD_{2005} 6.85 daily income per person in total population, as well as government expenditures on education, and the expenditures on health. Both latter are calculated as the percentages of GDP. The environmental indicators are water use and water pollution in m^3, fossil fuel use in MJ with pollution of CO_2 and NOx in kg, and the areas of forest and nature protection in m^2.

Those indicators are estimated per countries' GDP in USD_{2005}, calculated in a similar way to the income elasticities as mentioned in Appendix A. The calculation method is: the observed indicator in year t + 1 minus the observed indicator in the year t, divided by GDP in the year t + 1 minus GDP in the year t. This is followed by summing up and dividing by ten years, which are annual average income elasticities. For example, the number of poor people in 2015 minus the number in 2014 divided by GDP in 2015 minus GDP in 2014. Table C.1 shows results for high-, mid-, and low-income countries in columns and indicators in rows. Insofar data is available, these results for the period 2005–2015 are compared to the results for the period 1990–2015, which is not shown in this table. As the results are strongly influenced by only a few countries with extreme income elasticities of an indicator, 10 times

© The Editor(s) (if applicable) and The Author(s), under exclusive license to Springer Nature Switzerland AG 2025

Y. Krozer, *Economic Growth and the Environment*,
https://doi.org/10.1007/978-3-031-99181-3

Table C.1 Countries per capita performances in well-being, resource uses, and environmental impacts per GDP growth during the period 2005–2015; n—number of countries

Indicators (averages of n number of countries)	High-income $USD_{2005} > 12{,}000$ n = 75	Mid-income USD_{2005} 4000–12,000 n = 51	Low-income < USD_{2005} 4000 n = 81
GDP per capita	39,303	7263	1864
Poverty percentage	−0.000002	−0.001	0.001
Education expenditures	0.01	−0.1	2
Health expenditures	0.1	0.4	−1
Water uses	0.01	0.02	−1
Water pollution	−0.003	0.1	−0.4
Uses of fossil fuels	2	−1	2
Climate change	0.1	0.6	0.1
Air pollution	−0.1	−0.4	0.2
Forest areas	0.01	−3	−4
Nature areas	−1	3	4

larger elasticities than all others are excluded. This way, biased results caused a few unreliable data are avoided.

During the period 2005–2015, the average income per capita in high-income countries was about fivefold of mid-income ones, which was about fourfold of low-incomes countries. Given that incomes grew, the differences in incomes per capita usually decreased across countries. Per additional income, the percentages poverty in the population was low in high-income countries but hardly decreased, while poverty increased in Australia, Norway, Qatar, Germany, and a few other countries. Meanwhile, the poverty rate decreased stronger in mid-income countries. For example, poverty decreased significantly in Costa Rica, but increased a lot in Mexico. Poverty in populations increased along with growing incomes in many low-income countries, as in Ethiopia. Insofar data is available, poverty increased more during high fuel prices from 2005 to 2015 compared to low fuel prices during the period 1990 to 2004. Additional incomes enabled to increase the governmental expenditures on education in high-income and low-income countries. These expenditures decreased in mid-income countries, which can be compensated by more private expenditures on education, but this data is unavailable. Additional incomes enabled to increase total expenditures on health in high-income and mid-income countries, but these expenditures decreased in low-income countries as Egypt and Sudan. These findings illustrate trade-offs between income growth and well-being. Given an income, policies are often decisive for well-being but many policies neglect it. A burden shared through income transfers from high-income countries to lower income ones, as proposed in the 'degrowth', can cause counter-intuitive impacts unless the beneficiaries prioritise well-being, or donors demand this priority.

Environmental performance of an additional income varied from positive and negative across countries. Water use hardly increased in high-income and mid-income countries, while decreased in several low-income countries as Gambia, Tajikistan, and Mali. Water pollution decreased in high-income countries and low-income ones, while increased in mid-income Peru, Colombia, and others. Uses of fossil fuels increased in high-income countries along with differences between these countries. For example, fuel use increased a lot in Canada, Brunei, while decreased in the other countries. Fuel use decreased in South Africa, Jamaica, and several other mid-income countries, contrary to most low-income ones where fuel use increased. High fuel prices reduced fuel use in high-income countries, but changes in lower income countries varied. CO_2 emissions increased in most though not all growing countries. These increases were small in most high-income countries and low-income ones while they were large in mid-income countries as Serbia and Botswana. Air pollution caused by NOx emissions decreased in high-income countries and even more in mid-income countries as Uruguay, but NOx emissions increased a lot in low-income countries as Egypt and Togo. Forest areas hardly grew in high-income countries, but they decreased a lot in mid-income and low-income ones as Colombia and Guyana, respectively Cameroon and Zimbabwe. Meanwhile, the nature areas decreased in high-income countries as in Greenland and in Canada while increased in mid-income ones as Guyana and Belize, and low-income ones as Benin and Tanzania. Those experiences across all countries indicate that additional incomes can improve, or aggravate performances in well-being and environment depending on investments reflected in trends.

Appendix D
Capabilities in Capital and Labour

In the mainstream economic theory, economic growth is assumed to depend the scale of capital and labour and their productivity. The scale of capital tends to increase when savings grow faster than all forms of capital, and all capital grows faster than the capital fixed in machines, constructions, and other capital goods. These conditions enable allocations of capital for a higher value, meaning that productivity of capital can increase. The scale of labour is indicated by labour force, while labour productivity by GDP per worker. Changes in GDP, fixed capital and labour productivity based on the World Bank data are indexed in Graph 19 on the vertical axis for the period 1990–2015 (1990 = 100). Given labour productivity, the value addition above fixed capital indicates growing capabilities in societies. These capabilities are assumed to be driven by technological change, called 'Solow residue' after Solow seminal study the USA economy in the last century. In present service economies, labour skills could be as important.

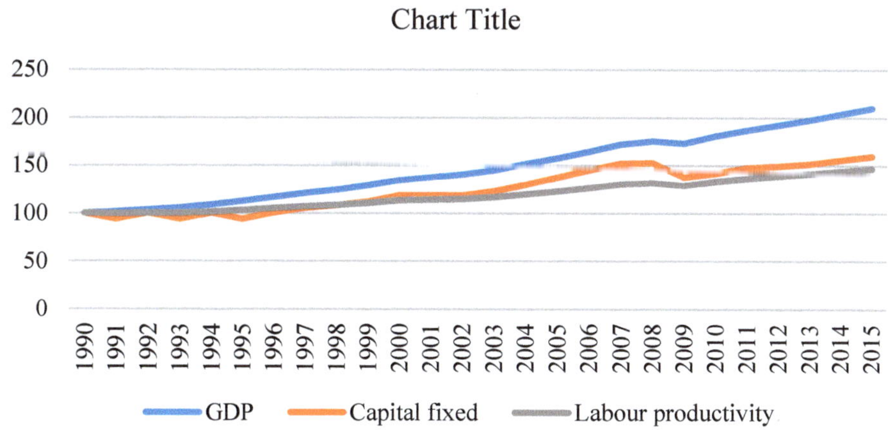

© The Editor(s) (if applicable) and The Author(s), under exclusive license to Springer Nature Switzerland AG 2025
Y. Krozer, *Economic Growth and the Environment*,
https://doi.org/10.1007/978-3-031-99181-3

While annual average GDP growth exceeded 3%, fixed capital grew below 2%, and labour productivity about 1.4% throughout the period 1990–2015. This implies a growing Solow residue, meaning increasing societal capabilities in using equipment and skills in services. Higher societal capabilities are partly lost by inefficient capital allocations. Global fixed capital grew slower than labour productivity during the early 1990s, presumably caused by the political collapses and transitions in the former Soviet Union and its satellites. This is followed by fast growth of fixed capital during the early 2000s, when information platforms expanded until burst of the 'internet bubble' entailing financial collapse in 2008 and economic recession. The societal capabilities differ across countries. For example, the societal capabilities increase in Mexico and Pakistan where GDP grows somewhat faster than labour productivity, whereas they decrease in Russia and Brazil, where GDP grew slower than labour productivity.

Appendix E
Performances in Innovation Processes

Countries performances in innovation processes are shown in Table E.1. These performances are indicated by the shares and growth rates of R&D in GDP, numbers and growth rates of intellectual property rights (IPRs), and number and growth rates of firm births, called startups. IPRs include patents, trademarks, copyrights, and designs. Those growth rates are annual averages during 2008–2017.

Table E.1 Indicators for performance in innovation processes in the focus countries, within the EU, and a few R&D-intensive countries

Annual average growth 2008–2017	R&D in GDP		IPR		Firm birth	
	2018 (%)	Growth (%)	2018	Growth (%)	2018	Growth (%)
Focus countries						
World	2	2	7930	4	3750	1
USA	3	2	1109	3	750	1
Japan	3	0.3	529	−1	29	16
EU28	2	1	653	1	1755	2
Russia	1	2	122	1	317	5
Brazil	1	5	235	6	189	−6
Mexico	0.4	−2	162	4	84	14
China	2	10	5381	15	285	11
Egypt	1	16	30	2	N.A	N.A
Indonesia	0.12	18	88	45	61	10
Philippines	0.1	8	41	7	20	6
Nigeria	0.1	2	32	−1	86	6
India	1	−0.4	387	9	124	8
Pakistan	0.4	−6	39	9	13	15

(continued)

© The Editor(s) (if applicable) and The Author(s), under exclusive license to Springer Nature Switzerland AG 2025
Y. Krozer, *Economic Growth and the Environment*,
https://doi.org/10.1007/978-3-031-99181-3

Table E.1 (continued)

Annual average growth 2008–2017	R&D in GDP		IPR		Firm birth	
	2018 (%)	Growth (%)	2018	Growth (%)	2018	Growth (%)
Bangladesh	0.1	−9	14	4	4	5
Ethiopia	0.4	13	2	13	31	20
European Union						
Belgium	2	4	25	−2	25	2
Bulgaria	1	7	7	−5	46	0
Czech Republic	2	4	11	−3	30	4
Denmark	3	2	6	−5	37	4
Germany	3	2	188	−1	73	1
Estonia	2	5	3	−5	20	6
Ireland	1	−1	4	−1	22	2
Greece	1	6	2	0	10	37
Spain	1	−1	76	0	95	−3
France	2	0	127	1	201	2
Croatia	1	1	4	−6	16	6
Italy	1	2	88	67	114	2
Cyprus	0.5	3	2	1993	15	−4
Latvia	1	2	4	−2	10	1
Lithuania	1	3	5	−1	6	1
Luxembourg	1	−1	0	28	7	22
Hungary	1	3	7	−4	24	1
Malta	1	2	2	7	6	16
Netherlands	2	1	3	0	72	8
Austria	3	2	11	−5	4	1
Poland	1	6	20	−1	37	10
Portugal	1	2	23	1	43	2
Romania	0.5	0.5	12	−3	94	1
Slovenia	2	3	4	−5	4	−1
Slovak Republic	1	7	5	−4	20	5
Finland	3	−2	6	−3	15	1
Sweden	3	0.2	12	−3	46	6
United Kingdom	2	−2	143	8	665	4
R&D intensive countries						
Israel	5	5	19	1	17	1
Korea, Rep	3	9	478	2	101	6
Singapore	42	5	42	2	43	6

Appendix F
Context of the Political Transitions

Rise and fall of the Soviet Union governance provide the context of political transitions. The Soviet Union was created on the territory of the former Russian Empire, governed by two dynasties of monarchs (tsars). While industries expanded in Europe and North America during the 1700s, the Russian Empire remained agrarian with absolute power of the tsar and hierarchic nobility that owned people (serfs) for work on land. Colonised populations in Siberia, Caucasia, Middle Asia, and Europe did slavery work. Huge army and security force oppressed discontent. Lost wars against Ottomans (Turkey) and Japan invoked social uprising, which constituted a parliamentary monarchy in 1905. This was followed by the army insurgence during 1st World War (1914–1920). It abolishes tsardom in 1917 with the help of revolutionaries that call themselves communist after works of Marx on Paris communards. It is often referred to as the October revolution. Their victory in bloody civil war across the Russian Empire (1917–1924) culminated in the constituting of the Union of Soviet Socialist Republics in 1922, called Soviet Union, while a few million Russians emigrated. Stalin, being keen on nationalism in the multicultural Russian Empire, envisioned the multinational governance based on the national rulers in service of communism many years before the Socialist revolution (Stalin, 1913). By the end of the 1920s, the Soviet republics of Ukraine, Russia, Georgia, Armenia, Azerbaijan, Turkmenistan, Kazakhstan, Uzbekistan, Tajikistan, and Kirgizstan were established, along with regional autonomies of the Chechen, Tuva, Komi, and other cultures. Nationalities were represented in the highest ranks of the Soviet governance, but the national aspirations were brutally oppressed by the local communist rulers. The tsarist institutions were supervised by the communist party, led by Lenin until his death in 1924. After four years of struggle for power within the communist party, which evolved along with liberalized economy and flourishing culture, Stalin took the leadership until his death in 1953.

Stalin regime appropriated production resources, imposed collective farms, controlled consumption and media, and purged, army, security forces, and institutions from criticism. The state directed production volumes and prices, workers' payments,

© The Editor(s) (if applicable) and The Author(s), under exclusive license
to Springer Nature Switzerland AG 2025
Y. Krozer, *Economic Growth and the Environment*,
https://doi.org/10.1007/978-3-031-99181-3

and other resource uses. Also, secular mass education was introduced, cultural and gender equality was promoted under the state control. Millions of prisoners were used for construction of infrastructure. Permanent military and ideological preparedness was enforced in education and at work. While the state enforced terror, millions of young Russians made careers in expanding industries and glorified communism. Civil wars continued: against farmers that opposed the collectivisation in Ukraine and Kazakhstan, as well as religious expressions on Caucasus, and nationalists in Turkmenistan and Uzbekistan. Presumably, more than 20 million of people died of persecution during thirty years of this ruling. In addition, Soviet Union lost about 20 million people during World War II (1939–1945). Soviet Union also invaded Finland, Poland, Estonia, Latvia, and Lithuania based on agreement with Nazi Germany about the division of Europe, called the Ribbentrop–Molotov pact in 1939. After the invasion of the Soviet Union by Nazi Germany I June 1941, the Soviet Union formed allied forces with the USA and United Kingdom in fights against the fascist states of Germany, Italy, Hungary, Romania, Slovakia, and Spain. By the end of this war, the Soviet Union captured Polish parts of Ukraine and Belarus, the Bessarabia region of Romania, similar to the present territory of Moldavia, and the Transcarpathian region of Hungary in the west. Territories of China and Japan in the east are also taken. It also controlled Poland, Czechia with Slovakia, Hungary, Romania, Bulgaria, Yugoslavia, Albania, and part of Germany in Europe, as well as Mongolia and part of Korea in Asia.

After Stalin death in 1953, that terror was relaxed in the Soviet Union and in its satellites captured during the WW2. Many political prisoners were released, but the communist party remained in control of politics, economy, and culture. Military expansion continued through the support of local revolutionaries as in Egypt, and direct interventions as in Iraq and Korea. The military production has grown, but civil production has stagnated during three decades after his death. The material-intensive basic industries were useful for the military expansion, but they did not meet consumer demands. Economy of the Soviet Union and its satellites stagnated, while economies in the USA and Western Europe grew rapidly along with decolonisation in Asia, Africa, and Latin America in the second half of the 1900s. Economic governance in Soviet Union and its satellites based on directives with fixed quantities, prices, and wages in production plans, caused endemic scarcities of consumer products in shops, along with the blooming of informal markets, persistent corruption, and perverted work morale. During nearly seventy years after the revolutions in 1917, The Soviet Union created a larger empire than the Russian Empire throughout three preceding centuries, but collapsed within several years of the late 1980s.

While the Soviet Union was admired by many experts and politicians in the 'West', many experts within the Soviet Union and its satellite countries observed decay from 1970s on, and published their observations in the internal notes. Experiments with decentralisation and price incentives were opposed by corrupted elites. The nomenclature alike feudal autocracy with imperial ambitions could not be changed. Losses in the Afghan war in the 1980s along with death of aging political leaders brought Gorbachev to power in 1985. Although the Afghan war was ended and freedom was allowed with the aim to prevent the collapse of economy, the Soviet Union governance decomposed rapidly and unexpectedly. By 1990, most of the satellite countries switched to a market economy. When the coup d'état by the Soviet security forces in August 1991 failed, Yeltsin took power thanks to the supportive Soviet army. By December 1992, the Soviet Union was officially dissolved and its republics became independent states. Shortly thereafter, several satellites of the Soviet Union and a few Soviet republics aiming for economic and military independence asked for membership in the European Union and the North Atlantic Treaty Organisation (NATO). These memberships are obtained after several years, but the timing varied. For example, Poland entered the EU in 2004, and Croatia as late as 2013. Some former Soviet republics joined the Confederation of Independent States (CIS) led by Russia, while a few others remained outside these blocks.

Appendix G
Economic Results of the Political Transitions

Whether the liberation from the Soviet Union was worth efforts can be underpinned by results. The following performance indicators are assessed: the average incomes per person in USD_{2015}, income distributions across countries, income-inequalities based on Gini coefficients, living conditions indicated by the average years of life, and economic restructuring measured by percentages industry in GDP. These indicators are shown for the years 1992, 2002, and 2012, which means right after the shifts, after the economic crisis and after political instability, respectively. Results in the transition countries that entered the EU (EU-entrants) are compared to the transition countries that did not enter it (EU non-entrants), as well as to the results in the EU, India, and China. Note that China also shifted from the state directly to a market economy, though still guided by the Communist Party. Table G.1 presents the indicators for 1992 and the indexes for 2002 and 2012 (1992 = 100). Income inequality within the countries is shown by coloured numbers. Green shows more equality, yellow minor change, red more inequalities, and black from lack of reliable data about the income distribution. Performances cover the EU-entrants followed by the non-entrants.

The average incomes of 11 countries that entered the EU in 1992 were about one-third of the EU average, but five times above the Chinese average and ten times above the Indian one. During the first decade of the political transition, incomes in these transition countries grew faster than the EU average, except in Bulgaria. The growth rates were higher than the Indian ones, but lower than in China while the Estonian economic growth approximated the Chinese one. After becoming EU members in the 2010s, incomes in all countries continued to grow above the EU average, which implies that the EU entry was beneficial for these transition countries. The income disparities between these countries in 1992increased during the first ten years of the political transitions. In 1992, the highest average income of the transit country that entered the EU, which was Slovenia, was about three times higher than the lowest one, which was Bulgaria. This spread increased before their entry to the EU, followed by decrease of the spread during the second decade after their entry into the EU. It indicates a moderating impact of the EU on incomes across the countries. Meanwhile,

© The Editor(s) (if applicable) and The Author(s), under exclusive license to Springer Nature Switzerland AG 2025

Y. Krozer, *Economic Growth and the Environment*,
https://doi.org/10.1007/978-3-031-99181-3

Table G.1 Performances of the countries after decomposition of the Soviet Union

	GDP per person			Average years of life			Share industry in GDP in 1992 and indexed 2012	
	USD2015 /person	Indexes of 1992		Years	Indexes of 1992			
	1992	2002	2012	1992	2002	2012	1992	2012
A few benchmark countries								
EU28	22048	122	134	75	103	107	25	85
China	1101	232	599	69	106	111	31	132
India	545	146	247	59	107	114	26	106
EU entrants								
Bulgaria	3837	111	174	71	101	104	20	119
Czechia	10238	127	162	72	104	108	30	112
Estonia	5745	199	283	69	103	111	25	96
Croatia	5643	177	205	71	105	108	28	71
Hungary	7363	134	156	69	105	109	24	103
Lithuania	4053	183	313	70	102	105	27	97
Latvia	4411	178	281	68	104	108	27	74
Poland	4849	157	238	71	105	108	37	79
Romania	4041	142	218	70	102	107	31	95
Slovakia	6655	145	226	72	103	106	22	124
Slovenia	11975	144	168	73	104	109	25	111
Non-entrants in the EU (presently in CIS shown italic)								
Armenia	872	186	380	69	103	107	28	108
Azerbaijan	2107	83	247	61	108	115	46	101
Belarus	2575	113	235	70	97	103	25	129
Georgia	1519	117	237	68	103	107	N.A.	N.A.
Moldova	1759	87	135	67	100	103	31	70
Russia	6346	93	149	67	97	105	35	81
Ukraine	2547	65	97	69	99	103	40	62
Kazakhstan	4887	114	201	67	98	103	42	76
Kyrgyzstan	928	80	107	68	100	103	46	54
Tajikistan	850	60	102	55	118	124	35	82
Turkmenistan	2734	86	192	64	102	108	N.A.	N.A.
Uzbekistan	1323	102	178	65	102	107	26	87

the inequality of domestic incomes decreased in six of these eleven EU-entrants, but increased in five of them throughout the transition period. The EU reduced the inequalities across countries, not within those countries. Life expectancy increased faster than in the EU in Estonia, Hungary, and Latvia with life expectancies below the EU average of 75 years in 1992. Meanwhile, India and China, which had shorter life expectancies, improved faster. Most transition countries were more industrialized than the EU and India in 1992, measured by the share of industry in GDP. Poland was even more industrialized than China in 1992, but the industrialisation declined. Opposite is observed in Bulgaria, Czechia, Slovenia, and Slovakia where industrial share was low in 1992, and increased during the transition period. The popular image of obsolete industries in former communist countries is largely misleading though more efficient, cleaner technologies are often introduced.

In 1992, twelve former Soviet republics that did not join the EU had a different start. Non-entrants' average income per person was about half lower than one of the EU entrants. During the first decade of transition, people in newly created countries lost income. For example, a typical Tajik lost nearly 40% of 1992 income and Ukrainian lost about 35% of it. Regarding these losses, social discontent, and violent changes of power in most countries, should not surprise. During the next decade, real incomes per person grew in all those new countries, but the growth rates of the EU-entrants were higher while the Ukrainian income did not reach the level of 1992. Although the Soviet Union advocated solidarity and equality, differences in the average income per capita across former Soviet republics were significant. In 1992, the highest average income in Georgia was eight times higher than in Tajikistan. For example, the average Tajik income was barely higher than the Indian average, while the Russian income was similar to the average of the EU-entrants, which was one third of the EU average. During the transition period, the spread of average income across the non-EU entrants increased, while the domestic income inequality decreased. The living conditions were lower in the non- entrants than in the EU entrants at the start of the transition in 1992, and they did not improve faster. Only Tajik lifespan grew fast, but it was short in 1992. Most non-entrants were more industrialised than the EU-entrants and the shares of their industries in GDP did not decline as fast as among the EU entrants.

Generally, the real incomes per capita increased in nearly all transitions after a period of deep economic crises, and their lifespan increased. Many people had to change skills and jobs as industries declined in many countries. Herewith, the EU entrants had a better start than the non-entrants, and these differences increased over ten and after twenty years of the political transitions. Overall, the results of political transitions are mixed. While prosperity in successful transition countries tangibly increased, slower improvements are achieved in less successful ones.

Appendix H
Indexes for Good Governance

Countries' ranking of successful transitions is compared to the ones on indexes for governance. Two indexes focus on 'democracy'. One is the Bertelmann Stiftung Transformation Index (BST), https://bti-project.org/en/downloads. Scores are based on 18 criteria in the categories: statehood, political participation, rule of law, stability of democratic institutions, political and social integration. Another index refers to the Economist Intelligence Unit (EIU). Our World Data show results in https://ourworldindata.org/grapher/democracy-index-eiu?tab=table. The economic liberties are addressed in the Index of Economic Freedom (IEF) with scores on 11 criteria. The criteria are Property rights, Government integrity, Judicial Effectiveness, Tax Burden, Government Spending, Fiscal Health, Business Freedom, Freedoms of Labour, Money, Trade, Investment, and Finance, https://www.heritage.org/index/pages/all-country-scores. The Corruption Perception Index (CPI) addresses integrity, which can be found at https://www.transparency.org/en/cpi/2023. Institutional performances are covered by the Worldwide Governance Indicators (WGI) with criteria for Voice and Accountability for civil participation, Political Stability and Non-Violence, Government Effectiveness, Regulatory Quality, Rule of Law, and for Control of Corruption, scoring on several properties per criterion; the average of scores per criterion is used www.govidindicators.org. People's responses to Gallup surveys in different countries are incorporated into the quality of life index (HAP), indicated by https://ourworldindata.org/happiness-and-life-satisfaction. Index for the business freedom refers to the Ease of Doing Business (EDB) with criteria for the Starting business, Dealing with construction permit, Getting electricity, Registering property, Getting credit, Protecting minority investors, Paying taxes, Trading across borders, Enforcing contract, and Resolving insolvency, and several scoring on a few attributes per criterion https://archive.doingbusiness.org/en/rankings. All of those indexes are expert opinions. Most recent indexes are used.

Table H.1 displays the rankings of the 23 political transitions. Country names are in column 1, ranking based on the transition factors in column 2. Rankings with the scores on democracy with BST in column 3, and with EIU in column 4. Rankings

© The Editor(s) (if applicable) and The Author(s), under exclusive license to Springer Nature Switzerland AG 2025

Y. Krozer, *Economic Growth and the Environment*,
https://doi.org/10.1007/978-3-031-99181-3

Table H.1 Lists countries with transition factors and indicators for good governance

Countries	Ranking factors	BTS	EIU	CPI	FREE	WB	HAP	BUS	COST
Czech	1	2	1	6	4	2	1	10	12
Lithuania	2	3	5	2	2	3	2	2	4
Poland	3	8	7	7	9	7	7	9	21
Romania	4	9	11	10	12	11	4	17	3
Estonia	5	1	2	1	1	1	6	3	8
Latvia	6	5	4	3	3	5	8	4	15
Slovenia	7	4	3	4	10	4	3	8	1
Slovakia	8	6	6	8	7	6	5	11	10
Hungary	9	12	8	13	15	9	11	16	19
Bulgaria	10	10	9	12	5	21	18	18	11
Georgia	11	14	15	5	6	10	22	1	16
Ukraine	12	11	14	17	23	16	23	19	6
Croatia	13	7	10	9	8	8	10	15	20
Kyrgyzstan	14	16	16	20	18	19	13	21	14
Armenia	15	13	13	11	11	14	19	12	7
Russia	16	17	19	19	19	20	16	6	9
Moldova	17	15	12	15	16	13	15	13	18
Tajikistan	18	22	22	21	20	22	20	22	22
Azerbaijan	19	20	18	22	14	18	21	7	13
Kazakhstan	20	18	17	16	13	15	9	5	2
Turkmenistan	21	23	23	23	21	23	17	23	23
Uzbekistan	22	21	20	18	17	17	12	20	17
Belarus	23	19	21	14	22	12	14	14	5
Correlation factor ranks		0.9	0.9	0.8	0.7	0.7	0.6	0.4	0.2

on economic liberties with IEF in column 5, on corruption with CPI in column 6. Rankings on the institutional performance with GWI in column 7, on quality of life with HAP in column 8, and on doing business with EDB in Column 9. The numbers in the table show the rankings of the countries. It is assessed if the ranking for successful transition correlated with the rankings on indexes. Higher regressions ($R^2 > 0.7$) indicate correlations, moderate regressions ($R^2 > 0.5$) indicate moderate links; and lower regressions show no links. In addition, number of matches between the ranking for successful transitions and the indexes are estimated. Table H.1 shows results with the colour green for successes, yellow for moderate successes, and red for low success. For the convenience of readers, rows are shown in the descending order of successful transitions and columns are in the descending order of the regressions from ($R^2 > 0.8$ to $R^2 < 0.4$).

MIX
Papier aus verantwortungsvollen Quellen
Paper from responsible sources
FSC® C105338

If you have any concerns about our products,
you can contact us on
ProductSafety@springernature.com

In case Publisher is established outside the EU,
the EU authorized representative is:
Springer Nature Customer Service Center GmbH
Europaplatz 3, 69115 Heidelberg, Germany

Printed by Libri Plureos GmbH
in Hamburg, Germany